Women's Entrepreneurship Policy

Women's Entrepreneurship Policy
A Global Perspective

Edited by

Colette Henry

Adjunct Professor, Griffith University, Australia

Susan Coleman

Professor Emerita, University of Hartford, USA

Kate V. Lewis

Reader, Newcastle University, UK

The editors and contributors to this book are members of the Global Women's Entrepreneurship Policy Research Network (Global WEP).

WOMEN'S ENTREPRENEURSHIP POLICY RESEARCH

Edward Elgar
PUBLISHING

Cheltenham, UK • Northampton, MA, USA

Cover image: Ambrose Chua on Unsplash

Published by
Edward Elgar Publishing Limited
The Lypiatts
15 Lansdown Road
Cheltenham
Glos GL50 2JA
UK

Edward Elgar Publishing, Inc.
William Pratt House
9 Dewey Court
Northampton
Massachusetts 01060
USA

Paperback edition 2024

A catalogue record for this book
is available from the British Library

Library of Congress Control Number: 2022948417

This book is available electronically in the **Elgar**online
Business subject collection
http://dx.doi.org/10.4337/9781800374652

ISBN 978 1 80037 464 5 (cased)
ISBN 978 1 80037 465 2 (eBook)
ISBN 978 1 3050 3900 6 (paperback)

Printed and bound by CPI Group (UK) Ltd, Croydon, CR0 4YY

Contents

Figures

Tables

About the editors

Colette Henry, PhD, is an Adjunct Professor, Griffith University, Australia, and Head of Department of Business Studies, Dundalk Institute of Technology, Ireland. Her previous roles include Norbrook Professor of Business & Enterprise (Royal Veterinary College, London), and President of the Institute for Small Business and Entrepreneurship (ISBE, UK). She is the founding editor of the *International Journal of Gender and Entrepreneurship*. She has published widely on entrepreneurship education and training, gender and entrepreneurship, creative industries and veterinary business. She is the founder and Chair of the Global Women's Entrepreneurship Policy Research network (GWEP), and she led the publication of 'Entrepreneurship Policies through a Gender Lens' (GWEP-OECD, 2021). Awards include the Diana International Research Project Trailblazer Award (2015) and the Sten K. Johnson European Entrepreneurship Education Award (2017) (Lund University, Sweden). Colette is a Fellow of the Academy of Social Sciences.

Susan Coleman, DPS, is a Professor Emerita of Finance at the University of Hartford (Connecticut) where she taught both graduate and undergraduate courses in entrepreneurial and corporate finance. Dr Coleman's research has concentrated on entrepreneurial finance with a particular focus on the ways in which women entrepreneurs secure financing for their firms. She has co-authored two books on women-owned firms: *A Rising Tide: Financing Strategies for Women-Owned Firms* (2012) and *The Next Wave: Financing Women's Growth-Oriented Firms* (2016). She has also published on social entrepreneurship and co-authored *Creating the Social Venture* (2016). In recognition of her scholarly contributions, Dr Coleman received the Humphrey R. Tonkin Award in 2016, the University of Hartford's highest award for research. She also received the 2019 Diana Changemaker Award for Research from Babson's Center for Women's Entrepreneurial Leadership.

Kate V. Lewis, PhD, is Reader in Entrepreneurship and Innovation at Newcastle University Business School, UK. Prior to that she was Reader in Entrepreneurship and Gender Studies at Manchester Metropolitan University and Associate Professor at Massey University, NZ. Kate is a former Consulting Editor for the *International Journal of Gender and Entrepreneurship*, Associate Editor of the *Journal of Small Business Management* and Editor in

Chief of *Small Enterprise Research*. As well as gender and entrepreneurship, her research interests include social entrepreneurship and the implications of work for identity.

Contributors

Helene Ahl, PhD, is Professor of Business Administration at the School of Education and Communication at Jönköping University, Sweden. Her discourse analysis of research texts on women's entrepreneurship in 2002 paved the way for her future research, which includes studies of women's entrepreneurship policy in Sweden, the UK and the USA, feminist analyses of how research formulates policy implications, the gendering of entrepreneurial narratives, and research on women's rural entrepreneurship. Her 2021 article on a postfeminist analysis of enterprise policy in the UK and Sweden co-authored with Professor Susan Marlow received the 'Paper of the year' award from *Human Relations.*

Karin Berglund is a Professor in Business at Stockholm University, Sweden. She has been attentive to the expansion of conventional entrepreneurship to new contexts and emerging forms of alternative entrepreneurship and innovation. Her research involves ethnographic studies of women's entrepreneurship, community development, social entrepreneurship, entrepreneurial learning and entrepreneurial practices in the public sector as well as policy studies and more experimental methodological approaches. Her overarching research interest lies in studying the emergence of novel forms of entrepreneurship to gain deeper insights into the emergence of entrepreneurial cultures and the power effects this entails. With feminist and other critical approaches, she is interested in contributing to a sociological understanding of entrepreneurship.

Naomi Birdthistle is an Associate Professor at Griffith University, Australia. Having worked in her family business for 20 years, she then established her own consulting business. Naomi has studied in Scotland (Stirling University – BA Hons), Ireland (University of Limerick – Masters and PhD) and the United States (Babson College [one-year undergraduate programme and an Executive Education programme] and Harvard University [summer school and Executive Education]). Naomi's research includes entrepreneurship education, women-owned and -led businesses, and the role women play in family businesses. She has recently secured two Department of Foreign Affairs and Trade (DFAT) grants focusing on empowering women entrepreneurs in Vietnam and in Japan.

Patrice Braun is an Action Researcher with a PhD in regional small business network development underpinned by ICT and a Master's in Research on the use of the Internet for environmental community information. She is Adjunct Professor in Research & Innovation at Federation University Australia and is Principal Consultant at Patrice Braun & Associates. Patrice's global research and consultancy work in sustainable regional futures and ICT-enabled development focuses on gender inclusion and entrepreneurship. She has published on gender-responsive ecosystems and trade practices, knowledge economy skills, and women's entrepreneurship as a path for economic empowerment and social change.

Candida G. Brush is the Franklin W. Olin Professor of Entrepreneurship at Babson College, USA. She is a co-founder of the Diana International Research Institute (DIRI), has authored 180 publications and 14 books, and is a Senior Editor for *Entrepreneurship Theory and Practice.* She is on the board of directors for Anchor Capital Advisors, LLC, Solo Coco (Dominican Republic), a member of the Boston Harbor Angels and Portfolia. She holds a doctorate from Boston University, and an honorary PhD from Jonkoping University. She is also a Visiting Professor at Nord University, Bodo, Norway and Dublin City University, Dublin, Ireland.

Gray Cavender is Professor Emeritus of Justice & Social Inquiry, School of Social Transformation, Arizona State University. His interests focus on corporate crime and regulation, punishment, gender and media studies. He serves on the international advisory board for *Crime Media Culture*, and is an Associate Editor for *the Oxford Research Encyclopedia on Crime, Media, and Popular Culture.* Academic books include *Corporate Crime Under Attack* (Taylor & Francis) and *Provocateur for Justice: Jane Tennison and Policing in "Prime Suspect"* (University of Illinois Press). His fictional books include *Death of the Ayn Rand Scholar* (Amazon) and *The Pandemic Casebook of Jillian Warne* (Amazon).

Evelyn Derera is an Associate Professor in the School of Management, IT & Governance at the University of KwaZulu-Natal (UKZN). Evelyn holds a PhD in Entrepreneurship from UKZN. She is passionate about entrepreneurship and has published her work in local and international journals. She has also presented her research at many local and international conferences. She currently teaches management and entrepreneurship courses at UKZN. Evelyn also holds a Diploma in Banking from the Institute of Bankers of Zimbabwe. Before joining academia, she worked in the banking sector in Zimbabwe. Her financial sector experience spans over ten years.

Antoinette Flynn is an Assistant Dean, Academic Affairs, senior lecturer, researcher and PhD supervisor at Kenny Business School, University of

Limerick, Ireland. Antoinette's PhD is in market-based accounting research and her Master's in International Business focused on international entrepreneurship, inspiring cross-disciplinary publications in the area of entrepreneurial finance and minority entrepreneurship. Antoinette has won a Best Paper award in the Entrepreneurship in Minority Groups track at the Institute for Small Business and Entrepreneurship conference and a number of teaching awards, including a National Teaching Hero award (National Forum for the Enhancement of Teaching and Learning in Higher Education), 2020.

Patricia G. Greene is Professor Emerita, at Babson College, USA, where she formally served as first dean of the undergraduate school then provost of the college. She is one of the five founding members of the Diana Project, a research group dedicated to studying women's entrepreneurship. She served as the 18th Director of the Women's Bureau of the U.S. Department of Labor. She is an educational advisor for Portfolia, a company with a new model for equity investing. Greene led the design, development and deployment of Goldman Sachs' *10,000 Small Businesses* and was Global Academic Director of *10,000 Women*.

Nancy C. Jurik is Professor Emerita of Justice & Social Inquiry in the School of Social Transformation, Arizona State University. Her interests focus on work organisation, entrepreneurship, and media constructions of gender and work. Her books include *Doing Justice, Doing Gender: Women in Legal and Criminal Justice Occupations* (Sage), *Bootstrap Dreams: U.S. Microenterprise Development in an Era of Welfare Reform* (Cornell University Press) and *Provocateur for Justice: Jane Tennison and Policing in "Prime Suspect"* (University of Illinois Press). She has received distinguished researcher and mentoring awards from Arizona State University as well as from several professional associations. She is a Global WEP member.

Alena Křížková, PhD, is Head of the Gender & Sociology Department of the Institute of Sociology, Czech Academy of Sciences. In 2014–2015 she received a Fulbright Fellowship to Arizona State University to conduct comparative CZ-US research on the entrepreneurship environment for disadvantaged populations and gender equality. Her research focus is on women's economic independence, economic and social justice, the gender wage gap, work-life balance, gender in organisations and in entrepreneurship and on violence against women. She is the Czech country expert in the 'Scientific analysis and advice on gender equality in the EU' (SAAGE) for the European Commission, and a member of the editorial board of the *Gender and Research* journal, and an executive team member of Global WEP.

Helen Lawton Smith is Professor of Entrepreneurship, Department of Management, Birkbeck, University of London. She is a Fellow of the

Academy of Social Sciences, a Fellow of the Royal Academy of Arts and a Senior Fellow of the Higher Education Authority. She is the Director of the Centre for Innovation Management Research (bbk.ac.uk/cimr). She was the principal investigator of the Birkbeck component of the European Union project *Transforming Institutions by Gendering Contents and Gaining Equality in Research* (TRIGGER) (2013–2017). Her current research on 'Addressing regional inequalities in innovation opportunities for BAME and disabled groups' is funded by the Regional Studies Association.

Dariusz Leszczyński received his Doctor of Social Sciences (PhD) degree in 2021 from the Warsaw School of Economics in the discipline of Management and Quality Science. He is the winner of the first prize awarded by the Warsaw School of Economics in the competition for the best doctoral thesis for 2020 in the discipline of Management and Quality Science. Dr Leszczyński is an alumnus of the Graduate School of Banking at Colorado (USA), holds an MBA from the Warsaw University of Technology (graduated with distinction) and earned a Master's degree in economic policy and finance from the Warsaw School of Economics. His research interests are focused on entrepreneurship, small business management, business models and strategies, the use of ICT technology in firms, and corporate finance.

Ewa Lisowska is Professor of Economy at SGH Warsaw School of Economics, Department of International Management. She conducts research on women in the labour market, women managers and entrepreneurs. Her teaching focuses on gender equality, gender diversity and the economy. She is a national expert in the field of female entrepreneurship. She is the author of many articles and book chapters on women entrepreneurs in Poland and in other countries of Central and Eastern Europe.

Mavis S. B. Mensah, PhD, is a Senior Lecturer and former Director of the Centre for Entrepreneurship and Small Enterprise Development, University of Cape Coast (UCC), Cape Coast, Ghana. She has 18 years of entrepreneurship teaching and research experience. Her research interests include entrepreneurship and small enterprise development, particularly the knowledge-based economy, the entrepreneurial university, innovation, youth and women's entrepreneurship, and entrepreneurship education and training. She holds a PhD in Development Studies from UCC, an MBA in Small and Medium-sized Enterprise Development from the University of Leipzig, Germany, and a Diploma in SMEs Management and Development from the Galillee College in Israel.

Barbara J. Orser is Professor Emerita at the Telfer School of Management, University of Ottawa, Canada. Advisory roles: Co-Chair, W20 Delegation of Canada and Executive Committee, Global Women's Entrepreneurship

Policy Research Network. She has co-authored/-edited over 120 publications, including *Entrepreneurship Policies through a Gender Lens* (GWEP/OECD, 2021) and *Feminine Capital: Unlocking the Power of Women Entrepreneurs* (Stanford University Press, 2015). Current studies focus on Gender-Smart Entrepreneurship Education and Training Plus (GEET+) and entrepreneurial feminism. She has been recognised as a feminist leader by *Canada 150 Women* (2017), the Women's Executive Network 100 Most Powerful Women in Canada (Champion Category), and The International Alliance of Women World of Difference 100 Award.

Beldina Owalla, PhD, is a Research Fellow at the Faculty of Business and Law, University of Portsmouth. Her research focuses on understanding the impact of gender and culture on entrepreneurship and innovation activities. Her research interests are in women's entrepreneurship, entrepreneurship education, business and social innovation, entrepreneurial leadership, SME growth and venture finance. She has worked on various projects exploring SME productivity, promoting diversity and inclusion in business innovation, and growth strategies of community businesses.

Katarina Pettersson, PhD, is an Associate Professor in Social and Economic Geography. Her research includes critically researching various aspects of entrepreneurship and different kinds of farming. A gender perspective is central in her research, and areas of particular interest include 'care farming', urban agriculture, rural policy and policy for women's entrepreneurship. Geographically her research is placed in Sweden, other Nordic countries, Rwanda and Tanzania.

Marie Pospíšilová is a postdoctoral Fellow at the Gender & Sociology Department at the Institute of Sociology of the Czech Academy of Sciences. She is interested in gender and entrepreneurship, co-preneurship and work-life balance. Currently, her research focuses on precarious aspects of entrepreneurship, the impact of the COVID-19 pandemic on small businesses and the self-employed, and analysing the social impact of pandemic-related economic restrictions. In addition, her work also covers gender aspects of extending working life and digitalisation.

Malin Tillmar is a Professor at the School of Business and Economics, Linnaeus University, Sweden. Her research covers entrepreneurship in various organisational and geographical contexts. A general theme is the room for entrepreneurial agency under various structural constraints – material, social and discursive. Her previous studies cover entrepreneurship in East Africa (Tanzania, Kenya and Uganda), in and through the Swedish public sector, intersectoral collaboration and women's entrepreneurship in various contexts. Currently, rural entrepreneurship and entrepreneurship for a sustainable and resilient society is her main focus. Professor Tillmar uses a broad range of methodological approaches, but her core competence is in ethnographically inspired studies and interactive research in collaboration with the surrounding society.

About Global WEP

The Global Women's Entrepreneurship Policy Research Network (Global WEP – www.globalwep.org) is a group of established researchers from over 30 counties. Its goal is to examine, internationally, support policies for women's entrepreneurship, and to identify explicit or implicit gender biases within public policies. Global WEP also seeks to identify effective policies or practices that are potentially beneficial to other countries in supporting women's entrepreneurial activities. Global WEP scholars exchange policy knowledge and share policy data for collective publications and report dissemination. In so doing, Global WEP adds value to extant policy scholarship and informs policy development.

Founded and launched by Colette Henry at a meeting of the Diana International Research Institute (DIRI) in Stockholm in 2014, Global WEP is supported by an Executive Team and an International Advisory Panel. Global WEP members comprise researchers from Africa, Asia, Australasia, Europe, North America and South America. Global WEP has published a number of internal reports, papers, books, book chapters and peer-reviewed academic journal articles. The Global WEP network and its members have also led several special issues in leading journals such as *International Small Business Journal, International Journal of Entrepreneurial Behaviour & Research* and *International Journal of Gender & Entrepreneurship*. Global WEP members have presented at various international research fora, including the Diana International Research Institute, the Institute for Small Business & Entrepreneurship (ISBE) and the United Nations Conference on Trade and Development (UNCTAD). We have also led and/or contributed to several webinars for the Organisation for Economic Co-operation & Development (OECD), the Diana International Research Institute, WEIForward, the Centre for Innovation Management Research (CIMR) at Birkbeck, and the International Council for Small Business (ICSB). In 2017, Global WEP published a comparative study of women's entrepreneurship policy in 13 countries in the *International Journal of Gender and Entrepreneurship* (Henry, Orser, Coleman and Foss, 2017). The research was based on analyses of 38 policy/policy-related documents, across Africa, Asia, Australasia, Europe and North America. This 13-country study was followed by more in-depth studies, such as that of Coleman, Henry, Orser, Foss and Welter (2019) in the *Journal of Small Business Management*. Drawing on institutional and feminist theories, this study provides a critique of policies and programmes to increase women entrepreneurs' access to capital in five economies: Canada, Germany, Ireland, Norway and the USA.

In 2021, in conjunction with the OECD, we published a report exploring entrepreneurship policies in 27 countries in Europe, Africa, Asia, North America, South America and Australasia.[1] Findings revealed countries with no dedicated women's entrepreneurship policy; countries where there were policies without programmes; and countries where there were programmes but no policies. Women-focused entrepreneurship policies often referred to women as a 'minority', 'lacking skills', 'in deficit' and needing to be 'fixed.' Access to financial capital was identified as one of the most significant barriers to women's entrepreneurship, and there was a general lack of monitoring and evaluation mechanisms.

Collectively, these studies reveal that authorship of women's entrepreneurship policy documents is often anonymous, is rarely gender-balanced, and sometimes is predominately by men. The analyses suggest that many government policies relegate women entrepreneurs to minority or disadvantaged group status, hence restricting access to resources or overtly privileging traditional male-dominated industry sectors. Few policy documents explicitly state a theoretical foundation or rationale for intervention nor describe evidence-based inputs and outcomes to inform future policy development. Many policies appear to be pilot or *ad hoc* initiatives. When such policies are considered within their national and institutional contexts, there is often evidence of a mismatch between official policies on the one hand, and practices and funded programmes on the other. Accordingly, many women's enterprise, small business and entrepreneurship policies have made only modest contributions to the economic welfare and security of women. Opportunities remain for policy makers to do more.

NOTE

1. OECD-GWEP. (2021). *Entrepreneurship Policies Through A Gender Lens*. Edited by Colette Henry, Barbara Orser, Susan Coleman (GWEP) and Jonathan Potter and David Halabisky (OECD, May). Retrieved 17 May 2022 at: https://www.oecd.org/industry/entrepreneurship-policies-through-the-gender-lens-71c8f9c9-en.htm.

1. Introduction to *Women's Entrepreneurship Policy*: taking stock and moving forward

Colette Henry, Susan Coleman and Kate V. Lewis

THE IMPORTANCE OF ENTREPRENEURSHP POLICY

Scholars recognise that policy is a powerful component of the entrepreneurial ecosystem and, as such, is necessary for economic growth (Mazzarol, 2014; Stam, 2015). As Foss et al. (2019) highlight, policy is also a context-specific force, embedded in a country's institutional framework. Accordingly, policy has considerable ability to influence entrepreneurial behaviour locally, regionally, nationally and globally (Welter & Smallbone, 2011).

Entrepreneurship policy also serves as a means for highlighting opportunities and encouraging innovation across a broad range of industries. Similarly, policy provides economic, social, cultural and regional flexibility in the sense that policies can be targeted towards specific industries, specific types of entrepreneurs and specific types of locations. Thus, entrepreneurship policy is not only a tool for stimulating innovation and economic growth, but also for breaking down barriers and enfranchising individuals, groups and communities that have been excluded, for whatever reason (OECD, 2020).

In addition to its role played in advancing economic development, job creation and innovation, entrepreneurship policy can also be used a means for creating social as well as economic benefits. Entrepreneurial firms provide their communities with new products and services while also providing jobs, thereby improving quality of life. Similarly, the presence of new firms contributes to a healthier and more competitive marketplace. In doing so, they benefit customers through lower prices and higher quality for their products and services. Importantly, entrepreneurial firms are part of the 'glue' that keeps communities dynamic through community engagement, and with that, contributions of time, talent and resources. In essence, policies that promote and support entrepreneurship also promote and support strong communities and, by extension, strong families.

It has also been acknowledged that entrepreneurship policy development is not without its challenges. Policy makers must differentiate between entrepreneurship and small business policies; appreciate that policy initiatives offered in isolation are likely to be ineffective; and realise that when it comes to developing women's entrepreneurship policy, 'one size does not fit all' (Mason & Brown, 2014).

WOMEN'S ENTREPRENEURSHIP POLICY

Women entrepreneurs make a significant contribution to economic development globally. According to the Global Entrepreneurship Monitor report (GEM, 2021), an estimated 274 million women globally are involved in business start-ups, 139 million women are business owners/managers of established businesses, and 144 million women are informal investors (p. 14). Women entrepreneurs predominate within government, health, education and social services sectors. Early-stage women entrepreneurs operate mainly in the wholesale/retail sector, which accounts for 51.3% of women entrepreneurs operating in this sector globally.

Scholars recognise that women's entrepreneurship is important because it provides a means to advance gender equality in industries, communities and counties around the world (GEM, 2021, p. 13). However, while the body of academic scholarship in the field of women's entrepreneurship has expanded significantly in recent years, the specific issue of *women's entrepreneurship policy* has not attracted concerted academic attention (Ahl & Nelson, 2015; Foss et al., 2019).

A report by the OECD, in conjunction with the Global Women's Entrepreneurship Policy Research network (OECD-GWEP, 2021), explored entrepreneurship policies with a gender lens across 27 countries in Europe, Africa, Asia, North America, South America and Australasia. The international policy insight notes within the report addressed women's entrepreneurship policy across several different themes, including, fostering a gender-sensitive entrepreneurship culture, strengthening the design and delivery of supports, building entrepreneurial skills, facilitating access to financial capital, supporting networks, and building a supportive regulatory environment. Findings revealed countries with no dedicated women's entrepreneurship policy, as well as some countries where there were policies without programmes or programmes without policies. This was considered by the research team to be a fundamental flaw in the women's entrepreneurship agenda globally. If governments are serious about encouraging and supporting women entrepreneurs, they need to have a dedicated women's entrepreneurship policy, embed this into their country's overarching policy framework and operationalise it by constructing relevant programmes on the ground. The report also found that, in those countries with a visible entrepreneurship policy focused on women, women are still referred to as a 'minority', 'lacking skills', 'in deficit' and needing to be 'fixed'. Access to financial capital was considered to be one of the most significant barriers to women's entrepreneurship and, in general, more support was being offered to high-growth, high-tech and export-oriented sectors where women do not typically predominate. There was recognition across the 27 country insight notes within the report that systematic monitoring and evaluation mechanisms were missing from most policies and programmes, and there was an acknowledgement that policies and programmes need to be linked to the wider entrepreneurial ecosystem if they are to be effective. One of the most significant conclusions from the report was that representatives from the target group, i.e. women, need to be involved in the design, delivery and management of women's entrepreneurship policies.

Such deficits in effective policy provision have also been highlighted by GEM (2021) researchers, who stress the need to develop policies that directly support women business owners:

> But public policies in many countries have still fallen short, with insufficient support for family care, schooling and small business impacts. Policies and relief programs that are best for women are also best for small business owners in general and for families … (GEM, 2021, p. 21)

In view of the above, we felt that women's entrepreneurship policy merited further academic attention, and that a book dedicated to this topic – that explores and critiques contemporary policy instruments as well as signposting towards potential policy solutions – would deepen understanding in this area. Ultimately, our goal was to contribute towards the already valuable body of scholarship in this field and help raise awareness among policy makers, programme managers and academics of the dangers associated with gender-blind entrepreneurship policies. Echoing our GEM colleagues (GEM, 2021), if we have one message to reiterate with this book it is that 'one size' entrepreneurship policies simply 'do not fit all' because they ignore the gender dimension and, as a result, do not actually support women entrepreneurs effectively.

OVERVIEW AND CONTRIBUTION OF CHAPTERS

In compiling this edited collection, we drew on scholars from the Global Women's Entrepreneurship Policy Research network (GWEP) – a group of scholars from over 35 countries, researching, critiquing and exchanging knowledge on women's entrepreneurship policy. We also drew on the broader international community of entrepreneurship policy scholars. Our aim was to address current gaps in policy scholarship by offering a collection of policy-related chapters on women's entrepreneurship from around the globe. We wanted to provide insights into how entrepreneurship policy is constructed and operationalised in different countries; the extent to which entrepreneurship policy may or may not be gendered; the different geographical, political, institutional and cultural contexts for women's entrepreneurship; and the challenges faced by policy makers in formulating entrepreneurship supports. Where possible, we also wanted to provide examples of effective policy solutions in practice. Accordingly, we designed our 'call for chapters' with a wide lens to capture the diversity of policy concepts, perspectives and practices on this topic. We invited conceptual and empirical contributions that addressed the issue of women's entrepreneurship policy regionally, nationally or internationally, and adopted a range of perspectives/theoretical lenses. We welcomed chapters with the potential to enhance our understanding of women's entrepreneurship policy, as well as those that could highlight the gendered nature of entrepreneurship policy in specific geographical contexts. Given the recent COVID-19 crisis, chapters that critiqued national policy responses to the pandemic as they relate to women's entrepreneurship were particularly welcomed. Our ultimate goal with this book was to use the various contributions to carve out an ambitious future research agenda for the field.

Following a rigorous review process involving assessment by the editorial team and by 'blind' peer reviewers, we settled on a total of eight chapters, in addition to our introductory chapter. We worked closely with the authors/author teams to refine their contributions, and we are grateful to them for their patience and diligence in finalising their chapters.

The first chapter in our collection – 'Exploring the Gender Gap in Women's Entrepreneurship: A Narrative Policy Analysis' (Chapter 2), by Patricia G. Greene and Candida Brush – acknowledges the positive impact women entrepreneurs have on economic growth and development but highlights a lack of understanding of the many challenges women entrepreneurs face. Such challenges include but are not limited to a lack of effective policies linked to access to credit, resources and assets related to economic participation and political empowerment. The authors review current indices that reflect the gender gap globally and use the United States as a case study. Their study utilises a narrative policy framework analysis that considers how narratives across macro, meso and micro dimensions influence policy. Such analyses show that current approaches often isolate and individualise problems for women entrepreneurs, which in turn leads to less effective policies.

Greene and Brush offer two key conclusions from their study. The first relates to what they term 'false narratives' – accepted discourses that create blind spots that in turn limit gender equality in both the workplace and entrepreneurship. Such narratives may be based on culture or history, may be inaccurate and have rarely been updated; yet they tend to persist. The second linked conclusion relates to the fact that, despite their inaccuracy and out-datedness, such narratives ultimately become mechanisms to interpret the foundation of policy, and subsequently illuminate future pathways for policy formation. The authors offer several suggestions for change with regard to the crafting of policies, the deconstruction of narratives, directing training towards lenders and other providers within the entrepreneurial ecosystem, updating definitions and more focus on dimensions of context, embeddedness and intersectionality.

In Chapter 3 – Strategies to Redress Entrepreneurship Gender Gaps in Canada Revisited – Barbara J. Orser outlines rationales for women-focused entrepreneurship policies. She uses recommendations advanced in Canadian taskforces and policy reports, as well as a review of small business policies conducted by the Organisation for Economic Co-operation and Development (OECD, 2017) to critique the *Women Entrepreneurship Strategy* (Innovation Science and Economic Development Canada, 2018). The strategy, which includes a CAN$5 billion investment by the Government of Canada, is targeted at women-owned and women-led small and medium-sized enterprises (SMEs). This chapter provides evidence of the importance of country context when constructing policies to support women-identified entrepreneurs. It also highlights the importance of intersectional data when reporting on the status of women-owned SMEs. The fragility of women's entrepreneurship policies is highlighted alongside shifting political agendas and a lack of empirical evidence to inform effective women-focused initiatives.

Based on the evidence she presents in her chapter, Orser concludes that without political leadership, bureaucratic will and rigorous analysis, advocacy has limited impact on enacting women-focused small business policies. In particular, reflecting the negative effects of the COVID-19 crisis, she suggests that post-pandemic policies to support women need to respond to gaps that have been identified by data. She calls for more evidence-based research, more equity in policy making, arm's length assessment of impact and an avoidance of government strategies focused solely on picking winners.

'Entrepreneurship as a Losing Proposition for Women: Gendered Outcomes of Neo-liberal Entrepreneurship Policy in a Nordic Welfare State' (Chapter 4) is by Helene Ahl, Malin Tillmar, Karin Berglund and Katarina Pettersson. Here, the authors analyse 20 years of empirical research on women's entrepreneurship in Sweden to provide the backdrop for the current status quo. They find that privatisation has resulted in oligopolisation and masculinisation of market(s), and that gendered public sector practices have been reproduced in the private sector. This has resulted in women turning from low-wage labour to low-profit entrepreneurship.

Ahl et al. demonstrate how the neo-liberal government reforms in Sweden originally intended to improve women's position in society had mixed and often negative results. While they may have resulted in more women-owned businesses, they also helped perpetuate traditional gender hierarchies. The authors conclude that this situation is due to an unrealistic belief in the market mechanism, a disregard of the role of entrenched gender roles and expectations, and the exclusion of men's responsibility for household work from policy design. The authors call on policy makers to amend policies to reflect these aspects.

In Chapter 5 – 'Mapping Ethnic Minority Women Entrepreneurs' Support Initiatives: Experiences from the UK' – Helen Lawton Smith and Beldina Owalla focus on mapping the support initiatives available to ethnic minority women entrepreneurs in the UK. The chapter compares the support provided by targeted initiatives to mainstream programmes with the aim of identifying possible gaps. The authors draw on evidence from previous research focused on promoting diversity and inclusion in business innovation and adopt an entrepreneurial ecosystem model to frame their analysis. Findings highlight the fragmented nature of existing ethnic minority women's support networks, and the need to further develop *intermediaries* and *networks* within entrepreneurial ecosystems.

In their chapter, while the authors demonstrate a demand for an inclusive entrepreneurial ecosystems framework that provides support for ethnic minority women entrepreneurs, they also highlight that a more integrated understanding of the experiences of this group across different parts of the country is needed. The development of intermediaries and networks within ethnic minority women entrepreneurial ecosystems is proposed to help address barriers to accessing finance and markets. Lawton Smith and Owalla conclude that a greater understanding of the socio-economic factors that constrain ethnic minority women entrepreneurs is needed alongside a shift in policy to not only create more entrepreneurs but also to offer better support to existing ones.

In Chapter 6 – 'Institutional Work in Czech and US Business Assistance Programmes and Implications for Entrepreneurial Inclusion' – Nancy C. Jurik, Alena Křížková, Marie Pospíšilová and Gray Cavender use the institutional work approach to examine how business assistance programme (BAP) workers approach male-centric business contexts. The chapter analyses interview data from the Czech Republic, a transitional economy, and the United States, an advanced market economy, to ask: does the institutional work of BAP staff and business experts foster increased entrepreneurial inclusivity or the reinforcement of male-centric business models? Findings reveal that although some BAPs took a business-as-usual approach and saw no need to tailor their services to women or other transitional entrepreneurs, others developed more inclusive assistance models including intersectional understandings and strategies to challenge barriers to entrepreneurship and economic well-being. Policy implications offered in the chapter include: the need to provide more stable support for BAP programming that addresses the diversity of entrepreneur needs including low- as well as high-growth businesses, start-ups and ongoing businesses; and the need for assessment of family and entrepreneurship policy effects on women and other transitional entrepreneurs. The authors further suggest that lessons could be learned from some of the temporary COVID-19 pandemic measures that were introduced. For example, in the Czech Republic, during the first wave of the COVID-19 pandemic, an allowance (ošetřovné) was offered for parents to care for sick children up to ten years of age. This was temporarily extended to entrepreneurs and self-employed groups that were not previously eligible, helping equalize conditions for employees and entrepreneurs. This type of policy could be made permanent. In the United States, while COVID-19 saw the introduction of temporary assistance monies for families it also highlighted the continued lack of a universal healthcare plan for SMEs and their employees.

Chapter 7 – 'Barriers to Women's Entrepreneurship in Poland and Institutional Support', by Ewa Lisowska and Dariusz Leszczyński – investigates the barriers that have been impeding the formation and growth of female-owned businesses in Poland from 1989. The authors review the literature and present an analysis of institutional supports for Polish women entrepreneurs, covering the period 2000–2020. Based on the classification of barriers and the results of their desk research analysis, they construct a theoretical framework of institutional support for female entrepreneurs in Poland. Their conceptual model, which builds on Scott's (2014) theoretical framework of three pillars underlying contemporary institutions, is used as a basis to make relevant recommendations for institutional support that is tailored to the specific needs of women-owned businesses; these are grouped into seven thematic areas. These areas include: promoting work-life balance; creating an entrepreneurial culture and mitigating socio-cultural barriers; developing entrepreneurship skills and capabilities; providing access to social protection support and benefits; teaching entrepreneurship and small business management skills; promoting female role models and building entrepreneurial networks; and counteracting negative social stereotypes about women's entrepreneurship. The chapter contributes to the literature on women's entrepreneurship by developing a classification of barriers that negatively affect the creation and growth of women-owned firms. Directions for future research that focuses on the progress of female entrepreneurship in Poland are also offered.

In Chapter 8 – 'Beyond COVID-19: Women Entrepreneurs and E-Commerce Policy in the Asia-Pacific', by Patrice Braun, Naomi Birdthistle and Antoinette Flynn – the authors investigate whether pandemic mitigation policy responses in the Pacific region have considered the gender aspects of e-commerce and international trade. The study is positioned in an entrepreneurial ecosystem framework, with a focus on policy support for female entrepreneurship. It offers an overview of the impact of COVID-19 on women entrepreneurs in a pandemic-driven digital business environment, exploring region-specific pandemic mitigation measures and questioning whether such measures really assist women entrepreneurs' recovery from the health crisis. The authors argue that Pacific region policy responses were unimaginative from a gender perspective and failed to build an inclusive recovery. Policy makers in both countries only superficially acknowledged gender disadvantages and failed to enact meaningful women-focused supports during the pandemic.

The study advances the intertwined and mutually reinforcing concepts of e-commerce and international trade, and contributes to the discourse on the gendered digital divide as well as the need for inclusive entrepreneurial ecosystems. Some future directions and policy recommendations are also offered, including the suggestion that regions would benefit from policies that recognise and support the interdependent capabilities of digital literacy, e-commerce and international trade. The authors conclude that women's entrepreneurship policy needs to evolve to comprise much more inclusive resilience measures capable of reacting to and embracing changes in the digital landscape.

Our final chapter – 'Analysis of Ghana's and South Africa's Women Entrepreneurship Policies' (Chapter 9) – by Mavis S. B. Mensah and Evelyn Derera, explores women's entrepreneurship policies in Ghana and South Africa, a topic on which there is a paucity of research. Two core research questions are addressed in the chapter: first, what kind of women's entrepreneurship policies exist in each of these two countries? Second, to what extent do the policies of each country address the normative, cultural-cognitive and regulatory institutional policy requirements? Drawing on the transformative research paradigm, the authors present a content analysis of 25 purposively sampled policy instruments using an analytical framework developed from Scott's institutional policy framework. Findings reveal that, although both countries have normative, cultural-cognitive and regulatory women's entrepreneurship policies, Ghana's policy prescriptions are limited and fragmented. This is in contrast to South Africa, where policies are comprehensive and co-ordinated with other national policy and strategic documents.

The authors argue that the Ghanaian government needs to devote adequate attention to women's entrepreneurship in its national entrepreneurship policy, or even consider developing a separate national policy. Normative and cultural-cognitive policies need to be broadened to include infrastructure development and leadership empowerment of women entrepreneurs. Notwithstanding South Africa's more comprehensive and co-ordinated policies, a separate women's entrepreneurship policy there could help bring together elements from current women's entrepreneurship policy prescriptions into one document to ease implementation and co-ordination.

CONCLUSIONS

The chapters in this book have contributed to the ongoing discussion related to the many challenges women entrepreneurs continue to face globally as they navigate their entrepreneurial journey. Collectively, the chapters have identified important issues that need to be considered when designing policy supports for women entrepreneurs; they also signpost towards possible policy enhancements and solutions. This has been achieved by focusing on multiple themes, such as highlighting the gender gap in entrepreneurship and critiquing strategies to redress that gap; supporting ethnic minority women entrepreneurs; inclusion considerations within business assistance programmes; barriers to women's entrepreneurship; and assessing COVID-19 entrepreneurship strategies from a gender perspective. Detailed policy reviews, narrative analyses, feminist analyses, ecosystem frameworks and institutional theory were used by our authors to uncover hidden biases, highlight policy failings and identify potential solutions. Geographical coverage of these themes spanned the USA, Canada, Sweden, the UK and Poland, including comparative studies between the Czech Republic and the USA, territories within the Asia-Pacific region, and Ghana and South Africa.

While great strides have been made by governments worldwide to support women entrepreneurs through structured policy interventions, for the most part these have been hindered by a disregard for women's actual requirements, a lack of evaluative measures to assess effectiveness and a general gender-blindness. The COVID-19 pandemic has been shown to disproportionately affect women entrepreneurs across the globe, in some cases reversing previous progress that had been achieved on the women's entrepreneurship agenda.

The design of entrepreneurial supports is not always based on evidence, nor is it based on direct input from women entrepreneurs. Hence, it is hardly surprising that 'one size fits all' and 'mainstream' policy approaches continue to be perpetuated. Some policies offer a semblance of fit and/or effectiveness yet – when reviewed and assessed – have been found to do little to help women entrepreneurs in practice; this was particularly evident in the chapters that explored the impact of COVID-19 strategies or those that considered seemingly positive policies that collectively and inadvertently created an entrepreneurial environment that ultimately proved to be 'a losing proposition' for women. All of this suggests that much more needs to be done. Below we offer some areas that policy makers might consider in their future design of policy interventions.

Moving Forward

We posit that more effective and less fragile policy supports could be developed if policy makers were to focus on the following areas:

1.   Evaluation – embedding data collection and evaluation into programme design

All too often, policies are developed, approved and put into practice without incorporating an evaluative framework to track and measure outcomes. There are several risks associated with an omission of this sort. First, it is difficult to argue that a programme has achieved its goals without having accumulated empirical data on progress and outcomes. Second, it is equally difficult to argue for a continuation of funding, resources or the programme itself without results. Alternatively, data collection throughout creates opportunities for a 'mid-course correction' if the process for implementing a given policy goes off track. This is an important consideration, because policies and practices often need to pivot over time in order to stay alive, to stay relevant and to achieve their goals. Finally, collecting data and evaluating outcomes makes it possible for decision-makers to identify and share 'best practice' policies and programmes across industries, regions and countries. Each of these points attests to the need for developing and embedding an evaluative framework into policy interventions from the outset. Consistent with that is a corresponding need to accumulate an evidence base to address the current lack of empirical data needed for sound decision-making.

2.   Developing a separate and dedicated national women's entrepreneurship policy

If there's one message that comes through loud and clear in the chapters included in this book, it is that 'one size does not fit all'. Similarly, 'gender neutral' policies assuming that what works for male entrepreneurs will also work for women are less than optimal. As our authors point out, gender neutral policies make it all too easy for women entrepreneurs to be ignored, overlooked or simply left out. Thus, their position on the policy grid is more fragile and less likely to garner the levels and types of support required. A lack of programmatic data gathering, analysis and evaluation which would clearly point out gender gaps and differences is partially to blame for this dilemma. It is also somewhat easier to underestimate the potential of women-owned firms because they tend to be smaller and in more competitive, less technology-focused industries than men (OECD/European Commission, 2021). Because of this, women entrepreneurs face different types of challenges and experience greater difficulty when it comes to gaining access to resources such as financial capital and networks comprised of other entrepreneurs and business people

(Halabisky, 2018). A dedicated national women's entrepreneurship policy would help women 'connect', while also ensuring that the contributions of women-owned firms are recognized and valued. Correspondingly, a national policy of this type would 'institutionalize' the importance of supporting women entrepreneurs in ways that will help them launch and grow their firms.

3. Directly involving women in the design, development, management, delivery and evaluation of entrepreneurship policies and programmes

Women entrepreneurs have been more severely impacted by COVID-19 due to their size and industry concentration, coupled with a greater need to address homecare responsibilities. Thus, their road back from the worst days of the pandemic will be more arduous. Many countries are already experiencing a gender gap in entrepreneurship and, for a number of these, that gap has grown in the wake of COVID-19 (OECD/European Commission, 2021). As they now work towards rebuilding their economies, these countries have an opportunity to harness the economic, social and innovative potential of women entrepreneurs by incorporating them into the policy creation and decision-making process. Providing women entrepreneurs with a seat at the policy table is a means for providing a pathway to better policy formulation, delivery and outcomes. Specifically, including women in the policy dialogue would help mitigate the current overreliance on outdated, inaccurate and often false narratives about women's entrepreneurship. Similarly, the direct involvement of women in the policy setting process could go a long way toward ensuring that the individual and intersectional contexts of women entrepreneurs are recognised and taken into consideration, resulting in more tailored and inclusive supports.

4. Linking women's entrepreneurship policy to the broader entrepreneurial ecosystem

The development of a dedicated national women's entrepreneurship policy has the potential to benefit women entrepreneurs at all stages of their entrepreneurial journey. Creation of such a policy says that women entrepreneurs and their firms are a priority, and that they merit commitment, support and resources that will increase the likelihood of their success. It is important to note, however, that women's entrepreneurship policy cannot survive or succeed in a vacuum. Rather, it is essential to position women's entrepreneurship policy within the broader entrepreneurial ecosystem in order to achieve alignment with other policies affecting women. Alignment of this type can provide policy leverage by simultaneously channelling mutually reinforcing benefits in the form of programmes and practices towards women entrepreneurs. In contrast, misaligned policies will have the opposite effect, as the chapter by Helene Ahl, Malin Tillmar, Karin Berglund and Katarina Pettersson points out. In their example, taken from Sweden, seemingly positive strategies created an unfavourable environment for women, thereby perpetuating gender hierarchies. In particular, strategies to increase the number of women entrepreneurs were not linked to other policies such as those related to family support and household work, the lesson being that policies within the broader ecosystem need to be aligned in order to achieve their desired results.

Finally, in addressing the above, we call on policy makers to engage more closely with the scholarly community and take advantage of the narrative, feminist and institutional theoretical lenses adopted by researchers to gain a much deeper understanding of the complex phenomenon of women's entrepreneurship. In so doing, we encourage policy makers to abandon outdated and traditional mainstream policy approaches in favour of revolutionary, targeted and effective strategies designed to truly support women entrepreneurs regardless of the conditions they face. While efforts along these lines will require an acknowledgement of policy failings alongside a readiness to learn from other countries and contexts, they will undoubtedly result in an enhanced environment for women entrepreneurs, a stronger entrepreneurial ecosystem and a more robust economy.

REFERENCES

Ahl, H. & Nelson, T. (2015). How policy positions women entrepreneurs: A comparative analysis of state discourse in Sweden and the United States. *Journal of Business Venturing*, 30(2), 273–291.

Foss, L., Henry, C., Ahl, H. & Mikalsen, G.H. (2019). Women's entrepreneurship policy research: A 30-year review of the evidence. *Small Business Economics*, 53, 409–429. https://doi.org/10.1007/s11187-018-9993-8

GEM – Global Entrepreneurship Monitor. (2021). *Women's entrepreneurship 2020/21: Thriving through crisis*. Published by GERA, London. Available from: https://www.gemconsortium.org/file/open?fileId=50841 (last accessed 16 March 2022).

Halabisky, D. (2018). Policy brief on women's entrepreneurship. *OECD SME and Entrepreneurship Papers*, No. 8. OECD Publishing, Paris. https://doi.org/10.1787/dd2d79e7-en

Mason, C. & Brown, R. (2014). Entrepreneurial ecosystems and growth-oriented enterprises. OECD LEED programme. http://www.oecd.org/cfe/leed/Entrepreneurial-ecosystems. pdf (accessed 28 November 2015).

Mazzarol, T. (2014). Growing and sustaining entrepreneurial ecosystems: What they are and the role of government policy. Seaanz, Australia: Seaanz White Paper.

OECD. (2017). *SME and entrepreneurship policy in Canada*. OECD Studies on SMEs and Entrepreneurship series. Paris: OECD Publishing. https://doi.org/10.1787/9789264273467-en

OECD. (2020). *International compendium of entrepreneurship policies*. OECD Publishing, Paris. http://doi.org/10.1787/338f1873-en

OECD/European Commission. (2021). *The missing entrepreneurs 2021: Policies for inclusive entrepreneurship and self-employment*. OECD Publishing, Paris. https://doi.org/10.1787/71b7a9bb-en

OECD-GWEP. (2021). Entrepreneurship policies through a gender lens. OECD, Paris, 17 May. Available from: https://www.oecd.org/industry/entrepreneurship-policies-through-the-gender-lens-71c8f9c9-en.htm (last accessed 16 March 2022).

Scott, W.R. (2014). *Institutions and organizations: Ideas, interests, and identities*, 4th edn. Thousand Oaks, CA: Sage Publications Inc.

Stam, E. (2015). Entrepreneurial ecosystems and regional policy: A sympathetic critique. *European Planning Studies*, 23(9), 1759–1769.

Welter, F. & Smallbone, D. (2011). Institutional perspectives on entrepreneurial behavior in challenging environments. *Journal of Small Business Management*, 49(1), 107–125.

2. Exploring the gender gap in women's entrepreneurship: a narrative policy analysis

Patricia G. Greene and Candida G. Brush

INTRODUCTION

> At the dawn of the 2020s building fairer and more inclusive economies must be the goal of global, national and industry leaders. (World Economic Forum, 2020)

> ... no country, community, or economy can achieve its potential or meet the challenges of the 21st century without the full and equal participation of women and men, girls and boys. (World Bank Group, 2021a)

> Gender inequality remains a major barrier to human development. (United Nations Development Programme, 2021)

Gender equality is a human rights issue, most often defined as 'women and men having the same opportunities, rights, and responsibilities within all areas of life' (Ahl, 2019, p. 1). From the economic perspective, advancing women's participation is a priority for global development organizations, given that this participation serves to improve economies for all. However, economic participation may mean very different things in different contexts. For instance, gender gaps are measured in a variety of ways, places and times, and using different theoretical approaches and methodologies (UN HDR, 2020; WEF, 2020). These indices typically compare men and women across countries based on certain factors, for instance economic empowerment, political leadership, health, knowledge, living standards and a variety of other factors. However, the focus is largely on women as employees or individuals in society. Currently, women make up 40 percent of the global work force (Kelley et al., 2015). Nevertheless, the status of women who are business owners and therefore employers, even if only employers of themselves, remains less clear.

Across countries, the importance of female entrepreneurship for economic development is widely accepted and numerous studies demonstrate the positive impact of female entrepreneurs on economic growth and development (Elam et al., 2019). Further, economies characterized by high levels of women's entrepreneurship are more resilient to financial crises and experience economic slowdowns less frequently (Elam et al., 2019; Meunier et al., 2017). Overall, entrepreneurship almost uniformly is presented as a pathway to provide economic stability for women, and subsequently their families, while also serving as a pathway to political, social and personal empowerment.

Missing is an approach that links gender gap issues and women business owners in a coherent manner that would allow for greater understanding of the current situation and future potentialities. Gender gaps continue to be pervasive and are certainly evident in women's entrepreneurial activities. Women face hurdles in cultural, political, legal and social factors as these constrain women worldwide, especially as they relate to economic participation and opportunity, and political empowerment (WEF, 2020). In summary, women-owned enterprises are smaller and disadvantaged in their access to credit, resources and assets (UN Secretary-General's High-Level Panel on Women's Economic Empowerment, 2016, p. 2). Given the importance of women's entrepreneurship and the implications of gender gaps, there is strong motivation to better understand the causes, and therefore possible solutions to these disparities around the world.

In this chapter we ask, 'How might a narrative analysis enhance policies addressing gender gaps in women's entrepreneurship?' We will first briefly review the indices used to assess gender gaps and to present where and how entrepreneurship is currently addressed. We will then present an overview of women as entrepreneurs. Using the United States as a case example, we review the current state of policy for women and entrepreneurship and introduce the Narrative Policy Framework Analysis as a means to explore possible applications to drive improved policy. We close with implications and next steps for our research.

GENDER GAP INDICES

The World Economic Forum defines the gender gap as 'the difference between women and men as reflected in social, political, intellectual, cultural, or economic attainment or attitudes' (Harris, 2017, p. 1). Perrin (2021) attributes the first gender gap analysis to Yllö (1984), who recognized the insufficiency of individual and interpersonal levels of analysis to fully explain gender equalities, hypothesizing that 'Males and females have different access to resources because of institutionalized inequalities' (Yllö, 1984, p. 3). Since then, numerous measures and methods have been developed and applied by organizations around the world to parse the gender gap, and these vary depending on definitions and metrics. In 1995 the UN Development Programme

(UNDP) introduced the Gender-Related Development Index (GDI) and the Gender Empowerment Measure (GEM) as complementary measures intended to raise awareness of gender inequality issues (Schüler, 2006). GDI was built from the Human Development Index and focuses on dimensions of a long and healthy life, knowledge and standards of living (http://hdr.uned dp.org/en/content/gender-development-index-gdi). GEM counts heads. As examples, for political empowerment GEM includes the number of parliamentary seats and for economic participation it looks at the share of administrative, professional, technical and managerial positions held by women and men, and then includes power over economic resources measured as the estimated earning income. To provide methodological improvements, in 2010 the UNDP released two new measures, the Gender Inequality Index (GII) which is another measure of gender inequality, also using the dimensions of reproductive health, empowerment and the labor market and the GDI New Gender Development Index (focusing on a long and healthy life, knowledge and standards of living: http://hdr.undp.org/en/content/gender-inequality-index-gii) (Schüler, 2006).

However, the UNDP is not the only program attempting to assess the gender gap (Branisa et al., 2014), with organizations including the OECD (SIGI), World Economic Forum (GGGI), Social Watch (GEI), the European Institute for Gender Equality (EU-GEI) and even the Global Gender Office of International Union for Conservation of Nature (EGI UNDP, 2015). Across these indices, the economic equality measures are consistently those of labor force participation and income.

Additional approaches to evaluating the gender gap have also emerged. In 2009 the World Bank launched Women, Business, and the Law, a regular study of the laws and regulations that impact women's economic inclusion. These studies document policies related to freedom of movement, decisions to participate in the workplace, pay, marriage, parents, assets, pension, and specifically consider entrepreneurship.[1] This program is particularly unique in that while the other indices mentioned here could be considered to inform policy, this one inventories policy.

While the gender gap indices may vary as to content and process, they share a common goal of gender equality. 'Gender equality is considered achieved when women and men have the same rights and opportunities across all sections of society, and when their behaviors, aspirations and needs are equally valued and favored' (Perrin, 2021, p. 3).

WOMEN AS ENTREPRENEURS

Globally, 252 million women around the world are entrepreneurs and another 153 million women are operating established businesses, according to the Global Entrepreneurship Monitor 2018/2019 Report on Women's Entrepreneurship

(Elam et al., 2019). In recent years, the rate of women's Total Entrepreneurial Activity (TEA) rose to an average of 10.2 percent closing the gender gap by 3 percent since the 2017 report, which provides an analysis of 59 economies (Kelley et al., 2017). This was approximately three-quarters of the rate for men. Within the same study, 17.6 percent of the women surveyed intended to start a business within the next three years. This is only about four points less than for men. And to continue the entrepreneurial spectrum, women's rate of business discontinuance was approximately 10 percent lower for women (2.9 percent) than for men (3.2 percent) (Elam et al., 2019).

There are many areas of similarity among women and men entrepreneurs. According to GEM data, the gender gap in terms of perceptions of opportunities, ease of starting a business and perceptions that entrepreneurship is a good career has narrowed significantly around the world. Despite positive trends in narrowing the gender gap and growth in entrepreneurial activity, however, there are some unique differences in how women entrepreneurs are doing entrepreneurship. First, women entrepreneurs are industrially segregated in the sense that they are more prevalent in wholesale and retail trade, government/health/education and social services and less prevalent in the information and communications technology sectors. Second, women are more likely to work as solo entrepreneurs. Third, women entrepreneurs may have lower growth aspirations, measured as expecting to add more than six employees in the next five years (Elam et al., 2019). And fourth, the last year has shown that context beyond institutional structures needs to be considered and expanded to include situations such as global pandemics.

In 2018 the US Small Business Administration reported that women were equal or majority owners of 45 percent of all US privately held businesses (12.3 million firms).[2] In 2019 the Global Entrepreneurship Monitor noted that women's participation in entrepreneurship marked an all-time high with Total Entrepreneurial Activity (TEA) rates of 18.3 percent for men and 16.6 percent for women, resulting in a narrowing of the gender gap to an all-time low of less than 2 percent (Kelley et al., 2020). Generally, the trends show increased levels of opportunity perceptions, growing confidence in perceived capabilities and more proactiveness in 2019/2020 on the part of women (Kelley et al., 2020). Thus, it appears that some of the gender gap between men and women entrepreneurs in the US as measured by TEA is narrowing, at least in part, because women are more likely to perceive opportunities, to have greater confidence in their capabilities and to be more favorably inclined toward starting a business. Nevertheless, women continue to start businesses in sectors that have lower entry barriers, are more highly competitive and are more often local in scope. Further, women have lower growth expectations than men in terms of adding employees.

Most recently, while early clinical evidence shows men are more heavily impacted by the health effects of the COVID-19 pandemic (Curley, 2020), the resulting economic crisis is affecting women entrepreneurs disproportionately hard (UN Women, 2020; Werner, 2020; WEF, 2021). In the absence of school, childcare, or eldercare services, women entrepreneurs bear most of the burden of family care (Manolova et al., 2020). The implication is that policy support for small businesses generally may not effectively address the challenges or needs of women entrepreneurs.

POLICY AND ENTREPRENEURSHIP

'Policy is the domain in which designated actors (legislators) propose and enact solutions to public problems' (Brush and Greene, 2016). To this end, countries worldwide have created policies to encourage, support and scale entrepreneurship and economic development. Overall, governments and NGOs around the world present messaging and promote activities to support women's entrepreneurial development as a key element for building economies. Some consider policy to be the most important component of an entrepreneurial ecosystem (Foss et al., 2019). As such, regulatory domains may be viewed quite broadly, including issues of taxation, financial services, telecommunications, transportation, labor markets, immigration, industry support, education and training, infrastructure and health (Mazzarol, 2014). In other words, basically any issue that can throw challenges at how we live our lives.

Despite the popularity and proliferation of policies for women entrepreneurs and women's entrepreneurship there are many challenges (Brush and Greene, 2016; Henry et al., 2017). The consideration of policies directed at women's entrepreneurship has been the focus of several recent articles, where scholars have questioned the underlying assumptions embedded in these policies. For example, Ahl and Nelson (2015) dove into the underlying question of how policies position women, by asking, 'What is the impact of policies on the overall position of women in the context of life opportunities and equality?' (p. 2). They concluded that there were six main assumptions, which they describe as 'historical' and 'embedded.'

1. Imperative of economic growth before gender equality
2. The male norm of entrepreneurship
3. The assumption of women as 'different'
4. The exclusion of men in the policy dialogue
5. The constitution of entrepreneurship as an individual undertaking
6. The exclusion of family and reproductive work as part of the entrepreneur's life commitment (pp. 2–3).

Alternatively, other scholars have noted some of the challenges resulting from policies directed to women entrepreneurs and women's entrepreneurship (Henry et al., 2017). Policy implications to date for women's entrepreneurship are 'mostly vague, conservative and centered on identifying skills gaps in women entrepreneurs that need to be fixed, thus isolating and individualizing any perceived problem' (Foss et al., 2019, p. 409). As noted by Foss et al. (2019), there are two approaches, individualizing and isolating, both potentially problematic for creating effective policy. We explore these two approaches in more detail below.

INDIVIDUALIZING

Individualizing the perceived problems keeps us in a deficit model that we, and others (Leitch et al., 2018; Marlow, 2014), have called out for years. To have a deficit of anything, you need to have an accepted amount of something that is considered desirable. It also means that the 'type' of something that matters is also relevant, as this guides what is actually measured. In the case of entrepreneurship, this can be looked at as having a desirable, or at least acceptable, quantity and quality of opportunities, all types of resources, and leadership. With the deficit model, if an individual woman does not have the defined basket of resources seen/specified as needed with the requisite skill set to put them together, her job is to see that she gains that skill set, resources, etc. Once she looks and acts in a manner to match expectations, her likelihood of being a success will increase. And success is also pre-defined in an economic model to match expectations.

The most significant underlying challenge with the deficit model is that the expectations are set from a world of work and home that developed and set role expectations centuries ago, and for which change has been slow. Understanding women in the context of entrepreneurship has also been slow. The first notable article on women's entrepreneurship appeared in the mid-1970s. This pioneering article, 'Entrepreneurship, A New Female Frontier,' was based on interviews with 20 female entrepreneurs (Schwartz, 1976). Following contemporary research in entrepreneurship at the time, Schwartz examined the traits, motivations and attitudes of women entrepreneurs, concluding that the primary motivators for women in this sample were the 'need to achieve,' job satisfaction, economic payoffs and independence, the same motivators as were found for male entrepreneurs (Collins and Moore, 1964). However, unlike their male counterparts, Schwartz found that women entrepreneurs reported experiencing credit discrimination during the capital formation stage. Given that the Equal Credit Act was not enacted in the United States until 1975, this was a sign of the times (Greene et al., 2004).

For the next three decades, the bulk of academic research about women business owners, or women entrepreneurs sought to uncover differences and disparities between men and women, considering whether or not they were equally likely to engage in entrepreneurial activity, or the extent to which organizational and management practices differed, if access to funding varied or whether there were performance differences (Jennings and Brush, 2013). Not only has the research been heavily focused on comparing men and women, but the vast majority of research, which some estimate to be more than 90 percent, is focused on populations of men entrepreneurs (Brush et al., 2020). As a result, the conclusions about differences from men entrepreneurs and their businesses led to implications about the deficits of women entrepreneurs and their ventures, and recommendation for education, training, policies and programs to bring women up to the level of their counterparts.

Only recently has research begun to focus on what might be learned from the business models that women entrepreneurs create, or to consider the positive influences of their businesses on ecosystems (Brush et al., 2019; Elam et al., 2019). There is evidence that social networking behaviors of women and men entrepreneurs vary within ecosystems, especially in the way that entrepreneurs construct their networks, with men being more aggressive in the process (McAdam et al., 2019; Neumeyer and Santos, 2018). Other research shows that women perceive different levels of social support in ecosystems (Sperber and Linder, 2019). Hechavarría and Ingram (2019) find that the prevalence of entrepreneurship is highest for women when the entrepreneurial ecosystem features low barriers to entry, supportive policy to women entrepreneurs, minimal commercial and legal infrastructure and a normative culture that supports entrepreneurship.

ISOLATING

A second major limitation has to do with how problems or challenges facing women entrepreneurs are perceived, which is as a singular, stand-alone, isolated problem. More specifically, the policy initiatives that are offered as supporting entrepreneurship focus on one aspect of women business owners' or women entrepreneurs' activities; for instance, helping women to develop start-up skills. This approach isolates both women and a particular aspect of start-up behavior. The reality is that start-up skills might be related to women's start-up circumstances (e.g., social support from their families, or household responsibilities). Governmental structures are designed to address an issue, or related area of issues, and as a result, often struggle with the idea of intersectionality, whether referring to groups of people or groups of challenges. Addressing women's entrepreneurship, we see silos related to women and entrepreneurship, an intersectionality that in both research and practice receives increased attention (Ahl and Nelson, 2015). These intersecting nodes are evident in the frameworks discussed above, pertaining to areas such as women, caregiving responsibilities and their businesses, or women, industrial access and their businesses. The challenge for policy makers is finding which intersecting node(s) to address, and how.

POLICY ON WOMEN'S ENTREPRENEURSHIP: THE CASE OF THE UNITED STATES

In order to best understand policy on women's entrepreneurship it is necessary to understand what policy actually exists. For the U.S., a review of Congress.gov's website provides the background for this type of exploration. Congress.gov is a federal website designed to provide up-to-date accounts of all policy activity for the U.S. Policy initiatives are monitored from the time of proposal through enactment. A search for entrepreneur + women for the time period covering the last ten years yielded 19 laws/resolutions that were enacted, and, for most of these, women entrepreneurs were included as only a tangential interest. These laws may be considered in four categories: see below: Appropriations, Disaster Recovery, Foreign Affairs, and Economic Advancement through Entrepreneurship (see Table 2.1).

Half of the policies created that included references to entrepreneurship and women were appropriations bills and/or resolutions. In each of these, more attention was paid to entrepreneurship in general and/or other types of women-related factors as opposed to focusing on women entrepreneurs specifically. One consistent inclusion was support for the Women's Bureau of the Department of Labor (although the amount of financial support has decreased recently). This office is dedicated to the support of working women but does include recognition of women business owners as part of its constituency. Appropriation laws have also mandated enhanced reporting on procurement goals related to women business owners and increased access to microfinance funds. Relatedly, STEM education for women was also supported.

The two disaster recovery laws were each prompted by a quite different type of disaster. The RISE Act (Recovery Improvements for Small Entities) after the Disaster Act of 2015 was prompted by superstorm Sandy and, most recently, the CARES (Coronavirus Aid, Relief and Economic Security) Act of 2020 was a reaction to the COVID-19 pandemic. Both Acts included support for the Women's Business Centers program of the Small Business Administration with the objective of providing counseling, training and other related services. In addition, the CARES Act directed the Administrator of the Small Business Administration to issue guidance for those provided loans in order to prioritize small businesses in 'underserved and rural markets, including veterans and members of the military community, small business owned by

Women's entrepreneurship policy

Table 2.1   *U.S. policy initiatives for women entrepreneurs 2010–2020*

Appropriations	Disaster recovery	Foreign aid	Economic advancement through entrepreneurship
115-245 Department of Defense and Labor, Health and Human Services, and Education Appropriations Act, 2019 and Continuing Appropriations Act, 2019	116-136 CARES Act Coronavirus Aid, Relief, and Economic Security Act	115-442 Protecting Girls' Access to Education in Vulnerable Settings Act	115-6 Promoting Women in Entrepreneurship Act
115-232 John S. McCain National Defense Authorization Act for Fiscal Year 2019	114-88 Recovery Improvements for Small Entities (RISE) After Disaster Act of 2015	114-24 Girls Count Act of 2015	114-38 Veterans Entrepreneurship Act of 2015
115-91 National Defense Authorization Act for Fiscal Year 2018	112-81 Middle Class Tax Relief and Job Creation Act of 2012	114-27 Trade Preferences Extension Act of 2015	113-128 Workforce Innovation and Opportunity Act
115-141 Consolidated Appropriations Act, 2018			111-358 America Competes Reauthorization Act of 2010
114-328 National Defense Authorization Act for Fiscal Year 2017			111-13 Serve America Act
113-76 Consolidated Appropriations Act, 2014			
112-55 Consolidated and Further Continuing Appropriations Act, 2012			
112-81 National Defense Authorization Act for Fiscal Year 2012			

social and economically disadvantaged individuals ... women, and businesses in operation for less than two years' (Congress.gov).

Part of U.S. foreign aid policy is to support entrepreneurial education on and training for women, especially in geographical areas of conflict. While this type of support is found throughout the appropriations bills over the years, the three bills cited in this category specifically called for the U.S. to support entrepreneurial training for girls and women.

The fourth category contains the six federal laws passed in the last ten years that specifically focus upon, or include as a category, women entrepreneurs.

- Promoting Women in Entrepreneurship Act (115-6) authorized the National Science Foundation to support entrepreneurial programs for women.
- Veterans Entrepreneurship Act of 2015 (114-38), while developed to amend a previous Small Business Act to increase access to capital for veteran entrepreneurs, also required a report assessing the level of outreach to female veterans by the Small Business Administration.
- Workforce Innovation and Opportunity Act (113-128) mandated improvement of employment training and education programs in the U.S. and specifically referred to the promotion of entrepreneurial skills training and microenterprise services. While women business owners were not a separate focus, the Act included a mandate that women should have an equal opportunity to participate. Notably, the Act also required a study on equivalent pay for women and men.
- The America Competes Reauthorization Act of 2010 (111-358) firmly connected STEM education with the teaching of innovation and entrepreneurship. The Act included the goal of increasing participation in STEM by women and underrepresented minorities.
- Serve America Act (111-13) was designed to update the National and Community Service Act of 1990, with one stated purpose of recognizing and increasing the impact of social entrepreneurs. The Act included the mandate of 'providing educational and work skill support for girls and empowering women to achieve independence' (Congress.gov).

Overall, these policy initiatives are limited by the isolation of the problem and individualism of the solutions noted earlier. Leaving aside the appropriations, where it is harder to determine exactly what funding was provided for women's programs, the majority of the other 11 programs heavily emphasize education and training for young women, disadvantaged women, women veterans, or women in areas of conflict. The disaster relief programs, which were short-term funds, did have the effect of serving women well, largely because they own a proportionately high number of businesses in retail, consumer services, professional services and foods. On the other hand, the four programs for economic advancement all focus on providing skill development, training and equal opportunity to participants. While there are benefits to all of these, the reality is that these policy initiatives do not address the challenges of growth or acquisition of growth capital. To do this, policy initiatives need to do training for stakeholders who control finances and allocate funding to women entrepreneurs in order to eliminate biases, stereotypes and other challenges (Brush and Greene, 2020; Foss et al., 2019).

The intersectionality of working women/women business owners raises some sets of questions. However, there is another layer of intersectionality around these problems to be considered, looking at not only women business owners/working women, but also demographics: such as sex with race and ethnicity. In this case, the challenges that women of color, or those from rural areas may have, cannot all be solved with business training and skill development. Many of the challenges here lie as much with access to opportunities as access to resources. And the overarching intersectionality is the ultimate miss – women entrepreneurs as working women, which can then be combined with other demographics. So how is it that policies are created that seem to miss the mark in solving the problems for women entrepreneurs? The next section explores a narrative policy framework.

NARRATIVE POLICY FRAMEWORK

Narrative has been a part of the field for entrepreneurship for some time and it has been applied broadly. Entrepreneurship researchers have looked at narrative as method (Hjorth and Steyaert, 2004; Larty and Hamilton, 2011), as well as by topics: demographics such as age (Clarke and Holt, 2010), sex (Sinisalo and Komulainen, 2008), identity (Jones and Betta, 2008; Phillips et al., 2013) and failure (Mantere et al., 2013). Most simply, Gartner (2007) describes narrative as simply 'an analysis of the stories that people tell' (p. 613), notably reminding us that narratives include not only how things are, but also how things should be, making them a combination of objective reporting and subjective considerations. Ahl and Nelson (2015) illustrated this approach with their use of discourse analysis in which they explored the underlying objectives to consider the impact of policies on women's lives.

In order to further explore the concept of policy along the intersections of women as entrepreneurs and women as participants in the workplace, we selected the Narrative Policy Framework (NPF) as a tool to guide our discussion. NPF is a means of studying policy process (Shanahan et al., 2018) and has been used across a variety of policy domains, including the Arab Spring (O'Bryan et al., 2014), Indian nuclear power debates (Gupta et al., 2014), fracking in Scotland (Stephan, 2020) and post WWII education policy (Veselkova and Beblavý, 2014). We were intrigued by the framework given that it is built on five key assumptions, each of which has the potential to advance our understanding on the relationship between public policy and women's entrepreneurship (Shanahan et al., 2018).

1. *Social construction.* Recognizes that both objective and subjective approaches are needed to understand public policy which is socially constructed while also existing within laws of nature (Jones and McBeth, 2010; Jones et al., 2014).
2. *Bounded relativity.* Meanings of social constructions vary, are bounded by beliefs and have some degree of stability over time. Meanings may also be revised for convenience (Jones and McBeth, 2010; Jones et al., 2014).
3. *Generalizable structural elements.* Narratives are made up of specific and identifiable structures.
4. *'Homo narrans'.* Stories are important to people, this recognizes the centrality of narratives in human cognition and communication (Shanahan et al., 2018).
5. *Narratives work at three interacting levels.* The macro (institutional/cultural), meso (social groups) and micro (individuals) (Shanahan et al., 2018).

The use of the levels allows for a more precise articulation of each narrative. Micro refers to the individual carriers and users of the rules, the economic actors. Within the context of our NPF application, micro refers to those individuals who form and shape policy narratives (Shanahan et al., 2018). Therefore, for our purposes, these are both the policy makers and women as entrepreneurs, and working women.

The meso level refers to the individual systems that become organized, building from Granovetter's classic recognition of the embeddedness of people in social structures at both the formal and informal levels (Granovetter, 1985 in Kim et al., 2016). These are the social groups which may serve as mediators or moderators in a social structure between the macro and micro level (Caldwell and Mays, 2012). While within entrepreneurship research the meso level has been studied, it has far less often been integrated into multilevel models (Kim et al., 2016). For NPF the meso level includes 'policy actors' – coalitions and organizations with a focus on policy construction and communication (Shanahan et al., 2018). For our case, this could be considered as working women's organizations such as Business and Professional Women and women's entrepreneurship groups such as Women's Business Centers.

The macro level consists of the population structure systems of meso (Dopfer et al., 2004), or in other works, macro is defined as the 'policy context' (Caldwell and Mays, 2012). When considering the Narrative Policy Framework, Ménard and his co-authors use the institutional perspective to consider the macro level as the ground rules for activities supporting produc-

Table 2.2   *The existing narratives – U.S.*

	Macro	Meso	Micro
Narrative examples			
Women in the Workplace	The increased percent of women in the workforce means that working women are no longer a segment needing support. Women have achieved parity with men in nearly all work roles.	Women need separate support organizations to support their professional advancement. There are not enough women with the qualifications to fill CEO and board positions.	Women are softer/gentler leaders. Women lack confidence and aspirations for growth.
Women in Entrepreneurship	A company must be owned 51% by a woman to be 'women-owned.' Women are in the 'minority' of small businesses.	Women have equal access to resources to grow their businesses, including financial. Women need sources of support and assistance that are separate from men.	Women business owners are a homogenous group. Women lack confidence to build and aspirations to grow.

tion and exchange (Ménard et al., 2018), as well as informal institutions such as customs, norms and beliefs. NPF is designed to be dynamic, calling out changes in institutions and the resultant impact or potential impact on policy (Shanahan et al., 2018). For our purposes, the macro level captures the institutional structures that impact women as entrepreneurs and as working women.

THE METHODOLOGY OF NPF

NPF has been applied using a variety of experimental and non-experimental methods, including surveys, interviews, focus groups and content analysis. Narratives themselves have been assessed through consideration of elements such as settings, characters, (heroes, villains and victims), plots, morals, belief systems, and strategies and solutions (Shanahan et al., 2018). Our preliminary use of NPF is to first identify which narratives, or stories, would be best suited to a second step of analysis for future research. As such, we launch this research project with a select summary of some long-standing narratives related to women entrepreneurs (Brush and Greene, 2021), together with the potential policy implications for each (see Table 2.2).

Using the core assumptions of the NPF as a structural guide, we identified representative narratives across the macro, meso and micro levels, for both women in the workplace and women in entrepreneurship. We considered the degree to which the narratives were socially constructed (both objective/ subjective aspects), bounded by beliefs, had specific identifiable structures and were important to people.

WOMEN IN THE WORKFORCE: NARRATIVE DISCUSSION

The macro-level idea is that a more equal percentage of women in the work-force suggests there is no need for tailored support. This is a narrative promulgated by The Heritage Foundation, a U.S. based conservative think tank, who included this thought in an annual report as a reason for suggesting that support for the Women's Bureau of the Department of Labor be discontinued. Further, even though there may be parity in numbers, the actual perceptions of equity in pay may be quite different. A recent PayScale salary survey of 27,000 workers in the U.S. showed that only 60 percent of all respondents believe that, in their workplace, men and women have equal opportunities.[3] More telling is the gender disparity whereby 74 percent of men and 48.9 percent of women believe opportunities are equal. The percentages are also different for Black (41.5 percent) and Hispanic (49.7 percent) women. When considering most workplaces, the PayScale responses suggest that 62.2 percent of men and 35.4 percent of women believe there is equal opportunity.

A 2010 report by the International Trade Union Confederation shows that there is significant occupational segregation, whereby women are concentrated in three industries: education and health services; trade, transportation and utilities; and local government.[4] The industries where women are employed (i.e., health and social services) are typically low-paid and wages have not risen substantially. Occupational segregation leads to career challenges, and disparities in decision-making in organizations. While the narrative that parity in numbers suggests there is no need for support of women, this single metric misses other important factors. The reality is that proportionality of women in the workforce does not translate into gender parity in income, power or benefits.

The second narrative, that women have achieved parity with men in nearly all work roles reinforces the message that the workforce is now inclusive and equitable, therefore policy attention and resources are best used elsewhere. By contrast, a recent study by McKinsey, reporting data for the sixth year on women in the workplace, indicates that women continue to lose ground at the very first step up to manager.[5] They found that for every 100 men promoted to manager, only 85 women were promoted, and this gap was even larger for

Black women (58) and Latinas (71). A counter narrative may be considered in the work of the Women's Bureau which identified 15 different ways in which women may differ from men in how they enter the workforce, their experiences within the workforce, and the rewards they take away with them (Greene, 2018). The current narrative also suggests that entities such as the Women's Bureau are too often siloed, working on issues in isolation, and instead suggests that someone in each agency or bureau be responsible for 'women's issues.' While the idea of wider representation may sound appealing, the reality is that these issues would be added to existing assignments, neglecting the fact that there is a necessary body of knowledge and practice related to women in the workforce and that expertise is necessary to guide change.

From the meso perspective, the narrative that women need their own support organizations evolved from the cultural and political challenges women had in moving into positions of executive leadership in the early 1990s (AAUW, 2016). Networking organizations, women's associations and groups sprang up to provide opportunities for job networking, contacts and social support. The number of organizations and coalitions supporting women in the workplace continues to grow, with many of these functioning at unexpected or at least previously unthought of intersections. For instance, the growth of apprenticeship programs for girls and women in nontraditional industries has led to organizations such as Women in Trade and Oregon Tradeswomen, Inc. (Hegewisch et al., 2014). In the U.S. and pre-pandemic (2018), military spouses (92 percent women) had unemployment rates of 13 percent, three times the national average (Women's Bureau, 2020), compared to a 4 percent unemployment rate for veterans overall (women and men). This difference has prompted groups such as Hiring Our Heroes, a group focused on veterans, to expand their work to include military spouses. When tracking back to the macro level, the enhanced awareness of this narrative has led to policy changes that explicitly include military spouses in many of the policies related to veterans' economic conditions.

A second meso-level narrative is that corporations and boards can't find enough qualified women to fill their upper-level seats. This narrative emerged from the historical requirement that individuals must have served as the chief executive of a publicly traded company in order to serve on the board of a publicly traded company. Given that so few women were CEOs of public companies, it was believed that there were not enough qualified women. However, 'board-ready' qualifications can also come from serving on a non-profit board, having C-suite experience or from other high-level leadership roles. As a result, for decades, the number of women on Corporate Boards of S & P 500 companies has hovered between 14–20 percent. Today the Russell 3000 reports that women comprise 20 percent of corporate boards.[6] In part, this increase, however slow, may be credited to efforts by the Women Corporate Directors organization which has expanded efforts to assist women's participation on boards.

Similarly, within the U.S. women make up a mere 5.8 percent of CEOs.[7] In contrast, more than 15 countries have passed legislation to increase women's representation on corporate boards. Although studies correlating gender diversity and performance are mixed, the larger point is that women have a voice in leading these organizations and they have greater career opportunities (Wang, 2020). Further, studies show that companies with diverse boards have more tolerance for intolerance of inequities and distribution of power, and that having women directors increases the likelihood that women will be in management and leadership roles in the company (Reddy and Jadhav, 2019).

At the micro level we consider individual skills and characteristics. For decades leadership has been associated with masculine traits: aggressiveness, decisiveness, willingness to engage in conflict, strength, etc. (Sczesny, 2003). In contrast, women have been described as softer, more caring and in many cases less effective leaders, which is often characterized as a 'women's leadership style'[8] (Fitzgerald, 2019). The narrative of women as softer leaders makes us think that those who hold forth on that narrative have never gone to high school in the United States or watched Game of Thrones, where in both cases the behaviors of girls and women vary greatly from each other. However, the narrative of women as more gentle, compassionate, etc., is pervasive and can be considered in two ways. First, it positions women as homogenous, all acting in the same manner. And, second, it automatically concludes that a softer management style is not as good and is seen as less effective. The positioning of all 'women' as having a single leadership style is completely unrealistic, especially considering the multiplicity of different leadership styles and approaches that have emerged over the decades (Eagly and Johannesen-Schmidt, 2001). A quick Google search will yield thousands of hits on different types of leadership styles, and none of them is considered to be 'feminine' or 'female.' Within a group of women, there will be a variety of leadership approaches, the same as would be the case for a group of men (Eagley and Johannesen-Schmidt, 2001). Further, the conclusion that a softer management style is a negative is in direct contrast to findings of research showing that women can be more cooperative, demonstrate greater concern for others and have a higher commitment to ensuring all parties are treated fairly in a negotiation (Kray and Kennedy, 2017).

WOMEN IN ENTREPRENEURSHIP: NARRATIVE DISCUSSION

The narrative about women and entrepreneurship at the macro level is tightly tied to definitions. In the U.S., a company must be owned 51 percent by a woman to be 'women-owned.' This is the defining statistic that positions a company as eligible for all federal programs offering any type of resource or assistance to companies by virtue of some special category of owner. A prime example is government procurement programs. The challenge this narrative carries is that as a women-owned company grows and acquires equity investors, the percent owned by the woman founder could fall below 51 percent, even though the founder may still be the primary owner, bear the risks of ownership and guide the direction of the company. As the narrative stands, business growth may limit the market opportunities of a woman owning such a business.

Women-owned businesses are also seen as the 'minority' of small businesses, as evidenced by state offices which are referred to as 'State Offices of Minority and Women Business Enterprises' which provide services for women and minorities together. Until recently, the percentage of women business owners reported annually using only the 51 percent ownership status was 36 percent. However, an additional 9 percent of U.S. businesses are equally owned by women and men.[9] The narrative often used is that men will put ownership of companies in their wives' names in order to benefit from government programs for women-owned businesses. There is no data to support this claim. A more accurate statement (and one now used by the U.S. Small Business Administration) is that 45 percent of businesses in the U.S. are owned at least 50 percent by women. The conclusion is that a narrative that accurately captures the macro structure of the U.S. economy drives better policy.

The meso level of consideration for women and entrepreneurship considers organizations that exist to provide resources to entrepreneurs. The narrative, increasingly similar to those about women in the labor force, is that women have equal access to resources to grow their businesses, including financial, because such resources are available to all entrepreneurs. Indeed, there is a prevailing narrative that funding, information, access to networks and access to labor are available in most ecosystems for all entrepreneurial ventures. The reality is that ecosystems are 'gendered' and, because of unconscious biases and stereotypes, women are less likely to receive growth capital, especially institutional venture capital (Brush et al., 2019). Data shows that less than 3 percent of the companies receiving venture capital have a women CEO, and only 15 percent have diverse teams. In part, this disparity is due to lack of network access, and also because the venture capital industry is dominated by partners of which 92 percent are male. The playing field for growth capital is not level, and despite great strides in new sources of funding, the investment industry needs disruption.

Entities such as Women's Business Centers exist largely due to narratives that women need sources of support and assistance that are separate from men.[10] Recent U.S. policy, prompted by the COVID-19 pandemic, reinforced that approach by providing financial assistance and concessions (temporarily removing requirements for matching funds) for Women's Business Centers. Limited research does support the idea that women may learn some subjects more effectively in sex segregated environments (Langowitz et al., 2006). Specifically, these programs build on research showing that 'women business owners tend to think and talk about their businesses, view their leadership roles, and operate their businesses in ways markedly different than those of their male counterparts' (Riebe, 2012, p. 243), including the pathways they take to entrepreneurship, their motivations and goals, and their ability to combine home and work (Greene et al., 2004; Merrill-Sands et al., 2005).

From a micro-level perspective, government, media and industry nearly always report the narrative of women business owners as a homogenous group. Despite a body of research that finds differences amongst women business owners and their businesses pertaining to demographics of the women (race, ethnicity, age, geography, educational level, etc.) and demographics of the business (industry, vertical, age, geography, etc.), narratives around women entrepreneurs from a policy perspective generally address these women in a more uniform manner, assuming a one-size-fits-all approach to opportunities and resources (Brush and Greene, 2020, 2021).

Part of the micro-level narrative for women entrepreneurs, similar to women in the labor force, is that women lack confidence to build and aspirations to grow their businesses. This narrative emanates from the cultural conversation around entrepreneurship which tends to focus predominantly on the (success-ful) male experience which evokes images of Mark Zuckerberg, Elon Musk or Bill Gates (Brush and Greene, 2020). The stereotype of the successful entrepreneur is young, white, male and in the high-tech business, who will create a unicorn company. In the first place, not all men aspire to grow their businesses or have the confidence to do so. Growth is a choice, and many men entrepreneurs prefer to keep their businesses small for various reasons, just like women entrepreneurs. Second, roughly 30–35 percent of the 63,730 businesses receiving angel capital last year were women-led,[11] while more than 207,000 women-led businesses have more than $1 million in sales.[12] The point is that there is a significant population of women entrepreneurs who do have the confidence and aspirations to grow their ventures. The stereotype that the normal entrepreneur is a 35-year-old male creates assumptions or biases to which women do not fit, and, therefore, makes women invisible or marginalized as the 'other' in the entrepreneurship field (McAdam, p. 12, in Brush and Greene, 2020).

CONCLUSIONS: THE IMPACT OF THE NARRATIVES ON POLICY

Our use of the Narrative Policy Framework proved to be a helpful approach for us to parse the existing narratives on women in the labor force and women in entrepreneurship from the levels of macro, meso and micro. We suggest two conclusions: (1) False narratives create blind spots which limit gender equality in the workplace as well as entrepreneurship opportunities and experiences and (2) Narratives are a means of interpreting and understanding the foundation of policy, as well as illuminating future pathways for policy formation. Our goal is now to illuminate blind spots and provide the space for actualizing those new ways of being.

Our initial analysis suggests several potential areas of change.

1. *The narratives themselves.* Some narratives are based on history, but have never, or at least rarely, been updated. Some narratives are based on cultural lore, or stereotypes, that were inaccurate, and out of convenience, they persist. Topics such as women considered as a homogenous group, access to capital and contracts, differential training needs, or even a women's likelihood to enter into entrepreneurial activities (Gherardi, 2011 in Brush and Greene, 2021) are data based, but they have not been updated to include the intersections of race, ethnicity, income or other factors. Regular and accurate reporting, taking into account the diversity of women's entrepreneurship, and challenges to dated and/or inaccurate narratives can help drive the new ones necessary for more effective participation by women in the economic system.

2. *The crafting of policies.* Using NPF to deconstruct policies helps to analyze those narratives at different levels, and therefore identify where best to address the education needed to update and revamp approaches. For instance, instead of focusing training and education on women to avoid deficits, it might be time to focus training and education on lenders, investors and others in the entrepreneurial ecosystems to help them become more aware of stereotypes and biases they may bring to investment decisions (Brush and Greene, 2020). Moving deeper into the NPF paradigm will help identify the policy actors best positioned to make a difference and help to avoid individualization and isolation.

3. *Accurate and updated definitions.* As we described, even the narrative around how many women are business owners in the U.S. is questionable. Up until recently (and a change prompted by questions to the

Small Business Administration by the authors), only majority-owned women-owned businesses were reported as women-owned. Those equally owned by women and men were not part of the discussion. It is not possible to have relevant policy when working from an inaccurate measure of ownership.

4. *Inclusion of context and embeddedness.* Perhaps the largest gap in policy for women's entrepreneurship, and related to the homogeneity narrative, is the lack of contextual concerns such as family issues and locational or geographic embeddedness. By ignoring cultural role expectations for women in households, family and childcare responsibilities and variations in location, policy implementation may miss entire populations of women and entrepreneurs.

5. *Individualizing, isolation and intersectionality.* These constructs are the driving motivators for this chapter. For a woman starting, growing, and sustaining a business, these activities are not separate from the rest of her life, nor do they represent a specific stage in her life. Given the economic imperative to encourage and support women entrepreneurs around the world as a means for building stronger economies for all, the related nature of these entrepreneurial behaviors must be recognized in narratives at all levels in order to create and enact effective policy.

LIMITATIONS AND NEXT STEPS/DIRECTIONS FOR FUTURE RESEARCH

In this chapter, we sought to address the question, 'How might a narrative analysis enhance policies addressing gender gaps in women's entrepreneurship?' Following the core question of the NPF about the role of narratives in the policy process, we worked from previous research to identify potential areas of study for specific narrative frameworks (Shanahan et al., 2018, p. 332). Our work is an early exploration of the use of NPF in looking at women business owners, particularly as a segment of the population of working women whose needs, opportunities, etc., are murky, or even lost in the consideration of the gender gap and the existent policy arena. Using the U.S. as a case study, we explore ten years of legislation. However, we approached our analysis by first contextualizing the policies, and exploring how gender gaps are measured, the existing state of women entrepreneurs and the relevant policies that are already in existence. The examination of narratives across levels allows for a more nuanced perspective on how policy matters because it takes into account the implications for individuals, groups and macro structures. We recognize that our analysis could be expanded with interviews and qualitative data that might highlight the sensemaking (bounded reality) and actual stories (homo narrans); clearly a future research possibility. Our choice of narratives was selective, but representative and pervasive. Other narratives might also be analyzed and explored using this framework; for instance, policies and programs at state levels, or those addressing women in particular industry sectors.

Future research might examine any of these narratives in more detail, selecting those with the greatest potential impact and then analyzing their implications for policy implementation and effectiveness. Alternatively, research might also dive deeper into the ways that these narratives are formed and disseminated. In other words, how do policy narratives originate, become accepted and shared? What is the role of the media, advocacy groups, scholarship and politics in this process? Finally, as noted at the beginning of this chapter, 'Gender inequality remains a major barrier to human development' (United Nations Development Programme, 2021). In order to move forward, it is essential that policy-making, policy analysis and policy implementation take into account not only the hard data, objective metrics and statistics, but also the narratives that shape beliefs and approaches.

ACKNOWLEDGMENT

The authors are grateful to Fyllis Berg-Elton for her editorial assistance.

NOTES

1. https://wbl.worldbank.org/en/wbl
2. https://www.sba.gov/sites/default/files/advocacy/Frequently-Asked-Questions -Small-Business-2018.pdf
3. https://www.payscale.com/data/equal-opportunity-perceptions
4. https://www.ilo.org/washington/areas/gender-equality-in-the-workplace/WCMS _159496/lang--en/index.htm
5. https://www.mckinsey.com/featured-insights/diversity-and-inclusion/women-in -the-workplace
6. https://2020wob.com/wp-content/uploads/2019/10/2020WOB_Gender _Diversity_Index_Report_Oct2019.pdf
7. https://www.catalyst.org/research/women-in-sp-500-companies/ and https://en .wikipedia.org/wiki/Gender_representation_on_corporate_boards_of_directors
8. https://www.apa.org/research/action/boss#:~:text=For%20example%2C %20women%20are%20slightly,in%20today's%20less%20hierarchical %20organizations
9. https://www.sba.gov/sites/default/files/advocacy/Frequently-Asked-Questions -Small-Business-2018.pdf
10. https://www.sba.gov/about-sba/sba-locations/headquarters-offices/office -womens-business-ownership
11. https://www.nhbr.com/unh-study-finds-fewer-angels-invested-more-in-2019/ #:~:text=The%20center%20found%20that%20total,of%203.6%25%20from %202018%20investments
12. https://www.forbes.com/sites/elainepofeldt/2018/09/28/how-more-women-can -break-the-1-million-mark/?sh=1be1ee107df1

REFERENCES

AAUW (2016), *Barriers and Biases: The Status of Women in Leadership*, Washington, D.C.

Ahl, Helene (2019), 'The equality work that needs to be done', in Helene Ahl, Ingela Bergmo-Prvulovic, and Karin Kilhammar (eds.), *Human Resource Management: A Nordic Perspective*, London: Routledge, pp. 105–118.

Ahl, H. and T. Nelson (2015), 'How policy positions women entrepreneurs: comparative analysis of state discourse in Sweden and the United States', *Journal of Business Venturing*, **30** (2), 273–291.

Branisa, B., S. Klasen, M. Ziegler, D. Drechsler and J. Jütting (2014), 'The institutional basis of gender inequality: the Social Institutions and Gender Index (SIGI)', *Feminist Economics*, **20** (2), 29–64.

Brush, C. and P. Greene (2016), *Closing the Gender Gap in Entrepreneurship: A New Perspective on Policies and Practices*, report prepared for the Organization for Economic Cooperation and Development (OECD), Paris, France.

Brush, C. and P. Greene (2020), *Catalyzing Change in Equity Investing: Disruptive Models for Financing Women's Entrepreneurship*, Diana International Impact Report, Wellesley, MA: Babson College.

Brush, C. and P. Greene (2021), 'Do women engage differently in entrepreneurship?', in T. Cooney (ed.), *The Palgrave Handbook of Minority Entrepreneurship*, Switzerland: Palgrave Macmillan (forthcoming).

Brush, C., P. Greene and F. Welter, (2020), 'The Diana Project: a legacy for research on gender in entrepreneurship', *International Journal of Gender and Entrepreneurship*, **12** (1), 7–25.

Brush, C.G., L. Edelman, T. Manolova and F. Welter (2019), 'A gendered look at entrepreneurship ecosystems', *Small Business Economics*, **53** (3), 393–408.

Caldwell, S. and N. Mays (2012), 'Studying policy implementation using a macro, meso and micro frame analysis: the case of collaboration for leadership in applied health research and care (CLAHRC) programme nationally and in North West London', *Health Research Policy and Systems*, **10** (32), 1–9.

Clarke, J. and R. Holt (2010), 'The mature entrepreneur: a narrative approach to entrepreneurial goals', *Journal of Management Inquiry*, **19** (1), 69–83.

Collins, O.F. and D.G. Moore (1964), *The Enterprising Man*, East Lansing: Bureau of Business and Economic Research, Graduate School of Business Administration, Michigan State University.

Curley, B. (2020), 'Why COVID-19 is hitting men harder than women', accessed 14 June 2020 at: https://www.healthline.com/health-news/men-more-susceptible-to -serious-covid-19-illnesses

Dopfer, K., J. Foster and J. Potts (2004), 'Micro-meso-macro', *Journal of Evolutionary Economics*, **14** (1), 263–279.

Eagly, A.H. and M.C. Johannesen-Schmidt (2001), 'The leadership styles of women and men', *Journal of Social Issues*, **57** (4), 781–797.

Elam, A., C.G. Brush, P.G. Greene, B. Baumer, M. Dean and R. Heavlow (2019), *Global Entrepreneurship Monitor 2018–2019 Women's Entrepreneurship Report*, London, UK: Global Entrepreneurship Research Association.

Fitzgerald, T. (2019), *Women Leaders in Higher Education: Shattering the Myths*, London, UK: Routledge.

Foss, L., C. Henry, H. Ahl and G.H. Mikalsen (2019), 'Women's entrepreneurship policy research: a 30-year review of the evidence', *Small Business Economics*, **53** (4), 409–429.

Gartner, W. (2007), 'Entrepreneurial narrative and a science of the imagination', *Journal of Business Venturing*, **22** (6), 613–627.

Greene, P.G. (2018, October), Personal Records. Women's Bureau. U.S. Department of Labor.

Greene, P.G., M.M. Hart, E.J. Gatewood, C.G. Brush and N.M. Carter (2004), 'Women entrepreneurs: moving front and center: an overview of research and theory', Coleman Foundation White Paper.

Gupta, K., J.T. Ripberger and S. Collins (2014), 'The strategic use of policy narratives: Jaitapur and the politics of siting a nuclear power plant in India', in *The Science of Stories*, New York: Palgrave Macmillan, pp. 89–106.

Harris, B. (2017), 'What is the gender gap (and why is it getting wider)?' World Economic Forum, accessed 5 March, 2021 at: https://www.weforum.org/agenda/2017/11/the-gender-gap-actually-got-worse-in-2017/

Hechavarría, D.M. and A.E. Ingram (2019), 'Entrepreneurial ecosystem conditions and gendered national-level entrepreneurial activity: a 14-year panel study of GEM', *Small Business Economics*, **53** (2), 431–458.

Hegewisch, A., J. Henrici, E. Shaw and T. Hooper (2014), 'Untapped resources, untapped labor pool: using federal highway funds to prepare women for careers in construction', Jobs for the Future.

Henry, C., B. Orser, S. Coleman and L. Foss (2017), 'Women's entrepreneurship policy: a 13-nation cross-country comparison', *International Journal of Gender and Entrepreneurship*, **9** (3), 206–228.

Hjorth, D. and C. Steyaert (2004), *Narrative and Discursive Approaches in Entrepreneurship*, Northhampton, MA, USA: Edward Elgar.

Jennings, J.E. and C.G. Brush (2013), 'Research on women entrepreneurs: challenges to (and from) the broader entrepreneurship literature?', *The Academy of Management Annals*, **7** (1), 661–713.

Jones, M.D. and M.K. McBeth (2010), 'A Narrative Policy Framework: clear enough to be wrong?', *Policy Studies Journal*, **38** (2), 329–353.

Jones, M.D., M.K. McBeth and E.A. Shanahan (2014), 'Introducing the Narrative Policy Framework', in M. Jones, M.K. McBeth and E.A. Shanahan (eds.), *The Science of Stories*, New York: Palgrave Macmillan, pp. 1–25.

Jones, R., J. Latham and M. Betta (2008), 'Narrative construction of the social entrepreneurial identity', *International Journal of Entrepreneurial Behavior & Research*, **14** (5), 330–345.

Kelley, D., C. Brush, A.C. Corbett and M. Majbouri (2020), *2019/2020 United States Report, Global Entrepreneurship Monitor*, Wellesley, MA: Babson College.

Kelley, D., C. Brush, P. Greene, M. Herrington, A. Ali and P. Kew (2015), *Special Report. Women's Entrepreneurship*. Babson College: Global Entrepreneurship Monitor Research Association.

Kelley, D., B. Baumer, C. Brush, P. Greene, M. Mahdi, M. Majbouri, M. Cole, M. Dean and R. Heavelow (2017), *Global Entrepreneurship Monitor: Women's Entrepreneurship 2016/2017 Report*, Wellesley, MA: Babson College.

Kim, P., K. Wennberg and G. Crodieu (2016), 'Untapped riches of meso-level applications in multilevel entrepreneurship mechanisms', *Academy of Management Perspectives*, **30** (3), 273–291.

Kray, L.J. and J.A. Kennedy (2017), 'Changing the narrative: women as negotiators and leaders', *California Management Review*, 60th Anniversary Issue: Haas Research on Leadership, **60** (1), 70–87.

Langowitz, N., N. Sharpe and M. Godwyn (2006), 'Women's business centers in the United States: effective entrepreneurship training and policy implementation', *Journal of Small Business & Entrepreneurship*, **19** (2), 167–182.

Larty, J. and E. Hamilton (2011), 'Structural approaches to narrative analysis in entrepreneurship research: exemplars from two researchers', *International Small Business Journal*, **29** (3), 220–237.

Leitch, C., F. Welter and and C. Henry (2018), 'Women entrepreneurs' financing revisited: taking stock and looking forward', *Journal of Entrepreneurial Finance*, Special Issue: New perspectives on women entrepreneurs and finance, **20** (2), 103–114.

Manolova, T., C. Brush, L. Edelman and A. Elam (2020), 'Pivoting to stay the course: how women entrepreneurs take advantage of opportunities created by the COVID-19 pandemic', *International Small Business Journal: Researching Entrepreneurship*, **38** (6), 481–491.

Mantere, S., P. Aula, H. Schildt and E. Vaara (2013), 'Narrative attributions of entrepreneurial failure', *Journal of Business Venturing*, **28** (4), 459–473.

Marlow, S. (2014), 'Exploring future research agendas in the field of gender and women's entrepreneurship', *International Journal of Gender and Entrepreneurship*, **6** (2), 102–120.

Mazzarol, T. (2014), 'Growing and sustaining entrepreneurial ecosystems: what they are and the role of government policy', Seaanz, Australia: Seaanz White Paper.

McAdam, M., R.T. Harrison and C.M. Leitch (2019), 'Stories from the field: women's networking as gender capital in entrepreneurial ecosystems', *Small Business Economics*, **53**, 459–474.

Ménard, C., A. Jimenez and H. Tropp (2018), 'Addressing the policy-implementation gaps in water services: the key role of meso-institutions', *Water International*, **43** (1), 13–33.

Merrill-Sands, D., J. Kickul and C. Ingols (2005), 'Women pursuing leadership and power: challenging the myth of the "opt-out revolution"' [CGO Insights, no. 20], Boston, MA: Center for Gender in Organizations, Simmons School of Management.

Meunier, F., Y. Krylova and R. Ramalho (2017), 'Women's entrepreneurship: how to measure the gap between new female and male entrepreneurs?', *World Bank Policy Research Working Paper*, (8242).

Neumeyer, X. and S.C. Santos (2018), 'Sustainable business models, venture typologies, and entrepreneurial ecosystems: a social network perspective', *Journal of Cleaner Production*, **172**, 4565–4579.

O'Bryan, T., C.A. Dunlop and C.M. Radaelli (2014), 'Narrating the "Arab Spring": where expertise meets heuristics in legislative hearings', in Michael D. Jones, Elizabeth A. Shanahan and Mark K. McBeth (eds.), *The Science of Stories: Applications of Narrative Policy Framework*, New York: Palgrave Macmillan, pp. 107–129.

OECD (2016), *Policy Brief on Women's Entrepreneurship*, European Union Publications Office: Luxembourg. ISBN 978-92-79-67995-7.

Perrin, F. (2021), 'Can the historical gender gap index deepen our understanding of economic development?', *Journal of Demographic Economics*, 1–39. Doi:10.1017/dem.2020.34.

Phillips, N., P. Tracey and N. Karra (2013), 'Building entrepreneurial tie portfolios through strategic homophily: the role of narrative identity work in venture creation and early growth', *Journal of Business Venturing*, **28** (1), 134–150.

Reddy, S. and A.M. Jadhav (2019), 'Gender diversity in boardrooms – a literature review', *Cogent Economics & Finance*, **7** (1), 1–11.

Riebe, M. (2012), 'A place of her own: the case for university-based centers for women entrepreneurs', *Journal of Education for Business*, **87** (4), 241–246.

Schüler, D. (2006), 'The uses and misuses of the gender-related development index and the gender empowerment measure: a review of the literature', *Journal of Human Development*, **7** (2), 161–182.

Schwartz, E. (1976), 'Entrepreneurship: a new female frontier', *Journal of Contemporary Business*, **5** (1), 47–76.

Sczesny, S. (2003), 'A closer look beneath the surface: various facets of the think-manager-think-male stereotype', *Sex Roles*, **49**, 353–363.

Shanahan, E.A., M.D. Jones and M.K. McBeth (2018), 'How to conduct a narrative policy framework study', *The Social Science Journal*, **55** (3), 332–345.

Sinisalo, P. and K. Komulainen (2008), 'The creation of coherence in the transitional career. A narrative case study of the woman entrepreneur', *International Journal for Educational and Vocational Guidance*, **8** (1), 35–48.

Sperber, S. and C. Linder (2019), 'Gender-specifics in start-up strategies and the role of the entrepreneurial ecosystem', *Small Business Economics*, **53**, 533–549.

Stephan, H.R. (2020), 'Shaping the scope of conflict in Scotland's fracking debate: conflict management and the narrative policy framework', *Review of Policy Research*, **37** (1), 64–91.

UN Secretary-General's High-Level Panel on Women's Economic Empowerment (2016), *Leave No One Behind: A Call to Action for Gender Equality and Women's Economic Empowerment*, United Nations.

UN Women (2020), 'Policy brief: the impact of COVID-19 on women', United Nations Secretariat, accessed 4 April 2021 at: https://www.unwomen.org/en/digital-library/publications/2020/04/policy-brief-the-impact-of-covid-19-on-women

United Nations Development Programme (2021), 'Gender Inequality Index', accessed 16 February 2021 at: http://hdr.undp.org/en/content/gender-inequality-index-gii

United Nations Human Development Report (2020), 'Gender Development Index (GDI)', accessed 28 April 2021 at: http://hdr.undp.org/en/content/gender-inequality-index-gii

Veselkova, M. and M. Beblavý (2014), 'From selectivity to universalism: how macro-level policy narratives shape meso-level policy outcomes?', in *ECPR General Conference, Glasgow*.

Wang, Y.H. (2020), 'Does board gender diversity bring better financial and governance performances? An empirical investigation of cases in Taiwan', *Sustainability*, **12** (8), https://doi.org/10.3390/su12083205

Werner, A. (2020), 'Why unemployment fueled by pandemic is hitting women harder than men', in CBSNEWSCOM, accessed 10 June 2020 at: https://wwwcbsnewscom/news/coronavirus-unemployment-women-us-economy/

Women's Bureau (2020), 'Military spouses fact sheet', accessed 6 March 2021 at: https://www.dol.gov/sites/dolgov/files/WB/mib/WB-MilSpouse-factsheet.pdf

World Bank (2021a), 'The World Bank in gender', accessed 21 February 2021 at: https://www.worldbank.org/en/topic/gender

World Bank (2021b), *Women, Business and the Law 2021*, Washington, D.C.: World Bank. Doi:10.1596/978-1-4648-1652-9. License: Creative Commons Attribution

CC BY 3.0 IGO, accessed 25 February 2021 at: https://openknowledge.worldbank .org/bitstream/handle/10986/35094/9781464816529.pdf

World Economic Forum (2020), 'Our recovery from the coronavirus crisis must have gender empowerment at its heart', accessed 10 June 2020 at: https:// wwwweforumorg/agenda/2020/05/industries-gender-women-coronavirus-covid19 -economic

World Economic Forum (2021), *Global Gender Gap Report 2020*, Geneva, Switzerland: World Economic Forum, accessed February 2021 at: http://www3.weforum.org/ docs/WEF_GGGR_2020.pdf.

Yllö, K. (1984), 'The status of women, marital equality, and violence against wives: a contextual analysis', *Journal of Family Issues*, **5** (3), 307–320.

3. Strategies to redress entrepreneurship gender gaps in Canada revisited

Barbara J. Orser

INTRODUCTION

This chapter presents rationales for policy interventions and an overview of women's entrepreneurship policies in Canada. Recommendations advanced in 23 illustrative Canadian reports, including a review of small- and medium-sized enterprise (SME) policies conducted by the Organisation for Economic Co-operation and Development (OECD, 2017), are used as a basis for an assessment of the *Women Entrepreneurship Strategy* (Innovation, Science and Economic Development Canada (ISED), 2018). In doing so, this chapter examines the research question: what is the rationale and structure of women's entrepreneurship policies in Canada?

This country-level study advances the literature in several ways. First, the critique describes the Government of Canada's portfolio of policies to support women-owned and women-led firms. The study also presents evidence about the importance of employing an intersectional lens in the design, implementation and reporting on women's entrepreneurship policies. These insights are relevant as Canada is perceived as being among 'best' practice nations with respect to entrepreneurial attitudes, infrastructure and opportunity-based entrepreneurship.

The *Global Entrepreneurship and Development Index* (2018), for example, ranks Canada third out of 137 countries with respect to entrepreneurial ecosystems. In Canada, entrepreneurship is perceived positively as a career, "… women entrepreneurs in Canada are 10% more likely than men to report opportunity as a motive for business start-up, suggesting that women's entrepreneurship is well supported in Canada" (Elam et al., 2018/2019, p. 23). The 2019 *Global Entrepreneurship Monitor* (Elam et al., 2018/2019) also reports that Canada is one of only five countries at gender parity in early-stage rates of entrepreneurial activity, with high rates of internationalization and favourable media coverage of women entrepreneurs. Moreover, the 2020 *Global Entrepreneurship Monitor* (Bosma et al., 2020) showcased strategies of the federal government to meet the United Nations Sustainable Development Goals (UN SDG). The findings are therefore relevant to government signatories to the UN calls to action.

Second, women's entrepreneurship policy research is a "relatively under-researched area" of entrepreneurship with "disparity between knowledge generated by academic researchers and that which can be usefully employed by entrepreneurs and policymakers" (Foss et al., 2019, p. 410). Most studies of women's entrepreneurship policies consider programme efficiencies and outcomes, and not the dynamic nature of policies (Arshed, Chalmers & Mathews, 2019). This study documents the evolution of rationales for, and priorities advanced in, reports, taskforces and forums in Canada between 1986 and 2020. The findings provide an historical perspective to help close the gap between knowledge generated by previous academic research and development of entrepreneurship policies.

Third, this study advances a dashboard of policy recommendations. Content is drawn from a large-scale review of small and medium-sized enterprise (SME) policies in Canada conducted by the OECD titled *SME and Entrepreneurship Policy in Canada* (2017). This study also references Canadian women-focused SME policy reports published between 1986 and 2020. The report recommendations serve as a framework to critique the Women Entrepreneurship Strategy (ISED, 2018). The study considers strategies to address instability among 'formulators' (such as politicians and bureaucrats) and 'implementors' of policy (such as, small business support organizations) (Arshed et al., 2019, p. 562). Insights inform next generation entrepreneurship policies.

To inform the research question, this chapter comprises several sections. The following section considers the evolution of rationales for women entrepreneurship policies. A profile of women-owned SMEs and self-employed women in Canada is then presented. A summary of Canadian and OECD (2017) SME policy recommendations follow. This information informs the critique of the Women Entrepreneurship Strategy (ISED, 2018).

EVOLUTION OF WOMEN-FOCUSED SME POLICIES

There is increasing interest in policies and other measures that seek to support women entrepreneurs. This is evidenced in academe through the acceleration of women's entrepreneurship policy studies (Foss et al., 2019), recent special issue journal publications about women's entrepreneurship (such as those featured in *Small Business Economics, Journal of Small Business & Entrepreneurship, International Small Business Journal, Strategic Entrepreneurship Journal* and *Journal of African Management Review*) and the development of academic consortia, such as the Global Women's Entrepreneurship Policy Research Group (Henry et al., 2017). Economic agencies are prioritizing strategies to support women entrepreneurs (W(omen)20, 2020; World Bank, 2020). Emergent think-tanks, such as Women's Economic Imperative (2020) and multi-agency initiatives such as WeEmpower (2020) also seek to advance policies to further gender equality and women's economic empowerment.

To inform measures to support women-identified entrepreneurs, this section presents an overview of the evolution of policy rationales, with a focus on the country focus of this study. Policymakers, academics and other stakeholders can employ this information to clarify rationales and to address market imperfections that warrant intervention. The information also helps to inform the context of Canadian SME policies.

Early Rationales for Women-focused SME Policies

During the 1970s to 1990s, mainstream SME policies presupposed that what works well for men worked well for women. Small business policies focused on offsetting the liabilities of newness and were predicated on assumptions that economic returns from SME growth offset the incremental expenditure of public funds (Storey, 2003).

Canada, like many countries, witnessed the unprecedented entry of women into self-employment between 1970 and 1990.[1] The period was also characterized by the introduction of women-focused and minority SME policies, typically from the context of niche assistance (Stevenson & Lundström, 2001). The OECD report *Policy Brief on Women's Entrepreneurship* (Halabisky, 2018), for example, states that policies to support women's entrepreneurship date back to the 1970s.

In a review of the literature, Mayoux (2001) has reported that most women-focused SME policies were grounded in one of two objectives: economic development or economic independence. The *economic development* objective assumes that women-owned SMEs are underutilized or underperforming, and that they are resources to be tapped for employment and economic growth. Neo-liberal feminist rationales that underscore this perspective presuppose that women entrepreneurs need to circumvent systemic barriers in order to grow their firms (Fischer et al., 1993). The *economic independence motive* aligns with the need for social justice, poverty reduction and women's self-sufficiency.

Early women's entrepreneurship studies in Canada mirrored these rationales for policy intervention (Stevenson, 1988; Belcourt, Burke & Lee-Gosselin, 1991; Orser 1991; Bérard & Brown, 1994), and mandates of several federal agencies. Since 1989, the mandate of international assistance in Canada has evolved to emphasize equality, poverty reduction, promotion of human rights, and sustainable development via micro-financing and sustainable development programmes – policies administered through [then] Canadian International Development Agency (Mackreal, 2013). Conversely, women-focused SME policies were driven by the economic development mandate of [then] Industry Canada and gender-equality mandate of [then] Status of Women Canada. Lack of consensus about the need for, and legitimacy of, women-focused SME policies characterizes this period. This was in part due to limited industry advocacy and the ghettoization of women's policy within Status of Women Canada (Orser, 2017).

Progressive Rationales for Women-focused SME Policies

In a multi-country assessment of policies to support women, the OECD (Halabisky, 2018) advances more nuanced rationales for women-focused SME policies, including: "women are under-represented in entrepreneurship relative to men and closing this gap would result in welfare gains for the economy, society and for individual women"; institutional barriers (e.g., attitudes that discourage women from creating businesses, market failures that make it difficult for women to access resources); lower awareness of support programmes; and programme in-take mechanisms that favour men entrepreneurs:

> While the specific policy aims of different governments vary, they tend to include: 1. Address under-representation among business owners; 2. Offer an option to integrate women into the labour force; 3. Increase economic independence through empowerment; 4. Promote job creation and economic growth; 5. Promote equity and social inclusion; 6. Reduce poverty; 7. Create more equal access to resources, skills and experience, opportunities, and business networks; and 8. Improve access to mainstream business support mechanisms. (Halabisky, 2018, p. 18)

Rationales for women-focused SME policies continue to evolve (Pettersson, 2012; Ahl & Nelson, 2015; Pettersson et al., 2017). Entrepreneurship policy documents increasingly emphasize the UN Sustainable Development Goals, goals underscored by the tenets of social feminism (Fischer et al., 1993), intersectionality (Crenshaw, 1989), emancipation to "bring about new economic, social, institutional, and cultural environments ... autonomy, expression of personal values, and making a difference in the world ..." (Rindova et al., 2009, p. 477), gender planning and development theory (Moser, 2012), anti-colonialism (Parpart, Connelly & Barriteau, 2000) and gender and entrepreneurial empowerment (Digan et al., 2019). For example, in a critique of Canadian *Feminist International Assistance Policy*, Grantham et al. (2019,

p. 3) report on why it is important that policymakers adapt feminist and inter-sectional approaches:

> Focusing on economic inclusion alone cannot guarantee women's broader empow-erment – we need feminist and intersectional approaches to transform unequal power relations, norms and structures in society. Promoting and investing in feminist collective organizing is key. So is addressing the intersection of social, economic and political disadvantages that women face – as workers, as members of different classes (in both urban and rural settings) or as members of specific groups (racialized women, Indigenous women, informal workers, immigrants, women with disabilities).

Similarly, Ravanera and Sultana (2020) cite the need for policies in Canada that prioritize equality, women's economic empowerment and LGBTQ2+ rights. Richard (2020) employs post-structuralist feminism to examine texts of the *Canada-United States Council for Advancement of Women Entrepreneurs and Business Leaders* (2015). Messaging was seen to position women as "other" and subordinate to men, hence sustaining a male norm. Three themes are observed, "women are objects of economic growth", "... barriers need to be removed before women can succeed" and "women entrepreneurs need to be fixed". The study recommends a shift in rationale from neo-liberal feminism to measures predicated on gender equality (Richard, 2020, p. 90):

> With a shift in wording from an interventionist poverty alleviation paradigm to a feminist empowerment paradigm it may help avoid putting women in a subordi-nate position to men when creating and measuring policy and support programs for women entrepreneurs. Given the long history of support for women entrepreneurs in Canada, dating back to 1995, the lack of any real evidence that the last 20 years of support has dramatically increased the government's mandated "economic growth by means of the woman entrepreneur", and a government who is focused on being seen as a leader in gender equality, now may be the time to try a radical shift in approach.

To further position intersectionality, an anonymous reviewer of this chapter wrote,

> Intersectionality dislodges the primacy of gender depending on the context. For example, Indigenous entrepreneurs of all genders may share more in common with each other than Indigenous and non-Indigenous women in some settings in Canada. An intersectional approach can help to illuminate these challenges and opportunities.

Positioning intersectionality within a feminist lens, Brydges and Hracs (2019, p. 513) draw on Gill (2014, p. 510) to explain that a *feminist intersectional approach* "seeks to understand the connections between multiple axes of oppression and exclusion, on the understanding that these are not simply 'additive' but constitute distinct experiences and subjectivities" (2014, p. 510). Importantly, the imperfect, often ambiguous and open-ended, nature of intersectionality is what makes it so useful (Davis, 2008).

In April 2021, the Government of Canada announced a feminist budget with the mandate to "ensure an inclusive, intersectional recovery that builds a truly equitable society". The plan identified agencies tasked with "modernizing and improving the quality of this analysis, with particular attention to the intersectional analysis of race, Indigeneity, disability, and gender identity" (Government of Canada, 2021, p. 413). The budget proposed $101.4 million over five years to Innovation, Science and Economic Development Canada (ISED) for the *Small Business and Entrepreneurship Development Program*. Investments are expected to consolidate, simplify and streamline the suite of "boutique" programmes to enhance consistency, management and reporting, including the *Women Entrepreneurship Strategy* (Government of Canada, 2021).

It is notable that the budget referenced "intersectionality" in the context of recommendations of a "Taskforce for Women in the Economy". The taskforce, however, does not include representation of women entrepreneurs, despite requests to do so from industry organizations (Canadian Women's Chamber of Commerce, 2021). The budget did, however, renew funding for the *Women Entrepreneurship Strategy* and *Black Entrepreneurs Program*. Investments include skills development, a national day care policy, and funding to "modernize federal procurement and create opportunities for specific communities by diversifying the federal supplier base". Targets include procuring from Black-owned businesses, a 5% federal target to contract with businesses managed and led by Indigenous peoples, data analytics and supplier diversity opportunities for "equity deserving groups" (Government of Canada, 2001, p. 138).

To date most budgets, women's entrepreneurship policies, reports, taskforces and forums are atheoretical, implicitly prioritizing economic goals predicated on a neo-liberal feminist rationale over equality, health, environmental, racial and other socio-economic goals. Few economies have enacted inclusive strategies. The OECD (2019) has reported that, "no Member State has a standalone 'inclusive entrepreneurship' strategy that covers a range of target groups, virtually all EU Member States include inclusive entrepreneurship policy objectives in national strategic documents and action plans". Such practices lead to loss of policy and funding support for underrepresented entrepreneurs, including women.

Shifting political agendas that support and then refute the value of women's entrepreneurship policies further erode the legitimacy of targeted measures. For example, in examining factors contributing to the instability in women's entrepreneurship policies in the United Kingdom, scholars cite the tendency of politicians to legitimize such policies among voters rather than entrepreneurial ecosystem stakeholders, and to make policy announcements without commensurate funding to support service delivery by stakeholders, such as regional small business support organizations (Arshed et al., 2019). The study observes how "passionate" arguments made for mainstream versus women-focused measures amplify negative judgements about women's entrepreneurship policies. Arguments are so profound they are "unlikely to attain 'taken-for-grantedness' with a critical mass of ecosystem stakeholders, including women beneficiaries" (Arshed et al., 2019, p. 577). The researchers conclude women's entrepreneurship policies will continue to struggle to achieve a "self-reinforcing" state given persistent bottom-up resistance.

Failure to state the rationale for intervention impedes policy assessment and can result in policies that favour privileged women (Coleman et al., 2019), and larger and older companies (Dalziel et al., 2014). Clarification of rationales is needed to better structure investments and address instability in women entrepreneurship policy reforms (Henry et al., 2017).

Figure 3.1 depicts the evolution of frameworks for small business policy interventions. The top row identifies alternative policy rationales. The bottom row presents illustrative principles that underlie these policies. The figure can be used to identify assumptions that underscore interventions and to map progress towards the UN Sustainable Development Goal 5 of gender equality and women's economic empowerment.

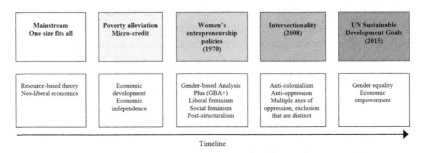

Figure 3.1   *Evolution of frameworks for small business/entrepreneurship policies*

STATE OF WOMEN'S ENTREPRENEURSHIP IN CANADA

To inform entrepreneurship and small business measures in Canada, an aggregation of Government of Canada (Statistics Canada) data is presented.

Collectively, the data demonstrate the need to align policy with evidence and for industry-specific interventions to support women-identified entrepreneurs.

In 2017, 15.6% of employer SMEs were majority women-owned, 20.9% were equally owned by men and women, and 63.5% were majority men-owned. These shares of employer firm by gender of ownership have remained stable over the past decade (Statistics Canada, 2019):[2]

> Women-owned businesses were more prevalent in service industries such as retail trade, accommodation and food services, and tourism, and less were prevalent in agriculture, forestry, fishing and hunting; mining, quarrying, and oil and gas extraction; construction; and manufacturing. They were also more prevalent among enterprises with fewer than 20 employees. (Statistics Canada, 2019)

Review of *Labour Force Survey* data shows that between 2000 and 2019, there were no gender differences in the change in absolute number of self-employed women compared to men (Figure 3.2).

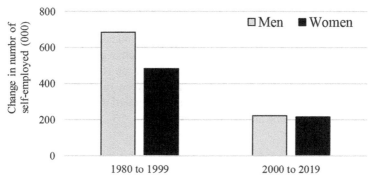

Source: Statistics Canada, Labour Force Survey, CANSIM 1410002601.

Figure 3.2   *Change in the number of self-employed individuals by gender (1980 to 2019)*

Employing longitudinal data on market entry among start-ups with less than 100 employees, majority women-owned start-ups demonstrated lower survival rates than men-owned and equally owned start-ups (2005 to 2013); while equally owned start-ups had the highest survival rate, controlling for firm size (Statistics Canada, 2020c).

Sector and concentration of women in sectors were associated with survival:

> Women-owned start-ups had a lower and statistically significant (at the 5% level) hazard rate of exit relative to men-owned firms in retail trade and accommodation

and food services. These service industries typically have a higher concentration of women-owned firms, whereas women-owned firms in industries with a lower concentration of women-owned start-ups were more likely to exit. These industries include construction; agriculture, forestry, fishing and hunting; administrative and support, waste management and remediation services; and transportation and warehousing. However, they were much more likely to exit in health care and social assistance, an industry in which they do have a large presence. (Statistics Canada, 2020c)

Growth in Annual Revenue, Net Income, and Employment

Statistics Canada (Rosa & Sylla, 2016) reports that, "In general, majority female-owned SMEs employed 25.1 percent fewer employees in 2011, and 19.5 percent fewer employees in 2014, than majority male-owned SMEs." ISED (2020b) has reported that between 2015 and 2017, 33.6% of majority women-owned SMEs experienced zero percent or less change in annual revenue, 47.9 experienced 1% to 10% annual revenue growth, and 18.5 experienced 11% or higher annual revenue growth. This compares to 34.2% of majority men-owned SMEs that experienced 0% or less change in annual revenue, 45.0% that experienced 1% to 10% annual revenue growth and 20.9% that experienced 11% or higher annual revenue growth (ISED, 2020b). Comparison of percentage change in annual revenue is, however, ambiguous as the absolute amount of revenue varies between majority women-owned SMEs and men-owned SMEs. This point is illustrated when growth is defined as change in net income and employment.

Access to Capital

Given access to capital is a frequently cited policy recommendation, data from ISED's *2017 Survey of Financing and Growth of SMEs* (ISED, Statistics Canada) are employed to illustrate the frequency of requesting capital (capital leasing, equity, trade credit, debt) by gender of firm ownership. Based on representative, large-scale survey data, significant gender differences in frequency in which majority men-owned and majority women-owned SMEs apply for all forms of financial capital are noted. Research is needed to disentangle confounding factors, such as firm age, size and sector. While there has been considerable social media, advocacy and government attention paid to external equity, most small business owners seek and secure debt to finance their businesses (Cosh, Cumming & Hughes, 2009). Research on equity finance is limited. In part, this is due to the fact that very few business owners seek this type of external capital. This therefore makes intersectional analyses of equity finance particularly difficult.

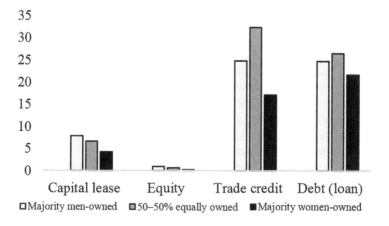

Source: Canada, Surveys of Financing and Growth of Small and Medium Enterprises (SFGSME).

Figure 3.3A   *Financing requested by gender of firm ownership, 2017*

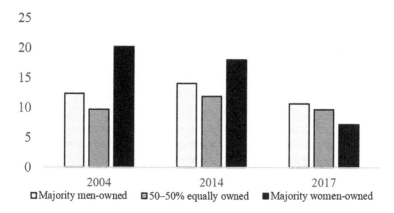

Source: Canada, Surveys of Financing and Growth of Small and Medium Enterprises (SFGSME).

Figure 3.3B   *Turndown rates on applications by gender of firm ownership, 2004, 2014, 2017*

POLICY RECOMMENDATIONS TO SUPPORT WOMEN ENTREPRENEURS IN CANADA

To inform the critique of the Women Entrepreneurship Strategy (ISED, 2018), this section presents a summary of recommendations advanced by the government-funded analysis and review of small business policies in Canada conducted by an international team of experts by the OECD (2017).[3] Other women-focused policy reports, taskforces and forums are summarized in Table 3.1. The OECD (2017) recommendations comprise the criteria used to assess the Women Entrepreneurship Strategy (2018).

Challenges identified in the OECD (2017) report included: scaling up small businesses; increasing the proportion of high-growth firms, increasing productivity and exporting among established firms; increasing bank lending volumes and easing restrictive lending practices; increasing angel, equity crowdfunding and institutional investment; and a national innovation system weighted towards basic rather than applied research. The OECD (2017, p. 17) prioritized "financing women entrepreneurs and increasing gender diversity in public and private procurement, replicate successful local women entrepreneurship support programmes in other regions and formulate a women's enterprise strategy." More specific recommendations included:

- Access to capital: creation of Business Development Bank of Canada (BDC) programme for women, quotas for women's participation in BDC programmes, gender disaggregated data on the use of BDC programmes, and provision of micro-finance.
- Access to mainstream and women-focused programmes: expansion of *local* women entrepreneurship support programmes, particularly the Women's Enterprise Initiative to other regions beyond Western Canada.
- Access to federal SME procurement: set-asides for women-owned enterprises and initiative to raise awareness of supplier diversity principles among government and private sector procurement officers.
- *National women's enterprise strategy*: setting out objectives, support measures, implementation mechanisms and government responsibilities for promotion of women entrepreneurship with procedures for coordination among federal and provincial/territorial governments.
- *Coordination of support services and advocacy*: creation of a specialized government agency to take the lead on women's entrepreneurship policy.
- *Gender and other owner profile data*: improve availability of gender-disaggregated data on SME activities, obstacles and programme use to support policy formulation.

Table 3.1   Canadian women-focused entrepreneurship policy reports, taskforces and forums (1986–2020)

Sources/author(s)	Increase access to SME financing	Networking, mentoring, training, advice, incl. financial literacy	Better coordination of services (e.g., horizontal, private/public partnerships, reduce red tape)	Increase awareness of economic contributions of women ENT's, address credibility gaps	Women-focused and targeted SME programmes and services	Promotion of entrepreneurship as a career option	Women-friendly training, advisory services, curriculum	Access to government programmes, services, grants, contributions	One-stop access to information	Income protection, self-employment training (benefits, insurance)	Increase access to federal SME procurement	Gender, race disaggregated programme reviews and data, Indigenous data	Internationalization support (e.g., export training, missions)	Reporting best practices to facilitate enterprise growth
British Columbia's Women's Programs (1986)[b]	✓			✓	✓	✓						✓		
Stevenson (1988)[a]			✓	✓							✓			
Baird (Small Business Secretariat, 1982)[b]	✓	✓	✓	✓			✓					✓		
Belcourt, Burke & Lee-Gosselin (1991)[d]	✓	✓	✓					✓	✓					
Bérard & Brown (Western Diversification, 1994)[b,d]	✓	✓			✓	✓	✓							
Canadian Federation of Independent Business (1994)[c]	✓	✓												
Hughes (Canadian Policy Research Networks, Inc., 1999)[b,d]										✓				
Foundation of Canadian Women Entrepreneurs et al. (2000)[a]	✓	✓	✓		✓	✓	✓	✓						
St. Onge & Stevenson (2001)[a]	✓	✓				✓	✓	✓	✓	✓				
Bates (Status of Women Canada, 2002)[d]	✓	✓				✓							✓	✓

Policy and programme recommendations

Policy and programme recommendations

Sources/author(s)	Increase access to SME financing	Networking, mentoring, training, advice, incl. financial literacy	Better coordination of services (e.g., horizontal, private/public partnerships, reduce red tape)	Increase awareness of economic contributions of women ENTs, address credibility gaps	Women-focused and targeted SME programmes and services	Promotion of entrepreneurship as a career option	Women-friendly training, advisory services, curriculum	Access to government programmes, services, grants, contributions	One-stop access to information	Income protection, self-employment training (benefits, insurance)	Increase access to federal SME procurement	Gender, race disaggregated programme reviews and data, Indigenous data	Internationalization support (e.g., export training, missions)	Reporting best practices to facilitate enterprise growth
Bulte et al. (PM's Taskforce on Women Entrepreneurs, 2003)[b]	✓	✓	✓	✓	✓	✓	✓	✓	✓	✓	✓		✓	
Rooney et al. (Status of Women Canada, 2003)[d]	✓	✓	✓	✓	✓			✓		✓				
Industry Canada (2004)[b,d]	✓	✓	✓	✓										
Aboriginal Women & Economic Development (INAC/SWC, 2009)[b]	✓	✓	✓	✓	✓							✓		
Orser (Canadian Taskforce for Women's Business Growth, 2011)[a,b]	✓	✓	✓	✓	✓	✓	✓	✓	✓		✓	✓	✓	✓
McKinsey & Company (2017, p.11)[a,b]	✓	✓	✓									✓		
OECD (2017)[b]	✓													
Institute for Competitiveness and Prosperity (2019)[a,c]		✓			✓			✓			✓	✓		
National Aboriginal Capital Corporations Association (2019, 2020a, b)[a,c]	✓	✓	✓					✓			✓	✓		✓
Grantham, Stefov & Tiessen (Oxfam Canada, 2019)[a]			✓		✓			✓			✓		✓	✓
Women's Entrepreneurship Knowledge Hub (2020a)[a,c]	✓	✓	✓				✓	✓			✓	✓	✓	✓

Policy and programme recommendations

Sources/author(s)	Increase access to SME financing	Networking, mentoring, training, advice, incl. financial literacy	Better coordination of services (e.g., horizontal, private/public partnerships, reduce red tape)	Increase awareness of economic contributions of women ENTs, address credibility gaps	Women-focused and targeted SME programmes and services	Promotion of entrepreneurship as a career option	Women-friendly training, advisory services, curriculum	Access to government programmes, services, grants, contributions	One-stop access to information	Income protection, self-employment training (benefits, insurance)	Increase access to federal SME procurement	Gender, race disaggregated programme reviews and data, Indigenous data	Internationalization support (e.g., export training, missions)	Reporting best practices to facilitate enterprise growth
Women's Chamber of Commerce (2020)[c,a]	✓									✓				
Ravanera & Sultana (uToronto, YWCA, 2020)[c,d,a]*	✓				✓		✓			✓	✓	✓		

Notes: a = private sector; b = government/sponsored; c = non-profit/non-governmental; d = academic. * Intersectional lens. Acronyms: PM, Prime Ministers; SWC, Status of Women Canada; uToronto, University of Toronto Gender and the Economy Institute (GATE).
Source: Adapted and update from Orser (2017).

The OECD's (2017) priorities are consistent with those advanced in other Canadian reports. Between 1986 and 2020 at least 23 reports, taskforces and forums have advanced recommendations with respect to women's entrepreneurship policy and programming (Table 3.1). The most frequently cited recommendations were to: increase access to SME financing ($n = 17$); enhance provision of networking, mentoring, training and advisory services ($n = 15$); improve coordination of services ($n = 13$); fund women-focused SME programmes ($n = 11$); ease access to government programmes, services and grants ($n = 9$); and assemble gender, sex and other data for programme assessment and reporting ($n = 9$).

Among the six reports published since the launch of the Women's Entrepreneurship Strategy (ISED, 2018), recommendations continued to advocate for measures to increase access to financing, networks, mentors, training, government programmes, services, grants, contributions and provision of data for programme review and reporting. Improved access to federal contracting shifted to the top five recommendations.[4]

Stevenson's (2004) recommendations for a national policy framework and advocacy arm in government for women's entrepreneurship mirror recommendations advanced by the Prime Minister's Taskforce for Women Entrepreneurs (Bulte et al., 2003), the Canadian Taskforce for the Growth of Women-owned Enterprises (Orser, 2011) and OECD (2017). The (2018) Women Entrepreneurship Strategy reflects Canada's first national women entrepreneurship policy framework. A permanent office to champion women's entrepreneurship has not been realized.

WOMEN-FOCUSED ENTREPRENEURSHIP POLICIES IN CANADA

In Canada, the period 2015 to 2020 ushered in unprecedented government focus on women-owned SMEs. Following the 2015 federal election, the Liberal government introduced Canada's first gender-balanced cabinet; in 2017, the government announced the Canada-United States Council for Advancement of Women Entrepreneurs and Business Leaders (Council) and the *Feminist International Assistance Program*. Subsequently, the 2018 budget announced the *Women Entrepreneurship Strategy* built on four initiatives:[5,6]

- Entrepreneurship fund and ecosystem fund;
- Improved access to federal programming;
- Funds for Statistics Canada and a Women Entrepreneurship Knowledge Hub;
- Related initiatives in other federal agencies.

In 2018, Statistics Canada launched the Centre for Gender, Diversity and Inclusion Statistics, and an online platform to aggregate databases, reports and tools (e.g., weblinks to OECD Gender Data Portal, UN Women, the International Labour Organization and the World Economic Forum). The Global Entrepreneurship Monitor (Bosma et al., 2020, p. 93) reported that the Canadian federal budget expanded support for inclusive entrepreneurship for women, youth, seniors and Indigenous peoples through a CAN$100 million Indigenous Growth Fund and a CAN$17 million Aboriginal Entrepreneurship Program over three years. The government allocated CAN$3 million to Futurpreneur Canada to support youth entrepreneurs.

To further support women and other equity seeking groups, in 2020 Canada's first woman Finance Minister delivered the *Fall Economic Plan* outlining a feminist pandemic recovery strategy. The plan specified that policies were to be evaluated and tracked based on how measures affect women, men, youth, members of the LGBTQ2+ community, persons with disabilities, racialized Canadians and Indigenous peoples. The plan profiled a gender-results framework that prioritizes education and skills development, equal and full participation in the economy, gender-based violence and harassment, security of person and access to justice, poverty and health outcomes and gender equality, including in leadership (Government of Canada, 2020a, p. xi).

Assessment of the Women Entrepreneurship Strategy

The objectives of the Women Entrepreneurship Strategy (Government of Canada, 2018) CAN$5 billion investment were to double the number of women entrepreneurs by 2025. The 2018 budget also referenced a 2017 McKinsey Global Institute study that projected that "... by taking steps to advance greater equality for women – such as employing more women in technology and boosting women's participation in the workforce – Canada could add $150 billion to its economy by 2026" (Government of Canada, 2018, p. 11). To date, there has been no public accounting of the impacts of the Women Entrepreneurship Strategy.

The OECD (2017) recommendations related primarily to the need to scale up small businesses, increase the number of high-growth firms, and enhance productivity and exporting among established firms. These recommendations reflect Government of Canada data that document gender differences in firm growth, survival and productivity of SMEs. Yet, an objective of the Women Entrepreneurship Strategy appears to be that of facilitating start-ups. Research is clear that job creation and economic development are disproportionately driven by the growth of new enterprises. Accordingly, it would appear that policy ought to pivot from an emphasis on promoting start-ups to one of supporting the survival and growth of existing women-owned SMEs. The disproportionate impacts of the COVID-19 pandemic on women-owned SMEs further increases the urgency of doing so.

Increase Access to Capital

Increased access to capital was operationalized through federal and crown corporation funds, such as: (1) Innovation Science and Economic Development (ISED) Women Entrepreneurship Fund; (2) Business Development Bank of Canada (BDC) Women in Technology Venture Fund; and (3) Export Development Corporation (EDC) women-focused programme. Each fund is discussed in the context of OECD (2017) and other Canadian report recommendations (Table 3.1).

Women Entrepreneurship Fund

The Women Entrepreneurship Fund allocated a portion of the total CAN$30 million investment to 321 projects by women entrepreneurs (including Indigenous-owned SMEs) in the form of up to $100,000 in non-repayable contributions and CAN$30 million to women-owned and women-led businesses to grow and reach new markets.[7]

Applicant evaluation criteria emphasized economic performance metrics: increased revenue, market share, jobs created, and improved production, process, technology or service. These criteria align with OECD (2017) recommendations to support SMEs in scaling-up, expanding, growing, pursuing market opportunities abroad and advancing commercial research to drive innovation.

Applicant eligibility specified firms of less than 500 employees, *women-owned* – where women have owned the majority of the company (more than 50%) for at least two years – or *women-led*, an enterprise with a woman or women with long-term control and management of the business, equity stake and active role in strategic and day-to-day decision making.[8] *Diverse* and *intersectional groups* were also specified. *Diverse* was defined as women with disabilities, Indigenous women, women in rural or remote regions, recent immigrants, visible minority women, and women from Official Language Minority Communities (OLMCs), LGBTQ+, youth, seniors. Applicant guidelines defined *intersectional* as individuals with overlapping or intersecting social identities (e.g., LGBTQ+ groups in rural and northern areas, or women in remote areas with disabilities).

It is not yet clear how awarding $100,000 in non-repayable contributions to fewer than 400 women-owned SMEs has impacted approximately 275,000 other women-owned SMEs, 231,000 equally-owned SMEs (Grekou, Li & Liu, 2018a) and 1,059,500 self-employed women (Statistics Canada, 2020a).

Interventions, according to widely accepted principles of economics, should address demonstrated capital market imperfections. Accordingly, the rationale for this investment is not justified.

The rationale for the Women Entrepreneurship Fund must be considered in the context of the problem it seeks to address. Federal data show that majority women-owned employer SMEs in Canada are less likely than counterpart men to apply for (any type of) external financing. Government data, moreover, reveal that women-owned enterprises are more likely to have loan applications approved than SMEs owned by men (Statistics Canada 2017 Survey of Financing and Growth of SMEs). Figure 3.3A (above) illustrates these points. In 2017, compared to majority men-owned and SMEs owned equally by men and women, majority women-owned SMEs were significantly less likely to apply for debt, equity, capital leasing or trade credit. Figure 3.3B illustrates that when majority women-owned SMEs did apply for debt, they were more likely to have their loan applications approved, a significant change from the previous survey periods. The rationale for non-repayable contributions needs to be based on recent evidence of a gender-related financing gap, an investment that is not supported by these federal data.

These points are supported by studies from Canada that show that *terms of lending* do not vary by gender of borrower, when confounding covariates such as firm size, sector and owner experience are controlled (Fabowale et al., 1995; Haines et al., 1999; Orser et al., 2006; Huang & Rivard, 2021). The 2017 finding from the *Survey of Financing and Growth of SMEs* is under-reported in reports about the state of women's entrepreneurship and access to capital in Canada. This is counterproductive because it likely discourages women from seeking needed financing. These observations speak to the value of studies enforced by means of blind, peer-review and sophisticated analytics that control for firm/other attributes for informing women's entrepreneurship policies.

The Women Entrepreneurship Fund approach also raises concerns about political opportunism, liabilities of 'cherry-picking' winners, and showcasing enterprises (e.g., deploying public funds to garner social media) versus investment in intermediaries with regional and sector reach. It has been said that government has trouble picking winners.

Next-generation policies to increase women entrepreneurs' access to and management of capital might be more effective if targeted at both demand and supply side change, including: enhancing access and use of trade credit, leasing and equity; addressing gender differences in financial literacy among small business owners (Scotiabank Women Initiative, 2020); informing ecosystem stakeholders about lending and investment practices in Canada; and clarifying venture capitalists and angel investor expectations.

Strengthening micro-loan adjudication capacities and sharing good practices, for example, may enhance provision of early-stage capital coupled with training and advisory services, particularly for those entrepreneurs whose firms are too new to secure capital from formal lenders. Investigation into provision of micro-loans, including to self-employed women, co-operatives and social enterprises is warranted. It is essential to position policy in the context of current Canadian banking and financing practices.

Women in Technology Venture Fund

Branded as "one of the world's largest venture capital funds dedicated to investing in women-led technology companies", the Business Development Bank of Canada (BDC), a crown corporation, has committed CAN\$200 million to the *Women in Technology Venture Fund.* This fund mandate is:

> To deliver a return on the investment and make a lasting impact on the Canadian tech ecosystem through: (1) direct investment in women-led tech companies; (2) indirect investment in emerging venture funds with at least one-woman partner which has also committed to investing in women-led tech companies; and, (3) ecosystem development with partners to support a self-sustaining ecosystem for women that provides mentorship, networking, and tools... .

The BDC (2020) website reports that the number of women entrepreneurs has quadrupled over the past 40 years.

Provisions in the BDC Women in Technology (WIT) Venture Fund respond to the observation that "domestic institutional investors are not playing the role that might be expected" (OECD, 2017, p. 15). BDC has not actioned an OECD (2017) recommendation of setting minimum quotas for women clients. Targeting the BDC Women in Technology (WIT) Venture Fund at women-led versus women-owned SMEs levels is inconsistent with the recommendations of OECD (2017) and the reports highlighted in Table 3.1.

The media criticism that ensued is noteworthy. In April 2019, an ad hoc assessment of fund recipients concluded that the profiles of some recipient firms did not meet fund guidelines. Irregularities included firms that listed senior women on the BDC website but not on the CrunchBase company profile, promotions of women timed with receipt of BDC funding, absence of women in leadership at the time of the assessment, and organizations on CrunchBase that indicated that they received Women in Technology (WIT) Venture Fund monies with no women in leadership positions (Mutch, 2019). The observations motivate disclosure of compliance to funding guidelines, and impact analysis of beneficiaries using an intersectional lens.

WEKH (2020) suggests that support for *women-led* or women-founded companies "... stems in part from the severe underrepresentation of women within high-growth technology companies, and in part from the implications for attracting venture capital". The WEKH (2020) report cites the Canadian Advanced Technology Alliance (CATA) that ironically argues, "51 percent equity definition for women owned businesses introduces yet another form of discrimination against women" (CATA, 2019). Industry accusations that policies to support majority women-owned SMEs are "discriminatory" fail to acknowledge historical gender inequalities and documented differences in the growth performance of majority women-owned SMEs.

To the best of the author's knowledge, there has been no public accounting or intersectional analysis of the Women in Technology Fund. Thus, it is unclear if, or to what degree, definitional criteria employed by the BDC Women in Technology (WIT) Venture Fund lead disproportionately to opportunistic behaviour by applicants. It is unclear how criteria pit investors, including women, against women founders for access to limited funding. It is unclear how the prioritization of women-led enterprises, without substantive consultation, impacts the work of supplier diversity organizations. Independent and rigorous analysis is implied.

In light of the government objective to double the number of women entrepreneurs by 2025, BDC's (2020) statement that the number of women entrepreneurs has quadrupled over the past 40 years – without clarification of the temporal context of *when* women entered self-employment – is misleading.[9] So too is the federally-sponsored *The State of Women's Entrepreneurship* (WEKH, 2020, p. 5) that asserts: "Self-employment among women is also growing faster than it is for men" (WEKH, 2020, p. 5).[10]

It is true that the growth in the number of self-employed women between 1975 and 2000[11] was unprecedented. By 2000, however, this growth had almost completely abated. As noted, between 2000 and 2019 Statistics Canada Labour Force Survey data revealed that self-employment increased by approximately 200,000 men and about the same number of women. There were few gender differences in the change in absolute numbers of self-employed women compared to men.

Embedded within these data is another observation: self-employed men are more likely than self-employed women to be incorporated and to have paid help. Women entering self-employment are less likely to incorporate or to have paid help: essentially, their businesses appear to be more precarious than those of men. Government policy should not be furthered by claims that are at variance with their own data. Rather than the overriding policy objective to create (double) the number of new (precarious) firms, the data support the need to sustain and grow existing women-owned enterprises in Canada. Furthermore, universal childcare and broader access to leave and employment insurance are not yet in place. The impacts of the pandemic have made clear the importance of such measures in supporting the self-employed and small business owners, particularly marginalized and racialized women entrepreneurs in Canada.

Export Development Corporation (EDC) Women-focused Programme

The EDC website indicates that the programme seeks to create "$2 billion in trade by 2023 – eight times more than the $250 million target set in 2018; 1,000 unique customers by 2023, up from 381 in 2018; and increased investment of $100 million, up from $50 million in 2019". The objectives are again impressive. It is not clear what problem is to be solved by this investment. Statistics Canada (2019) reports that majority women-owned SMEs have progressed in export activity, their "share of these SMEs that exported increased from 5.9% in 2007 to about 11.2% in 2017, while the share for men-owned SMEs remained largely unchanged, from 11.1% to 12.2%, over the same period (2017)" (Government of Canada, 2017; Industry Canada, 2015). It is too early to assess the 2023 target.

Increase Access to Mainstream and Women-focused Programmes

The federal government invested CAN$85 million in the WES Ecosystem Fund with objectives to "strengthen capacity within the entrepreneurship ecosystem and close gaps in service for women entrepreneurs led by non-profit organizations". Project-based funds were awarded through two streams: seven national/multi-regional projects totalling CAN$15 million, and 45 regional projects totalling CAN$70 million. The government allocated additional investment of CAN$100 million to existing projects in response to the COVID-19 pandemic.

This pillar reflects significant investment in ecosystem supports for women and is an innovative approach to industry-specific measures. Recipients are to focus on creating inclusive incubators and accelerators, training women in start-ups and growth, networking and matchmaking. Programmes target specific sectors and demographic groups, such as: the Canadian Film Centre and women-led digital media firms; the Saskatchewan Food Industry Development Centre Inc., women entrepreneurs in food processing; the Elizabeth Fry Society and marginalized women who may have struggled with mental health issues or have had conflict with the law; and Groundswell Education Society which supports social enterprises and underserved women, including LGBTQ+, newcomer, Indigenous peoples and low-income clients.

This approach is relevant given Statistics Canada (2020c, n.p.) evidence about the associations between firm size and industry concentration with respect to firm survival and productivity of women-owned SMEs:

> ... with equally owned start-ups having the highest survival rate when controlling for firm size but not industry. Women-owned start-ups also exhibited lower labour productivity than equally owned and men-owned start-ups, with men-owned start-ups having the highest overall labour productivity when controlling for capital but not industry. Interestingly, when industry differences were accounted for, women-owned start-ups were more productive and more likely to survive than men-owned start-ups in those industries in which women-owned start-ups had a large presence (i.e., retail trade, accommodation and food services but not health care and social assistance).

Next-generation policies should be directed at increasing productivity, targeting all sectors versus those perceived to be underrepresented (e.g., sectors under the Innovation Superclusters Initiative). Investment in management information and financial software, financial and digital literacy, and other measures to enhance productivity should continue (e.g., digital main street training to transition services to online delivery formats).

Increase Access to Federal SME Procurement

Public Services and Procurement Canada (PSPC), Canada's central purchasing agency, has been mandated by the Prime Minister to increase the participation in federal procurement of businesses led by members of underrepresented groups, including women. While there is funding allotted to a set-aside for Black entrepreneurs, women-focused SME set-asides have not yet been established.

Initiatives focus on outreach and awareness of SME contracting opportunities. PSPC is pilot testing approaches that incorporate social procurement measures (e.g., small pilot in temporary services; selection methods for architects, engineers and catering services):

> PSPC is also partnering with professional organizations that support under-represented communities to encourage participation in government procurement among their membership. These include the Gay and Lesbian Chamber of Commerce (GLCC), Women Business Enterprises (WBE) Canada and the Inclusive Workplace and Supply Council of Canada (IWSCC). (PSPC, 2020)

The government continues to lag large municipalities (such as City of Toronto) and large corporations in supporting supplier diversity procurement initiatives. This slow response is despite multiple reports that have called for public procurement programmes to support women-owned SMEs (see Table 3.1) and the recommendations of the Standing Committee on Government Operations and Estimates to:

> make federal procurement more inclusive for SMEs, women-owned businesses and other socially disadvantaged groups. (Lukiwski, 2018, p. 1)

Pilot initiatives with a sector focus and set-aside for Black-owned and -led enterprises provide evidence about the limited impact of decades of advocacy for women-focused procurement programmes. Prioritizing pilot projects in sectors in which women and people of colour are overrepresented perpetuates stereotypes. The announcement of the Black Entrepreneurship Strategy suggests the need for an integrated strategy to support underrepresented groups, one that includes set-asides for all equity seeking groups.

Coordination of Support Services and Advocacy

The government has established an interdepartmental committee of senior policymakers that meet to discuss the Women Entrepreneurship Strategy. Global Affairs Canada has also established a Gender and Trade Advisory Group comprised of external and internal experts who meet periodically. ISED Canada has not established an agency to lead women's entrepreneurship policy or coordinate cross-federal policies and programmes. The committees are not mandated to continue and can be disbanded through a policy decision.

This study found limited evidence of substantive infrastructure to support the long-term viability of women-focused policy. An interdepartmental committee to advise women-focused SME policies reflects historical practice, an approach evidenced through four previous and disbanded committees on women entrepreneurs between 2000 and 2015 (Orser, 2017). Evidence suggests that committees are highly vulnerable to changes in federal priorities and political leadership.

Women Entrepreneurship Knowledge Hub

The third pillar allotted CAN$9 million to a Women Entrepreneurship Knowledge Hub (at Ryerson University Diversity Institute). The Hub, which was initially expected to become self-sustaining (as specified in ISED 2018 requests for proposals) links together:

> ... the elements of the ecosystem, advancing research and the sharing of best practices, promoting a gender and diversity lens across all elements in the innovation ecosystem not just women entrepreneurship organizations but also financial institutions and investors, incubators and business support organizations, educational institutions and large organizations, which procure services from entrepreneurs.

WEKH is organized around 9 regional hubs and brings together more than 100 researchers, 75 partner organizations, as well as stakeholders across the ecosystem. (Cukier & Chavoushi, 2020, n.p)

An arm's-length assessment of the incremental impacts of, and participation within, the WEKH have not yet been reported.

Expert Advisory Board

The fourth pillar of the WES is an Expert Advisory Board that is comprised of seven external and three ex officio members. The board does not reflect diverse "policy-smart" advisors from grassroots, feminist, women-owned enterprises, and underrepresented communities of diverse women entrepreneurs. To bolster outreach, to seek views that challenge policy assumptions, and to enhance inclusive decision making, ISED might usefully benefit by moving to a robust advisory process.

An independent advisory board with the explicit mandate to support entrepreneurs and small business recovery among equity seeking groups should be struck and managed independently of federally funded recipient intermediaries. Input should be sought by diverse communities of stakeholders, recognizing that many majority women-owned SMEs do not retain the assets to participate in consultations. Advisory processes should enlist women in paid advisory roles given that compared to industry advocates, many women entrepreneurs do not retain the financial cushion or employees to offset the time and other resources necessary in order to participate in advising government.

Gender and Other Owner Profile Data

Since 2018, multiple federal government agencies have released reports employing gender-disaggregated data to report on the statistical profiles of entrepreneurs and self-employed Canadians. The implications for research are now considered.

IMPLICATIONS FOR RESEARCH

To inform women-focused measures, the government is encouraged to clarify the rationale for millions of dollars in non-repayable contributions and to report on the incremental impacts or outcomes of these investments. Statistics Canada retains the capacity to undertake such analyses, including the ability to directly compare, by matching funded and non-funded firms and tracking performance using Canada Revenue Agency business identifiers (e.g., tracking and comparing cohort changes in survival, growth and jobs created). This recommendation is consistent with assessments of the *Canadian Small Business Financing Program* that is also administered by ISED (2020c).

Similarly, to benchmark outcomes, a comparison of large-scale mainstream initiatives regarding women-owned SMEs and all SMEs is recommended (such as CAN$950 million *Innovation Superclusters Initiative* led by ISED). Comparative analyses of incremental performance will strengthen understanding about the efficacy and rationales for targeted (women-focused), mainstream (innovation) and sector-specific interventions. Such analyses will inform debate about the legitimacy of these policies and programmes.

These research recommendations are important given that a lack of empirical evidence (Foss et al., 2019) stymies progress in the development of women's entrepreneurship policies and motivates policies predicated on political ideology, perceptions and opportunism rather than evidence-based measures (Arshed et al., 2019).

The literature reports on rapid shifts in policy agendas and deviations between the *intent* of policies targeted to SME policies and *implementation*, deviations that further dilute the legitimacy of women-focused policy (Arshed et al., 2016; Pettersson et al., 2017):

> … how macro-level policy objectives, when refracted through multiple layers of localized interpretation, tend to deviate (sometimes dramatically) from their original ostensive purpose (Arshed et al., 2016; Burch, 2007). Thus, while policies are representative of certain normative ideas, they are also changeable during the social processes of enactment, and their institutional maintenance is ultimately beholden to the ever-shifting agendas of diverse participating actor groups (Lascoumes & Le Gales, 2007). (Arshed et al., 2019, p. 555)

Research is needed to report on localized programmes and the unintended consequences of measures targeted at *women-owned* versus *women-led* enterprises, including schisms among bureaucrats, investors, advocates and supplier diversity support organizations.

To strengthen stakeholder input in informing policies, the Government of Canada is encouraged to construct a standing pan-Canadian panel of self-employed workers and SME owners. Similar to the monthly *Labour Force Survey* managed by Statistics Canada, a standing panel of women-owners could respond (in a timely manner) to periodic survey questions, gauge issues and provide rapid arm's-length feedback on policies to support entrepreneurs. The need for such a panel, one that enables rapid access to a large, representative sample of non-employer and employer SMEs, is evidenced in the limited impact of periodic federal consultations (e.g., *Canada-United States Council for Advancement of Women Entrepreneurs and Business Leaders* and *Feminist International Assistance Program*) and a seven-person Expert Advisory.

Academic research and industry consultations are also needed to understand the policy development processes, including role of political influence [interference] and adjudication protocols to operationalize policies. Most women-focused SME policy studies have focused on the efficacy of interventions and policy design, framed as:

> a monolithic, static discourse (e.g. Ahl & Nelson, 2015) and not as a distributed social institution. To address information gaps, there is a need to examine policy from the perspective of the diverse actors that constitute the policy enactment ecosystem. (Arshed et al., 2019, p. 555)

It is encouraging that the government has introduced a Black Entrepreneurship Program that includes a procurement set-aside. The set-aside, however, fails to support all equity seeking groups. It is notable that the Black Entrepreneurship Program and Aboriginal Entrepreneurship Program are designed to redress historical inequities with different social, cultural and economic origins. Clarification about why and how federal investments redress such differences is warranted.

There is almost no intersectional data to report on federal WES beneficiaries or the impact of mainstream and targeted programmes to support women, LGBTQ2+, Black people, disabled and Indigenous peoples. The practice of comparing underrepresented entrepreneurs *to each other* downplays the roots of inequity. Federally funded small business programmes should mandate intersectional reporting on impacts. It would be informative to understand how the government has addressed limitations of the Aboriginal Entrepreneurship Program (Lukiwski, 2018).

In summary, to move beyond ad hoc women-focused to inclusive small business policies, this study aligns with calls for research to understand further the rationale and policy development process, implementation of policies, and the assessment criteria for evaluation protocols of women-focused and mainstream SME support programmes.

Study Limitations

Study limitations are noted herein. This study was limited to one developed country. Given the limitations of a single-country methodology, findings cannot be generalized to other geo-political contexts. The author's perspective is from the viewpoint of an established, White, academic, settler and cis woman. The author was an advisor to the OECD (2017) SME policy review. She is a participant in the Global Affairs Canada Gender and Trade Advisory Group and the Principal Investigator of an unsuccessful proposal for the

Women Entrepreneurship Knowledge Hub. While these roles provide insight into policy decision processes, the critique likely reflects experiential bias.

This study does not examine provisions within the feminist international assistance programme or gender-based trade negotiations in Canada. Both portfolios fall outside of the pillars of the Women Entrepreneurship Strategy. The critique therefore provides an incomplete assessment of all Government of Canada measures to support women entrepreneurs. Finally, the scope of analysis does not consider regional women-focused policies. To access databases of women-focused programmes, see the Government of Canada,[12] the Women's Enterprise Organizations of Canada[13] and the Women Entrepreneurship Knowledge Hub.[14]

CONCLUSIONS

The Women Entrepreneurship Strategy (ISED, 2018) addresses two challenges identified by *the Global Women's Enterprise Research Group*: lack of women entrepreneurship policies and women's entrepreneurship policies without programme funding (Henry et al., 2017). This study presents evidence that without political leadership, bureaucratic will and rigorous analysis, advocacy has limited impact on enacting women-focused small business policies.

The literature review identifies a number of factors associated with the fragility of women's entrepreneurship policies, including shifting political agendas, lack of consensus on policy rationale and limited empirical evidence to inform debate about women-focused versus mainstream measures. The 2020 Fall Economic Statement that profiles a *gender-results framework* to prioritize equal and full participation in the economy (Government of Canada, 2020a) is encouraging and suggests that women entrepreneurs will be a target for future government investment.

Post-pandemic policies to support women and other underrepresented entrepreneurs must clarify further the rationale and respond to evidence-based gaps that are informed by data (e.g., target investment at existing versus potential small businesses). A transparent procurement strategy for equity seeking groups is needed, one that takes into account the complex intersections of power that reproduce inequities. As an anonymous reviewer of this chapter cautioned, an integrated approach to entrepreneurship funding should not minimize historical inequities and power structures that impact people differently. "An equity-based approach helps people access the resources they need to be successful, rather than giving everyone the same resources. An equity-based approach is critical where *equal* treatment may reproduce systemic inequities, including racism, sexism, heterosexism, ableism, and more."

Arm's-length advisory and assessment of the impacts of investment in policies targeted to women are needed to enhance the legitimacy of women's entrepreneurship policy in Canada, and thus avoid instability of these measures as evidenced in the UK (Arshed et al., 2016, 2019). At this time, the policy development processes and impacts of the Women Entrepreneurship Strategy remain a "black box". Research is needed to enhance transparency, avoid governments cherry-picking winners and to understand further the influences of politics, bureaucratic will, mass protests and other influences in policy development processes. This study offers insights to encourage further research and policies to support diverse entrepreneurs.

NOTES

1. For example, Industry Canada (1998) reported that "although women entrepreneurs comprise only one-third of all self-employed, their numbers are growing at a rate that is twice that for self-employed men" (44.4% for women versus 20.0% percentage change for men (net increase in self-employment of 190,780 for women and 212,265 for men)). Sources: Census of Canada (1991, 1996).
2. In 2017, 40% of SMEs were majority owned by members of the same family, 12.2% by visible minorities, 1.4% by Aboriginal persons and 0.5% by person(s) with a disability (ISED, 2020b).
3. The methodology of the 2017 OECD *SME and Entrepreneurship Policy in Canada* report included a questionnaire by government authorities and study mission to Canada by the OECD Secretariat and international experts. Comments on a draft report by steering group members of the OECD *Working Party on SMEs and Entrepreneurship*, stakeholders in Canada and a peer review of the draft report by government were also undertaken. This report assessed policies before a federal election in 2015.
4. Illustrative studies include: The Institute for Competitiveness & Prosperity (2019); National Aboriginal Capital Corporations Association (2019, 2020a, 2020b); Grantham, Stefov and Tiessen (on behalf of Oxfam Canada), 2019; Women's Entrepreneurship Knowledge Hub (2020); Women's Chamber of Commerce (2021), Ravanera and Sultana (Gender and the Economy (GATE), University of Toronto and YWCA, 2020).
5. In 2020, the Black Entrepreneurship Program (ISED, 2020a) was announced. Similar to the Women Entrepreneurship Strategy (ISED, 2018), the portfolio includes: a Black entrepreneur loan fund; ecosystem funding; and a Black entrepreneurship knowledge hub. The government also committed to increasing Black entrepreneurs' access to federal contracts through a procurement set-aside programme.
6. The Government of Canada 2018 Budget (p. 110): https://www.budget.gc.ca/2018/docs/plan/budget-2018-en.pdf
7. Subsequent investment (CAN$10 million) included as set-aside of $2.5M for Indigenous women projects.
8. Additional criteria included: "*Long-term control and management of the business* – have been engaged in the operation, management and ownership of the business for at least two years. *Active role in strategic decision making* – involved in elements related to the establishment of priorities, objective and goals for the business; overall operations of the business. *Day to day decision making* – involved in elements related to the financial management, human

resources, supply management, logistics or customer services. *Equity stake –* demonstrates an ownership in the company."

9.   Since 2000, the annualized average rate of increase of women's particpation in self-employment is approximately 1.5 percent per year (Statistics Canada, *Labour Force Survey*, various years).

10. Between 2000 and 2020 the increase in the number of women in self-employment was almost equal to the increase in number of men in self-employment (Statistics Canada, *Labour Force Survey*, various years).

11. Statistics Canada (2018) reports that "The number of women-owned enterprises increased to over 300,000 in 2013, from 232,800 in 2005 ... or by 33%. The employment in women-owned enterprises increased by 20% to nearly 900,000 in 2013. Equally owned enterprises experienced a similar growth in business count (32%), but with a slower growth in employment (12%). By contrast, men-owned enterprises grew the least, 22% for business counts, and 8% for employment."

12. Accessed at: https://www.ic.gc.ca/eic/site/csbfp-pfpec.nsf/eng/la03285.html

13. Accessed at: https://wekh.ca

14. Accessed at: https://weoc.ca

BIBLIOGRAPHY

Aboriginal Women & Economic Development (Indian and Northern Affairs Canada & Status of Women Canada (2009). *Evaluation of INAC's Economic Development Programs – Follow-up Status Update as of September 30, 2009*, Government of Canada. Access at https://www.rcaanc-cirnac.gc.ca/eng/1307037190438/1542996957702#archived

Ahl, H. & Nelson, T. (2015). How policy positions women entrepreneurs: A comparative analysis of state discourse in Sweden and the United States. *Journal of Business Venturing*, 30(2), 273–291.

Arshed, N., Chalmers, D. & Matthews, R. (2019). Institutionalizing women's enterprise policy: A legitimacy-based perspective. *Entrepreneurship Theory and Practice*, 43(3), 553–581.

Arshed, N., Mason, C. & Carter, S. (2016). Exploring the disconnect in policy implementation: A case of enterprise policy in England. *Environment and Planning C: Government and Policy*, 34(8), 1582–1611.

Baird, B. (1982). *Canadian Women Owner/Managers*. Policy Research and Formulation Unit, Small Business Secretariat, Queen's Park, Toronto, January.

Belcourt, M., Burke, R. J. & Lee-Gosselin, H. (1991). *The glass box: Women business owners in Canada*. Ottawa: Canadian Advisory Council on the Status of Women.

Bérard, J. & Brown, D. (1994). *Services to women entrepreneurs: The Western Canadian case*. Manitoba Office, Western Economic Diversification Canada.

Bobiwash, H. (2020a). *Indigenous women entrepreneurs in Canada. Summary of National Survey Findings* (2020b). National Aboriginal Capital Corporations Association. https://nacca.ca/wp-content/uploads/2020/07/NACCA-IWE-Survey-Report.pdf

Bobiwash, H. (2020b). *Indigenous women entrepreneurs in Canada. Valuable investments in their businesses, families and communities*. National Aboriginal Capital Corporations Association. https://nacca.ca/wp-content/uploads/2020/07/NACCA-IWE-Summary-Report.pdf

Bosma, N., Hill, S., Ionescu-Somers, A., Kelley, D., Levie, J., Tarnawa, A. and the Global Entrepreneurship Research Association (2020). *Global Entrepreneurship Monitor 2019/2020 Global Report*. https://www.babson.edu/media/babson/assets/global-entrepreneurship-monitor/2019-2020-GEM-Global-Report.pdf

British Columbia's Women's Programs (1986). *Survey of women business owners in British Columbia: Major findings and policy implications. British Columbia: The Programs*. (Author's archives.)

Brydges, T. & Hracs, B. J. (2019). What motivates millennials? How intersectionality shapes the working lives of female entrepreneurs in Canada's fashion industry. *Gender, Place & Culture*, 26(4), 510–532.

Bulte, S., Callbeck, C., Duplain, R., Fitzpatrick, K., Redman, K., & Lever, A. (2003). *The Prime Minister's task force on women entrepreneurs*. Ottawa: National Liberal Caucus Research Bureau, Information Management.

Burch, P. (2007). Educational policy and practice from the perspective of institutional theory: Crafting a wider lens. *Educational Researcher*, 36(2), 84–95.

Business Development Bank of Canada (2020). Women in Technology Venture Fund. https://www.bdc.ca/en/bdc-capital/venture-capital/strategic-approach/women-tech-fund. Also see https://www.bdc.ca/globalassets/digizuite/10308-changing-face-of-women-entrepreneurs.pdf

Canada-United States Council for Advancement of Women Entrepreneurs and Business Leaders and the Feminist International Assistance Program (2017). *Advancing women in business*. https://advancingwomeninbusiness.com/

Canadian Advanced Technology Alliance (CATA) (2019). *51 percent equity definition for women owned businesses introduces yet another form of discrimination against women*. https://cata.ca/2019/feds-51-percent-equity-definition/

Canadian Federation of Independent Business (CFIB, 2004). *Report on Trade*. Toronto: Canadian Federation of Independent Business.

Canadian Women Chamber of Commerce (2021). *What women entrepreneurs need from Canada's 2021 budget*. https://canwcc.ca/wp-content/uploads/2021/04/Budget-2021-Report_R.pdf

Coleman, S., Henry, C., Orser, B., Foss, L. & Welter, F. (2019). Policy support for women entrepreneurs' access to financial capital: Evidence from Canada, Germany, Ireland, Norway, and the United States. *Journal of Small Business Management*, 57(Supp 2), 296–322. https://doi.org/10.1111/jsbm.12473

Cosh, A., Cumming, D. & Hughes, A. (2009). Outside entrepreneurial capital. *The Economic Journal*, 119(540), 1494–1533.

Crenshaw, K. (1989). Demarginalizing the intersection of race and sex: A Black feminist critique of antidiscrimination doctrine, feminist theory and antiracist politics. *The University of Chicago Legal Forum*, Article 8, 1989(1), 139–167.

Cukier, W. & Chavoushi, Z. H. (2020). Facilitating women entrepreneurship in Canada: The case of WEKH. *Gender in Management*, 35(3), 303–318.

Dalziel, M., Cumming, D. & Wolfe, D. (2014). Report of the expert panel examining Ontario's business support programs. Ontario Minister of Finance and the Ontario Minister of Economic Development, Employment and Infrastructure. DOI: 10.13140/RG.2.2.26302.69440

Davis, K. (2008), Intersectionality as buzzword: A sociology of science perspective on what makes a feminist theory successful. *Feminist Theory*, 9(1), 67.

Department for Women and Gender Equality Act (2018). Overview of the departmental mandate and legislation. https://cfc-swc.gc.ca/trans/briefing-information/transition/2019/tab-a-en.html

Digan, S. P., Sahi, G. K., Mantok, S. & Patel, P. C. (2019). Women's perceived empowerment in entrepreneurial efforts: The role of bricolage and psychological capital. *Journal of Small Business Management*, 57(1), 206–229.

Elam, A., Brush, C., Greene, P., Baumer, B., Dean, M., Heavlow, R., Babson College, Smith College, and the Global Entrepreneurship Research Association (GERA) (2018/2019). *Global Entrepreneurship Monitor (GEM) Global 2018/2019 Women's Entrepreneurship Report*. https://www.gemconsortium.org/file/open?fileId=50405

Export Development Corporation (EDC) (2020). EDC creates more opportunities for women in trade. https://www.edc.ca/en/about-us/newsroom/edc-women-trade-2020.html

Fabowale, L., Orser, B. & Riding, A. (1995). Gender, structural factors, and credit terms between Canadian small businesses and financial institutions. *Entrepreneurship Theory and Practice*, 19(4), 41–65.

Fischer, E. M., Reuber, A. R. & Dyke, L. S. (1993). A theoretical overview and extension of research on sex, gender, and entrepreneurship. *Journal of Business Venturing*, 8(2), 151–168.

Foss, L., Henry, C., Ahl, H. & Mikalsen, G. H. (2019). Women's entrepreneurship policy research: A 30-year review of the evidence. *Small Business Economics*, 53(2), 409–429.

Foundation of Canadian Women Entrepreneurs, Business Development Bank of Canada, & Kartini International Consulting (2000). *Best Practices for Women Entrepreneurs in Canada*, May.

Gill, R. (2014). Unspeakable inequalities: Post feminism, entrepreneurial subjectivity, and the repudiation of sexism among cultural workers. *Social Politics: International Studies in Gender, State & Society*, 21(4), 509–528.

The Global Entrepreneurship and Development Institute (2019). *Global Entrepreneurship Index*. https://thegedi.org/global-entrepreneurship-and-development-index/

Government of Canada (2017). *Survey on financing and growth of small and medium enterprises* (SFGSME). https://www.ic.gc.ca/eic/site/061.nsf/eng/03087.html

Government of Canada (2018). *Equality + Growth. A strong middle class*. Table in the House of Commons by the Hon. William Francis Morneau, Minister of Finance, 27 February 2018. https://www.budget.gc.ca/2018/docs/plan/budget-2018-en.pdf

Government of Canada (2020a). *Supporting Canadians and fighting COVID-19: Fall economic statement 2020*. News release. https://www.canada.ca/en/department-finance/news/2020/11/government-of-canada-releases-supporting-canadians-and-fighting-covid-19-fall-economic-statement-2020.html

Government of Canada (2020b). *Overview of federal government services for small business*. https://www.ic.gc.ca/eic/site/csbfp-pfpec.nsf/eng/la03285.html

Government of Canada (2021). Budget 2021. *A recovery plan for jobs, growth, and resilience*. https://www.budget.gc.ca/2021/home-accueil-en.html

Grantham, K., Stefov, D. & Tiessen, R. (2019). A feminist approach to women's economic empowerment: How Canada can lead on addressing the neglected areas of WEE. Oxfam Canada. https://giwps.georgetown.edu/resource/a-feminist-approach-to-womens-economic-empowerment-how-canada-can-lead-on-addressing-the-neglected-areas-of-wee/

Grekou, D., Li, J. & Liu, H. (2018a). *Women-owned enterprises in Canada. Economic insights*. Ottawa: Statistics Canada. https://www150.statcan.gc.ca/n1/pub/11-626-x/11-626-x2018083-eng.htm

Haines Jr., G. H., Orser, B. J. & Riding, A. L. (1999). Myths and realities: An empirical study of banks and the gender of small business clients. *Canadian Journal of Administrative Sciences*, 16(4), 291–307.

Halabisky, D. (2018). *Policy Brief on Women's Entrepreneurship, OECD SME and Entrepreneurship Papers*, No. 8, Paris: OECD. https://doi.org/10.1787/dd2d79e7-en

Henry, C., Foss, L. & Ahl, H. (2016). Gender and entrepreneurship research: A review of methodological approaches. *International Small Business Journal*, 34(3), 217–241. DOI: 10.1177/0266242614549779

Henry, C., Orser, B., Coleman, S., Foss, L. & Welter, F. (2017). Women's entrepreneurship policy: A 13-nation cross-country study. In Manolova, T. S., Brush, C. G., Edelman, L. F., Robb, A. M. & Welter, F. (eds), *Entrepreneurial ecosystems and growth of women's entrepreneurship: A comparative analysis.* Cheltenham: Edward Elgar, pp. 244–278.

Huang, L. (2020). *SME profile ownership demographics statistics.* Ottawa: Innovation, Science and Economic Development Canada, Small Business Branch, Research and Analysis Directorate.

Huang, L. & Rivard, P. (2021). *Financing of women-owned small and medium-sized enterprises in Canada.* Ottawa: Innovation, Science and Economic Development Canada, Research and Analysis Directorate, Small Business Branch. http://www.ic.gc.ca/eic/site/061.nsf/%20eng/h_03138.html

Hughes, K. (1999). *Gender and self-employment in Canada: Assessing trends and policy implications.* Ottawa: Canadian Policy Research Networks.

Industry Canada (2005). *Summary report from sustaining the momentum. An economic forum on women entrepreneurs.* Ottawa, Canada. https://www.ic.gc.ca/eic/site/061.nsf/eng/h_rd01306.html?Open=1&

Industry Canada (2014). *Innovation Canada: A call to action. Special report on procurement. The scope for using procurement to enhance innovation.* Catalogue no: Iu4-149/2-2011E-PDF. https://www.ic.gc.ca/eic/site/iccat.nsf/eng/07047_5.html

Industry Canada (2015). *Majority female-owned small and medium-sized enterprises. Special Edition: Key small business statistics.* https://www.ic.gc.ca/eic/site/061.nsf/eng/h_02966.html

Innovation, Science and Economic Development Canada (ISED) (2018). *Women entrepreneurship strategy.* https://www.ic.gc.ca/eic/site/107.nsf/eng/home

Innovation, Science and Economic Development Canada (ISED) (2020a). *Black entrepreneurship program.* https://www.ic.gc.ca/eic/site/150.nsf/eng/home

Innovation, Science and Economic Development Canada (ISED) (2020b). *SME profile: Ownership demographics statistics.* http://www.ic.gc.ca/eic/site/061.nsf/eng/h_03115.html#bookmark5-2

Innovation, Science and Economic Development Canada (ISED) (2020c). *Canada small business financing program: Guidelines.* https://www.ic.gc.ca/eic/site/csbfp-pfpec.nsf/eng/h_la03133.html

Institute for Competitiveness and Prosperity (2019). *Gender Equality, Diversity and Inclusion in Innovation: Roundtable Summary Report.* Accessed at https://www.empowerwomen.org/en/resources/documents/2019/04/gender-equality-diversity-and-inclusion-in-innovation-roundtable-summary-report?lang=en

Lever, A. (2004). *Best practices to support women entrepreneurs.* Toronto: Foundation of Canadian Women Entrepreneurs.

Lukiwski, T. (2018). *Modernizing federal procurement for small and medium enterprises, women-owned and Indigenous businesses.* Ottawa: House of Commons

Canada. https://www.ourcommons.ca/Content/Committee/421/OGGO/Reports/RP9
996115/oggorp15/oggorp15-e.pdf

Mackreal, L. (2013, 27 June). Ottawa's elimination of CIDA brand signals end of a foreign-aid era. *Globe & Mail.*

Mayoux, L. (2001). *Jobs, gender and small enterprises: Getting the policy environment right, in-focus programme on boosting employment through enterprise development, job creation and enterprise development.* International Labour Office (ILO), Geneva. https://www.ilo.org/empent/Publications/WCMS_111394/lang--en/index .htm

McKinsey Global Institute (2017). *The power of parity: Advancing women's equality in Canada.* S. Devillard, T. Vogel, A. Pickersgill, A. Madgavkar, T. Nowski, M. Krishnan, T. Pan, and D. Kechrid. https://www.mckinsey.com/featured-insights/ gender-equality/the-power-of-parity-advancing-womens-equality-in-canada

Moser, C. (2012). *Gender planning and development: Theory, practice and training.* Routledge.

Mutch, P. K. (2019, 26 April). Where are the women in Canada's women in tech venture fund? https://liisbeth.com/where-are-the-women-in-canadas-women-in-tech -venture-fund/

National Aboriginal Capital Corporations Association (2020a). *Indigenous Women Entrepreneurs in Canada. Summary of National Survey Findings.* Access at https:// nacca.ca/wp-content/uploads/2020/07/NACCA-IWE-Survey-Report.pdf

National Aboriginal Capital Corporations Association (2020b). *Indigenous Women Entrepreneurs in Canada. Valuable Investments in Their Businesses, Families and Communities.* Access at https://nacca.ca/wp-content/uploads/2020/07/NACCA -IWE-Summary-Report.pdf

Organisation for Economic Co-operation and Development (OECD) (2017). *SME and entrepreneurship policy in Canada.* OECD Studies on SMEs and Entrepreneurship Series. Paris: OECD Publishing. https://doi.org/10.1787/9789264273467-en

Organisation for Economic Co-operation and Development and the European Union (2019). *The missing entrepreneurs 2019: Policies for inclusive entrepreneurship.* Paris: OECD Publishing. https://doi.org/10.1787/3ed84801-en

Orser, B. (1991). Methodological and theoretical issues of research on home-based business. *Journal of Small Business & Entrepreneurship*, 8(2), 21–38. DOI: 10.1080/08276331.1991.10600369

Orser, B. (2011). Taskforce roundtable report. Action strategies to support Canadian women-owned enterprises. University of Ottawa, Telfer School of Management. http://sites.telfer.uottawa.ca/womensenterprise

Orser, B. (2017). Strategies to redress entrepreneurship gender gap in Canada. In Henry, C., Nelson, T. & Lewis, K. (eds), *Companion to Global Female Entrepreneurship.* London and New York: Routledge, pp. 95–115.

Orser, B., Riding A. & Manley, K. (2006). Women entrepreneurs and financial capital. *Entrepreneurship Theory and Practice*, 30(5), 643–665.

Parpart, J. L., Connelly, M. P. & Barriteau, V. E. (2000). *Theoretical perspectives on gender and development.* Ottawa: International Development Research Centre (IDRC). https://www.idrc.ca/sites/default/files/openebooks/272-4/index.html

Pettersson, K. (2012). Support for women's entrepreneurship: A Nordic spectrum. *International Journal of Gender and Entrepreneurship*, 4(1), 4–19. DOI: 10.1108/17566261211202954

Pettersson, K., Ahl, H., Berglund, K. & Tillmar, M. (2017). In the name of women? Feminist readings of policies for women's entrepreneurship in Scandinavia.

Scandinavian Journal of Management, 33(1), 50–63. https://core.ac.uk/download/pdf/196586405.pdf

Public Services Procurement Canada (PSPC) (2020). *Opportunities for under-represented groups.* https://www.tpsgc-pwgsc.gc.ca/app-acq/ma-bb/groupsousrep-undrepgroup-eng.html

Ravanera, C. & Sultana, A. (2020). *A feminist economic recovery plan for Canada: Making the economy work for everyone.* Toronto: The Institute for Gender and the Economy (GATE); YWCA Canada. https://www.tpsgc-pwgsc.gc.ca/app-acq/ma-bb/groupsousrep-undrepgroup-eng.html

Richard, T. (2020). Everything to offer or something to prove? The othering of women in the newly formed Canada-United States Council for Advancement of Women Entrepreneurs and Business Leaders. *Workplace Review*, Spring, 84–95.

Rindova, V. P., Barry, D. & Ketchen, D. J. (2009). Entrepreneuring as emancipation. *Academy of Management Review*, 34(3), 477–491.

Rooney, J., Lero, D., Korabik, K. & Whitehead, D. L. (2003). Self-employment for Women: Policy Options that Promote Equality and Economic Opportunities. Ottawa: Canada: Status of Women Canada. www.swc-cfc.gc.ca

Rosa, J. & Sylla, D. (2016). *A comparison of the performance of female-owned and male-owned small and Ottawa*: Statistics Canada, Centre for Special Business Projects. https://www.ic.gc.ca/eic/site/061.nsf/eng/h_03034.html#employm

Sawchuk, G. & Whewall, L. (1998). *Shattering the glass box: Women entrepreneurs and the knowledge-based economy.* Industry Canada – Micro-Economic Monitor. ISSN 1206-260X

Scotiabank Women Initiative (2020). Financial knowledge & financial confidence-closing gender gaps in financing Canadian Small Businesses. Scotiabank Knowledge Centre. https://www.scotiabank.com/women-initiative/ca/en/knowledge-centre/all.html

Statistics Canada (2019, 3 April). *Research Blog: Women-owned businesses in Canada.* https://www.statcan.gc.ca/eng/blog/cs/wob

Statistics Canada (2020a). Table 14-10-0027-01. Employment by class of worker, annual (x 1,000). DOI: https://doi.org/10.25318/1410002701-eng

Statistics Canada (2020b). *StatCan COVID-19: Data to insights for a better Canada. Impact of COVID-19 on businesses majority-owned by women.* By J. Bossé, S. Sood and C. Johnston. https://www150.statcan.gc.ca/n1/pub/45-28-0001/2020001/article/00056-eng.htm (see Statistics Canada – Canadian Survey on Business Conditions: Impact of COVID-19 on businesses in Canada, May 2020.)

Statistics Canada (2020c). *Survival and performance of start-ups by gender of ownership: A Canadian cohort analysis.* Analytical Studies Branch Research Paper Series No. 450, 10 September 2020. https://www150.statcan.gc.ca/n1/pub/11f0019m/11f0019m2020013-eng.htm

Statistics Canada (2020d). Labour Force Survey, December 2020. https://www150.statcan.gc.ca/n1/daily-quotidien/210108/dq210108a-eng.htm

Stevenson, L. (1988). Some methodological problems associated with researching women entrepreneurs. *Proceedings, Women in Management Research Symposium.* Mount Saint Vincent University, Halifax, Nova Scotia.

Stevenson, L. (2004). Policy framework for women's entrepreneurship in Canada. Presentation to Sustaining the Momentum Conference, Ottawa, 27–29 October 2004. Ottawa: Carleton University; Industry Canada.

Stevenson, L. & Lundström, A. (2001). *Patterns and trends in entrepreneurship/SME policy and practice in ten economies* (Vol. 3). Sweden: Swedish Foundation for Small Business Research [Forum för småföretagsforskning].

St. Onge, A. & Stevenson, L. (2001). *Creating an entrepreneurial environment foster the start-up and growth of women-owned entrepreneurs: Best practices from Atlantic Canada.* Unpublished. Presented at Durham University, UK, 2001.

Storey, D. J. (2003). Entrepreneurship, small and medium sized enterprises and public policies. In Acs, Z. J. & Audretsch, D. B. (eds), *Handbook of entrepreneurship research.* Boston, MA: Springer, pp. 473–511.

WeEmpower (2020). *Strengthening support for women entrepreneurs during COVID-19 – Advocacy tool launch and consultation on the definition of women-owned businesses.* https://www.empowerwomen.org/en/community/events-opportunities/2020/07/empowering-women-entrepreneurs-to-drive-economic-growth--presenting-the-advocacy-tool

Women Entrepreneurship Knowledge Hub (WEKH) (2020). *The state of women's entrepreneurship in Canada 2020.* https://wekh.ca/research/the-state-of-womens-entrepreneurship-in-canada/

Women and Gender Equality Canada (2019). 2018–2019. *Departmental Results.* Catalogue No. SW1-12E-PDF. ISSN 2562-9220. https://cfc-swc.gc.ca/trans/account-resp/pr/dpr-rmr/1819/1819-en.pdf

Women's Chamber of Commerce (2020). *Falling Through the Cracks. Immediate Needs of Canada's Underrepresented Founders.* Access at https://canwcc.ca/covid-survey/

Women's Economic Imperative (2020). *What we do.* https://weiforward.org/what-we-do/

W(omen)20 (2020). *W20 final report – If not now when.* https://www.w20saudiarabia.org.sa/publicationsblog/w20-communique-and-annex

Wood, S. (2019). How Minister Ng plans to double the number of women entrepreneurs in Canada. *Canada's National Observer*, 1 August 2019. https://www.nationalobserver.com/2019/08/01/features/how-minister-ng-plans-double-number-women-entrepreneurs-canada

World Bank (2020). *World Bank Group launches initiatives supporting women entrepreneurs.* Press release, 16 February 2020. https://www.worldbank.org/en/news/press-release/2020/02/16/world-bank-group-launches-initiatives-supporting-women-entrepreneurs

4. Entrepreneurship as a losing proposition for women: gendered outcomes of neo-liberal entrepreneurship policy in a Nordic welfare state

Helene Ahl, Malin Tillmar, Karin Berglund and Katarina Pettersson[1]

INTRODUCTION

As argued by many scholars, it is not sufficient to study entrepreneurship as a phenomenon isolated from its societal context (Welter, 2011); context varies greatly between countries, making any country-specific findings hard to generalise globally (Ahl, 2004). Contextual factors include legislation and public policies regarding entrepreneurship, but also the specific division of state and market in any country (Esping-Andersen, 1990, 2009). Contextual factors also include how the public/private divide is configured which, as feminist scholars point out, tends to impact men and women's life chances differently (Folbre, 1994).

Our case country, Sweden, has a comparatively large state or government sector. Comparatively more of the 'private' responsibilities (such as childcare) are organised by the state than in many other countries, making it easier for both parents to join the labour market (Lancker and Ghysels, 2012). The public sector has also provided many job opportunities for women, but more so in the past than at present, since the Swedish public sector has been subject to downsizing and privatisations over the last few decades (Svanborg-Sjövall, 2014).

Government policies in Sweden have aimed to increase women's entrepreneurship (or, rather, self-employment and small business ownership), not least in sectors previously organised and owned by the public sector. While entrepreneurship in its broad meaning is about realising and implementing an innovative idea or combination in any organisational form (Schumpeter, 1934/1983), both scholars and policy makers focus on business ownership.

A country's level of entrepreneurial activity is, for example, measured by the start up of businesses, including self-employment (GEM, 2020). Policies to increase women's entrepreneurship are included in several policy fields in Sweden. Sundin (2016) mentions enterprise and innovation policy, regional development policy, gender equality policy, policy for reorganising the public sector and labour market policy, all of which are finding an increase in women's entrepreneurship useful for attaining their policy goals.

Policies to increase women's entrepreneurship were claimed to result in many benefits, including: the revitalisation and improved quality of public sector services, and more chances for women to start businesses in their areas of expertise (Proposition, 1993/1994: 140); a variety of providers giving customers real choice; competition for qualified labour giving women and immigrants a better job market with better working conditions and higher wages (Proposition, 2008/2009: 29); making the 'black' cleaning market 'white', and opportunities for women to buy household services they would otherwise do themselves, thus making it easier to combine family and career (Proposition, 2006/2007: 94). These policies were claimed to ultimately result in increased gender equality (Henrekson, 2004). However, we ask whether entrepreneurship, which is claimed as a highway to an improved position in society for women (Henrekson, 2004; Orser & Elliott, 2015), is necessarily so in the context of a developed welfare state (Ahl & Nelson, 2015, Sundin, 2011).

Our theoretical perspective and research interest is feminist. We are first and foremost interested in the effects in terms of changes in women's position in society, for example, changes in the gender/power order as indicated by gendered divisions and by symbolic representations of gender (Acker, 1990, 1992). Will women fare better relative to men than before? Has entrepreneurship contributed to women's standing in society, to women's financial and other well-being, and has it improved the valorisation of the feminine vis-à-vis the masculine? We use official statistics and empirical evidence from studies on women's entrepreneurship in Sweden and elsewhere to substantiate our discussion, thus addressing recent calls for contextualising entrepreneurship research (Brush et al., 2014; Welter, 2011).

The chapter accomplishes the following aims: It identifies and describes specific, neo-liberal policies related to women's employment; marketisation of public sector operations in women-dominated fields and the policy for tax deductions of household services. It describes how policy for women's entrepreneurship was argued in conjunction with this. It further analyses how said policies position women, and it describes and analyses the material outcomes for women. This forms the basis for a discussion of the gendered outcomes of neo-liberal entrepreneurship and welfare state policies.

We hold that the Swedish case is appropriately chosen for studying what happens when the state steps down from direct control of welfare provision and looks to entrepreneurship to step in. This change, labelled the neo-liberal turn (Harvey, 2005; Larner, 2000), has been, and is, present in most Western welfare states, not least in Sweden. The country's very large and encompassing public sector made the effects of this 'turn' to private enterprise especially cogent and noticeable.

The chapter is structured as follows: It first relates the theoretical approach and describes the material used. As a background, we then describe the development of the so-called women-friendly Swedish welfare state. The next section discusses how it was affected by policy changes in the aftermath of the financial crisis in the 1990s. The analysis focuses on policy changes of particular relevance for women: *privatisation of services, care and health care, the school voucher system* and *tax deductions for household services*. Thereafter, we relate the arguments of ensuing policy calls for entrepreneurship, focusing especially on initiatives to interest more women in starting their own businesses, and we analyse how these policies position women. Following this, we draw together the results of empirical studies to discuss material outcomes and the result for women's position in society. In the final section, we draw conclusions in terms of the resulting gender/power orders and discuss how the policies position not only women vis-à-vis men, but also women vis-à-vis other women.

THEORY AND METHOD

Feminist theory is explicitly value-based and inherently political. *Feminism* is defined as the recognition of women's subordination in society and the desire to rectify this (Weedon, 1999). *Feminist theory* may then be defined as descriptions, interpretations and analyses of women's subordination – what forms does women's subordination assume, and why (Wahl, 1996). Knowledge derived from feminist theoretical analyses may then aid a feminist cause. Feminist theory has developed over a long period – more than a century – and in different national and political contexts. This is reflected in theory development; rather than one uniform theory, several strands of feminist theory are concurrently used (see Calás & Smircich, 1996 for a useful overview).

One dividing line is political: While *liberal* feminist theory stresses equality of opportunity, *socialist* feminist theory stresses equality of results. The idea of the former is that if all roadblocks are removed (suffrage, access to education, property rights, etc.), women will fare as well as men, if they only work hard enough. Since this has yet to be proved, *socialist* feminist theory says that removing roadblocks, while keeping the perceived way of organising work, family and society unchanged, will not suffice. Women's unpaid work at home must be accounted for, and structural change, including redistribution of income, is necessary to achieve gender equality (Calás et al., 2009; Fraser,

2009). While much of the entrepreneurship discourse focuses on the exploitation of opportunity, in this chapter we are specifically interested in studying the
outcomes or results for women.

Another dividing line is the view of gender: Much feminist research is
empiricist and has an essentialist view of gender. It treats gender as a dichot-
omous variable, i.e. equivalent to biological sex. It is useful in describing
women's representation and women's conditions, but somewhat limited in
analysing gendered practices. Social constructionist, or *post-structuralist*
feminist theory regards gender as a relational concept and as a process or an
accomplishment; one *does* gender, or gender is *performed* (Butler, 1990; West
& Zimmerman, 1987). A social constructionist view widens the study object
from men and women to anything gendered – policy, for example, may be
gendered (Bacchi, 1999). We take the latter perspective but use information
from empiricist research to substantiate our argument.

Acker (1992: 251) writes that *gendered processes* 'means that advantage
and disadvantage, exploitation and control, action and emotion, meaning and
identity, are patterned through and in terms of a distinction between male and
female, masculine and feminine'. Detailing a process view of gender, Acker
(1990: 146) distinguishes between:

1. The production of gender divisions, including allocation of power and
    resources.
2. Symbols and images that 'explain, express, reinforce, or sometimes
    oppose those divisions'.
3. Gendered patterns of interaction between people.
4. Gendered components of individual identity.
5. Gendered patterns in fundamental, ongoing processes of creating and
    conceptualising social structure.

While originally developed for and most frequently used for organisational
analysis, the framework is, as Acker suggests, just as useful for organisation of
social life on a larger scale.

The present study uses material from the following sources: Policy texts
and government information (decisions, reports, programme information,
etc.) – these are used to describe and analyse the content of policy, the arguments of policy, and its symbolic representation of women; publicly available
statistics – these are used to assess the effects of policy changes in terms of
gender divisions. We also make use of the results of prior Swedish studies of
the specific policy areas discussed in the chapter – these are studies concerning
gender divisions as well as studies on symbolic representations. The authors
have a long research trajectory on women's entrepreneurship, not least policy,
so we use our own prior studies, but also that of colleagues in the Swedish

research community. The source material is referred to throughout the article and detailed in the reference list.

The method may best be described as a feminist reading of our material, using Acker's theory as an interpretative frame of reference. Given the material at hand, the study focuses on two of Acker's processes – number one and two above – and makes inferences about process number five. We detail: (i) changes in gender divisions due to policy changes, and (ii) how policy itself positions women. The latter is studied by analysing the arguments for policy as well as how policy describes women and women's roles.

THE WOMEN-FRIENDLY SWEDISH WELFARE STATE

One of the most cited welfare state typologies is that of Esping-Andersen (1990, 2009). He was interested in the effects of different welfare state regimes on social stratification. He distinguished among them according to their degrees of *de-commodification*, i.e. the degree to which a person can maintain a livelihood without relying on the market. He modelled three versions: The most commodified is the *liberal* welfare state which relies on the market to provide welfare services. Two incomes are usually necessary to support a family, but childcare must be bought in the marketplace. The USA is an example of a liberal welfare state. The *conservative* welfare state, such as Germany, relies on the family to provide individual support, and benefits are means tested against family income. Women are primarily seen as caretakers and depend on their husbands' incomes. In Esping-Andersen's typology, Sweden is organised according to the *social democratic* (or Nordic/ Scandinavian) model, in which the state takes full responsibility for the well-being of its citizens. Sweden has universal, publicly funded health care, elder care and social care, a social assistance system and unemployment insurance. The state also takes responsibility for children, with public day care centres subsidised by the state, public schools, and universities free of tuition. Parents can take 18 months paid maternity or paternity leave, and they have the statutory right to paid leave when children are sick – all financed through the tax system. This system makes it easier to combine paid work with family responsibilities than in many other countries. Benefits are in principle the same for the self-employed, even if taking time off from one's business may be more difficult (Annink et al., 2015; Arenius & Kovalainen, 2006; Neergaard & Thrane, 2011). This has resulted in high labour market participation for women – 85 per cent of women versus 90 per cent of men were in the labour force in 2019 (Statistics Sweden, 2020), and, at least until recently, a comparatively low degree of social stratification (Scruggs & Allan, 2008).

Part and parcel of this system is a very large public sector in education, day care and health care which provided many employment opportunities for women. In 1987, before the privatisation of education, care and health care began, 55 per cent of all employed women worked for the public sector. In 2019, this figure was reduced to 46 per cent. Statistics Sweden (2020: 58) explains the change by reductions in the public sector with concomitant privatisation of public utilities in the 1990s. Employees in former public sector operations are now included in the private sector. But this system has also created a highly gender segregated labour market. Women are concentrated in lower paid jobs, primarily in the service sector and in the public sector, and women still take the primary responsibility for childcare and household work, resulting in a double shift for women – one paid and one unpaid. Women are also more likely to work part time, which reduces future pension payments (Statistics Sweden, 2020). Women are also heavily underrepresented in leadership positions in the private business sector. Only ten per cent of listed companies had a woman CEO or a woman chairperson in 2018 (Statistics Sweden, 2020).

Women's subordination was not addressed by Esping-Andersen's typology. He was concerned with social stratification according to class, but not gender. To address the shortcomings of gender-blind welfare state theorising, feminist scholars have developed alternative or modified typologies using alternative empirical indicators, such as women's unpaid work in the family (Boje & Ejrnaes, 2012; Budig et al., 2012; Folbre, 1994; Lewis, 1992; Melby et al., 2009; O'Connor, 1993; Orloff, 1993; Sainsbury, 1994, 1996, 1999). None of these models can explain all possible country variations (O'Reilly, 2006), but they all predict that the construction of the welfare state will have consequences for women's life chances.

Even if much work remains before Sweden can be counted as a fully egalitarian society, Sweden stands out in international comparisons (Tillmar et al., 2022). The generous family friendly policies, individual taxation and women's high labour market participation have made it fully possible for a woman to become financially independent from a significant other. This, in combination with women's high representation in public elective bodies, has earned Sweden a consistently high position in international gender equality indices (EIGE, 2019; UNDP, 2020).

The Swedish – or rather Nordic – welfare state has been called the women-friendly state (Hernes, 1987). In contrast to the situation elsewhere (MacKinnon, 1989) Swedish feminists worked *through* the state and the elective system, rather than in opposition to it; a so-called *state feminist* approach (Kantola & Outshoorn, 2007). Women have held between 40 and 47 per cent of the seats in the Swedish parliament since 1994 (Statistics Sweden, 2020). Working through the political system entailed political compromises, of course, but also small, reformist steps forward, which eventually created the 'women-friendly' welfare state which sets Sweden and the other Nordic countries apart from much of the rest of the world. However, economic globalisation and political trends brought about challenges for the social democratic welfare state model, which are further discussed below.

SWEDISH WELFARE STATE RETRENCHMENT

The Swedish welfare state expanded steadily until the mid-1970s; it was increasingly questioned during the 1980s and it came to a definite halt when the country was hit by the financial crisis in the early 1990s (Blomberg, Hedlund & Wottle, 2011). The tax base eroded with increasing unemployment, and an income taxation among the highest in the world reduced consumption too much to sustain the economy. Large cut-backs in public spending ensued, and also the restructuration of the public sector according to the neo-liberal 'new public management' ideology of US and UK politics of the 1980s (Hood, 1995; Solli & Czarniawska, 2014). These changes were largely carried through by a social democratic government, but they were consolidated by the 2006–2014 liberal/conservative government coalition (Tillmar et al., 2022). The social democratic/green party coalition, which took office in 2014 did not reverse the changes. The first changes concerned the privatisation of publicly owned companies. Businesses within banking, forestry or pharmaceuticals were sold during the 1990s, and public real estate, the railroad and telecommunications were privatised during the following decade (Gratzer et al., 2010). State monopolies in pharmacies and motor-vehicle inspection were dismantled as late as 2009 and 2012 (Proposition 2009/10; SOU 2008: 4).

Privatisation of Schools

Not only businesses, but also operations traditionally considered as firmly belonging to the public domain were privatised, beginning with the public school system. Except for a handful of privately owned compulsory schools, available only for the very wealthiest, all education was public and non-tuition in Sweden. School reforms up until 1992 aimed at creating an egalitarian system with the same standard of education available everywhere and to everyone (Dahlstedt & Fejes, 2019). But in 1992 a school voucher system was introduced. Politically, it was argued to increase the diversity of education offers, and to give parents and students freedom of choice. To counteract risks of increasing inequality, it was accompanied by a prohibition to charge tuition for education. So, in this system, privately owned schools are financed by the school voucher, paid for by tax money.

The reform has resulted in many private providers of pre-school and compulsory and secondary education, and enrolment has grown steadily. According to national, official statistics compiled by the Swedish Association of Independent

Schools, in 2020 there were 4,100 private schools in Sweden, comprising 26 per cent of about 16,000 schools and pre-schools, enrolling 384,000 students. Twenty per cent of pre-schoolers, 15 per cent of primary school students and 28 per cent of upper secondary school students were enrolled in a privately owned school. The corresponding figure for teachers and school personnel was 18 per cent in 2019 (Friskolornas riksförbund, 2021b). Students and parents are generally happy to be able to choose a school that suits them (Friskolornas riksförbund, 2021b). However, allowing for-profit, privately owned schools that are financed by tax money has caused much debate, since several private equity firms based in tax havens have invested in Swedish schools with the aim of selling them at a profit (Skolverket, 2014). Four of the largest school concerns were listed on the stock exchange in 2017 (Friskolornas riksförbund, 2017). Another much-debated result is increased segregation among students – already privileged parents choose schools accordingly, while the underprivileged tend not to exercise the same choice (Beach & Sernhede, 2011; Dahlstedt & Fejes, 2019; Östh et al., 2013). The system has also been criticised for causing grade inflation, since published school results are a marketing tool for schools (Wennström, 2020). Recently, the government has suggested remedies to some of these shortcomings, but still within the system of private ownership (SOU, 2020: 28). With the exception of a study by Sköld (2015), little attention has been given to the issue of gendered ownership structures in former public sector operations.

Privatisation of Services, Health Care and Elder Care

School reform was followed by the partial privatisation of public health care according to a similar logic – private providers may open businesses that are publicly financed. Services such as cleaning or catering for municipalities, hospitals and care centres were first outsourced. This was followed by the outsourcing of healthcare and care services. Two different models were employed. One was regulated by the *Public Procurement Act*, which allowed private firms to tender bids for public contracts (Swedish Public Procurement Act, 1992). The other was the *customer choice systems* in care and health care, which allowed the customer or patient to choose their service provider freely. The service provider was then reimbursed by the municipality, based on how many customers they attracted (SOU 2008, 2008: 4). A tax-funded public 'market' resulted. Since 2009, such a system, in accordance with *The Act on System of Choice in the Public Sector* (2008), is advocated and stimulated for use in municipal care services in the 290 municipalities (Swedish Association of Local Authorities and Regions, SALAR).

It should be noted that Sweden has a three-tiered government system. Most of the tax money is collected by the 21 regional and the 290 municipal bodies. Of relevance to the present discussion is that the national government is responsible for legislation and national programmes; the regions deliver hospital and primary care, and the municipalities are responsible for childcare, elder care and for schools. The uptake of the reforms was at first voluntary and varied between regions and municipalities, much depending on the local political rule. In primary health care, the Swedish government made it mandatory in 2010 to introduce such systems in all Swedish regions. The result is a mix of private and public providers, reimbursed by the county councils and municipalities. Private alternatives are more common in the larger cities than in rural areas. For example, while 40 per cent of all primary care centres were privately owned in 2019, in Stockholm the figure was 68 per cent, whereas in one of the northern regions – Västerbotten – it was only 13 per cent (Ekonomifakta, 2020). Politically, the reforms were argued in much the same way as the school reforms – more and better providers, better access, increased quality with small-scale operations and control, and freedom of choice for patients and clients.

Tax Deductions for Household Services

Another reform of relevance for our discussion was the introduction of 'RUT', a 50 per cent tax deduction of labour costs for services performed in the home, such as cleaning, by a registered company (Proposition, 2006/2007: 94). RUT is an acronym for the Swedish words for cleaning, maintenance and washing (and a woman's name), and the companies providing these services are labelled 'RUT-companies'. The reform was intended to make a largely black market white and was also seen as a way to create business opportunities as well as good and secure entry-level jobs for people far from the ordinary labour market. It was further argued to enable working women to avoid working double shifts by making household help more affordable (Proposition, 2006/2007: 94). The reforms were accompanied by tax breaks on income from employment or self-employment (but not on pensions or other incomes). The tax breaks were constructed in such a way that those with full-time, well-paid employment gained the most. People with just enough income to support themselves would not be able to afford the purchase of household services anyway (Thörnquist, 2014). There were no tax breaks for the unemployed, the sick or the retired, contributing to sharply increased income inequality in Sweden since 2006 (OECD, 2014).

THE INVOCATION OF ENTREPRENEURSHIP IN PUBLIC SECTOR REFORMS

Part and parcel of the reforms detailed above was an expectation that the private sector would step in where the state stepped out. While 'entrepreneur' was rather something 'the cat dragged in' in the rhetoric of the 1960s and 1970s (Czarniawska-Joerges & Wolff, 1991), the status of this figure was greatly enhanced towards the end of the century when the entrepreneur entered the stage as the envisioned saviour of the economy (Sørensen, 2008). Igniting this change was the path breaking finding of Birch (1979) that most new jobs were not created by large multi-national corporations, but by the many small and new firms.

Entrepreneurialism

However, the emerging discourse on entrepreneurship was not only about job creation, but also about deregulation, privatisation and exposing the public sector to private sector competition (Ahl et al., 2016). It was argued to make the public sector more cost-effective as well as to increase the quality of services. The discourse also entailed a major transformation in the way the individual was conceptualised. People were no longer primarily perceived as citizens, but as producers, entrepreneurs and consumers (ibid.). Du Gay (2004) speaks of a new ideology, *entrepreneurialism*, infusing all sectors of society. Neo-liberal ideas of private enterprise and the primacy of the market meant that ideas of individual freedom were re-conceptualised as freedom of choice, or perhaps, rather, freedom to consume (Harvey, 2005; Lemke, 2001).

In Sweden, this discourse gained traction in the 1980s when the right-wing opposition and the Confederation of Swedish Enterprise and other business organisations or representatives argued that the solution to bureaucracy and inefficiencies in a very large and encompassing public sector was deregulation and marketisation. Exposing public operations to private sector competition would make them more efficient (Blomberg, Hedlund & Wottle, 2011). This discourse gained further momentum when Sweden joined the European Union in 1995, not least through its very large structural funds programmes that supported regional development through entrepreneurship initiatives through regional private/public partnerships. The EU mandated that the programmes should attend to gender equality, which invited projects for women's entre-preneurship. Incidentally, the partnership model also introduced a new form of governance – multi-level governance – which 'bypassed' the national level, thus weakening Sweden's state feminist model (Hedlund & Lindberg, 2012) and de-politicising both gender equality and regional development (Hudson

& Rönnblom, 2007). While not the topic of the current chapter, it should be noted that scholars have found the partnerships to essentially recreate a male-dominated governance structure, in Sweden (Hedlund, 2011) and elsewhere (Bock, 2015).

These developments also entailed a change to how the feminist project was conceived. Gender equality policy in Sweden had been firmly focused on the labour market, and focused on achieving *equality of result* through proactive measures. The new discourse focused on gender as *equal opportunity* and on entrepreneurship as a way for women to profitably exploit opportunities and thereby achieve gender equality (Blomberg, Waldemarson & Wottle, 2011). The new discourse put the onus on women, rather than on policy, to improve women's situation, and it entailed a change from the redistribution of resources to the recognition of women's potential (Berglund et al., 2018; Fraser, 2014). The public sector was, in this discourse, seen not as a guarantor of job opportunities for women, but as 'locking in' women. Breaking up the public sector monopolies was seen as a way to provide women with opportunities for entrepreneurship and self-employment (Blomberg, Waldemarson & Wottle, 2011).

The Role of Women's Entrepreneurship

How did women enter this equation? The entrepreneur is a decidedly male figure in both public and scientific discourse. Women entrepreneurs are typically conceptualised as the exception or as 'different' from an unstated male norm (Ahl, 2006; Ahl & Marlow, 2012). Such exceptionalism is also present in Swedish political discourse on women's entrepreneurship. The Swedish government has run programmes to support women's entrepreneurship since the early 1990s. Financing for these programmes has represented a fraction of general entrepreneurship support which, due to its design and the gendered business landscape, largely benefited male owned businesses (Nutek, 2007; Tillväxtverket, 2012). But since the programmes were specifically tailored to women, they nevertheless garnished much publicity and debate. The programmes entailed business advice (with women advisors), special resource centres for women, business training, role model programmes, prizes, competitions, a 'beautiful business' award, project financing and micro loans (Pettersson, 2015). There was also an ambassador programme in which women entrepreneurs visited schools to inspire girls to become entrepreneurs. The ambassadors were not paid but expected to volunteer their time (Nilsson, 2010).

Elsewhere, we have analysed the political argumentation for these programmes (Ahl & Nelson, 2015; Berglund et al., 2018; Pettersson et al., 2017). The most salient outcome of these analyses was that arguments of gender equality came very far down the list, if at all, and further there was a shift over time. The very first text, commissioned by the government to suggest forms and purposes for resource centres for women, included formulations about entrepreneurship as a way for women to gain financial independence and freedom of patriarchal control:

> The goal could be to promote women's independence so that women ... can live a dignified life measured by women's standards. This means equal conditions for women and men regarding education, income, and influence in society. It means that society's resources – ownership, right of disposition – would be equally divided between the sexes. It means freedom from patronising, abuse, and other violations by men. (Friberg, 1993: 49, our translation)

As time went by, however, arguments of gender equality vanished and were replaced by arguments centring squarely on economic growth and job creation. Women owned only around 25 per cent of businesses at the time and were, therefore, conceptualised as an underutilised resource in economic growth. Throughout the policy texts we analysed (see Ahl & Nelson, 2015; Berglund et al., 2018; Pettersson et al., 2017, for details), women were also seen as able to make a unique, gender-specific contribution, in which the privatisation of the women-dominated public sector was made part of the solution. The government proposition in 1993, which followed as a result of the text cited above, suggested that more women-owned businesses in services previously dominated by the public sector would provide both jobs and essential services; this was deemed particularly necessary to retain the attractiveness of geographic areas subject to depopulation. At the same time, they would ensure population renewal by making it financially viable for women to stay in these areas (Proposition, 1993/1994: 140). There were clear expectations that women employed in the public sector would be particularly fit to run businesses in the fields that were now becoming open for private sector competition. By starting a business, they would solve their own upcoming unemployment problem in the making. In the decision to finance regional resource centres for women, the government listed as one of many tasks for the centres participation in the regional development work carried out in public-private partnerships. The resource centres were supposed to increase the partnerships' level of proficiency in gender issues (Proposition, 2001/2002: 4), and they were expected to do it for free, by volunteering their time and services (Stenmark, 2012); in effect, appropriating women's free labour.

The introduction of tax deductions for household services in 2007 was also tied to the entrepreneurship discourse. The motion to the parliament argued for these deductions as a way to alleviate working women's double burden, and thus improve their health, for professionalising cleaning, for making black market jobs white and contributing to business growth. It was further proposed that it would be a means for job creation for women, both as business owners and as employees (Motion, 2003/04: Sk426). As Sundin (2016) notes, women's entrepreneurship was constructed as a solution to a whole range of different societal problems. So, in summary, women seemed eminently useful: They were seen as good for economic growth, for job creation, for the privatisation of services, for population renewal, for informing civil servants on gender issues and for voluntary service work. But women were not, in the first instance, considered as prime targets for starting firms in sectors with high-growth and high-earning potential such as high tech or life sciences, and men's contributions to unpaid household work were not discussed. Were all these expectations met? The next section draws together available research and statistics to discuss the question.

THE GENDERED OUTCOMES OF MARKETISATION

In the following sections, we detail the outcomes for women of gendered processes (Acker 1990, 1992) related to the restructuration of the public sector and the ensuing call for entrepreneurship. As a background for the discussion we begin with general labour market statistics.

Women's Self-employment

As mentioned earlier, women's labour market participation in Sweden is high. In 1987, before the privatisation of education, care and health care began, 55 per cent of all employed women worked for the public sector. In 2019, this figure was reduced to 46 per cent (Statistics Sweden, 2020). The labour market was, and is, highly gender divided – according to Statistics Sweden (2020), 66 per cent of all working women worked in occupations that are dominated by women such as nursing, childcare or teaching in 2018. The most female-dominated occupation in 2018 was pre-school teachers, with 96 per cent women and 4 per cent men. Regarding men, 66 per cent worked in male-dominated occupations. They constituted 99 per cent of all carpenters and woodworkers, for example.

Women's self-employment has increased over the years. From historical figures of around 25–30 per cent (Svanlund, 2011), women's self-employment had risen to 39 per cent in 2018 (Statistics Sweden, 2020). But the pattern of gendered divisions in self-employment were the same as in employment, and there has been very little change over the years. Women constituted 79 per cent of those self-employed in health and social care, whereas men constituted 96 per cent of those self-employed in construction in 2018. Other women-dominated sectors were personal and cultural services, and education. Only financial business services was roughly gender equal (Statistics Sweden, 2020).

In sum, there has been a notable decrease in public sector employment, an increase in women's self-employment, and very little change in gendered divisions of employment patterns. However, these are overall statistics. To get more detailed knowledge, we need to look at the results of in-depth studies.

Women's Business Ownership in Former Publicly Owned Sectors

Sköld (2015) conducted a longitudinal analysis of individual level census data over a 25-year period starting in 1993, focusing specifically on women-dominated industries that were affected by the transformation of the public sector in Sweden. She studied changes in men's and women's small business ownership and found that politicians' wishes for more women-owned small businesses were met on an aggregate level, but on close inspection men still increased their business ownership more than women did in ten of the 16 studied sectors, and women were still underrepresented as business owners in relation to their representation as employees in 14 of the studied sectors in 2008. Only in 'childcare' and 'other health care' (such as a private physiotherapathy) did women's representation as business owners equal their share as employees (Sköld & Tillmar, 2015).

A further enquiry into the childcare sector, where women comprised 90–95 per cent found, however, that men employed in this sector still started businesses to a greater extent than women, and that there was also an influx of men from other lines of businesses into the childcare industry. Men were more likely to start a limited company and more likely to sell it for a profit after a few years. Women with small children, but not men, were also more likely to start a childcare business in order to combine work and family. The author labels the business owners 'businessmen in childcare' versus 'self-employed women childcare workers', noting that the male norm of entrepreneurship seemed to reproduce itself even in the most genuinely feminine gendered business of them all (Sköld, 2015).

Privatisation procedures (or the creation of a public market) also involved structural constraints that worked against the opportunities for women employed in the public sector to start their own firms in all but three of the studied sectors. In 'other health care', 'open health care' and 'dentistry' there was already a pattern of small business ownership and a private market, combined with a professionalisation of services, which offered legitimacy and acceptance for new small businesses. But in sectors such as 'hospital care', 'secondary schools' and 'nursing homes' the result was instead few but large new businesses that operated on economies of scale (Sköld, 2015).

Structural Obstacles for Women in Municipal Outsourcing Procedures

As mentioned above, the creation of public markets in Swedish municipalities follows either the Public Procurement Act where companies bid for contracts, or a customer choice system, where customers choose freely from a list of approved providers that get reimbursed from the municipality depending on the number of customers. Since the uptake of the reforms varies between the municipalities, we now turn to case studies.

Several detailed case studies have been carried out in Linköping, a large Swedish municipality, on the implementation and outcome of these reforms. Sundin & Rapp (2006) examined what happened to the municipality's 500 janitors when cleaning was made subject to private sector competition. Two companies were started – one by a man, who cut costs, developed the services, marketed them successfully to the private market and later cashed in on his investment when he sold the firm to a large cleaning company. The other company was started by a personnel cooperative (mostly women) that faced one difficulty after another, made a loss and ended up selling to a larger private firm at a loss. Why? The municipality gave these two firms different conditions at start-up – they favoured the man (Sundin, 2011; Sundin & Rapp, 2006). The cleaning business competes on price, and has by now become oligopolised in Sweden, which means that large businesses can offer a low bid to corner a market. The public procurement procedure thus disfavours start-ups by small and medium-sized companies in several industries – they cannot compete when large units are outsourced with tough price competition and short contract periods (Tillmar, 2004).

So, if public procurement is not conducive to more women-owned businesses, perhaps the customer choice system works better? Sundin & Tillmar (2010) followed the same municipality's 2007 introduction of the customer choice system in home-based elder care. The municipality aimed for a multitude of providers and many options to choose from for the elderly, while also aiming for favourable outcomes in quality and cost. They also thought that a customer choice system would favour small companies, since they did not have to go through a cumbersome bidding process. Reimbursement was fixed, so companies were to compete on quality. However, the design of the system mandated that people who did not make an active choice would be assigned to the company which maintained services for the municipal service flats in the area in which they lived – and these contracts were still given through the Public Procurement Act. The result was that one large international company made a zero-sum bid for the service flats in the city, and hardly any of the 4,000 elderly made an active choice. They wanted to choose a person, not a company. So, the contracts for the city-dwellers were consequently assigned to the previously mentioned zero-sum bidder. In the end, five of 14 businesses were owned by men, and these businesses accounted for about 97 per cent of the service hours provided. The authors concluded that even if the municipality was earnest in its wishes for many women-owned SMEs, the bidding procedures they set up favoured large-scale businesses, resulting in a masculinisation of the sector, both in terms of numbers and kind. A rationality of care was replaced by a rationality of economic efficiency (Sundin & Tillmar, 2010).

Thörnquist (2014) adds that in the customer choice system, in which remuneration is set at a low level and companies are to compete on quality in order to get authorised, there is a tendency for underbidding and for the use of cheap, often less-qualified labour as well as hard working conditions. Small companies also have difficulties competing with larger companies with better administrative resources.

So, neither public procurement nor customer choice resulted in a variety of women-led SMEs, quite the contrary. Economies of scale, high transaction costs, short contract periods, tough price competition, complicated rules for tenders and in some cases highly regulated professions created very difficult entry obstacles (Forssell & Norén, 2006; Sköld & Tillmar, 2015; Sundin & Rapp, 2006; Thörnquist, 2014; Tillmar, 2004, 2009).

Oligopolization and Masculinization in the School Market

The privately owned schools constituted 26 per cent of all schools in Sweden in 2020 (Friskolornas riksförbund, 2021b). At the introduction of the reform, schools were often started to promote a certain pedagogy, like Montessori or Waldorf, or certain sports, or different religious faiths, and ownership was spread widely, including staff or parent cooperatives (Lindgren, 2001). Later on, entrepreneurs with a business motif took advantage of the new market opportunity and started regular schools, and they often bought up other schools. Consolidation is ongoing, so the ownership structure is a bit of a moving target, and it is also differently structured at the different school levels.

In Sköld's (2015) analysis described earlier, most *pre-schools* were still many, small, often owned by women or run as parent cooperatives, and more so in small towns than in the big cities. An analysis from 2013 found consolidation of ownership at the *compulsory school* level – 36 per cent of students in private schools were enrolled in schools owned by the ten largest owners. The typical owner had a limited company, and some of the largest ones were owned by private equity funds (Skolverket, 2014). At the *upper secondary school* level limited companies dominated completely, and over half belonged to educational concerns. The ten biggest owners had half of the market in 2013. Unlike at the pre-school level, fewer owners were directly engaged in education – there was a substantial component of private equity firms, some of which were foreign based (Skolverket, 2014).

According to the Swedish Association of Independent Schools, 20 owners had five or more compulsory and upper secondary school units in 2018, enrolling 128,140 students (Friskolornas riksförbund, 2018). Based on the information provided, we calculated that these 20 owners comprised only three per cent of all school owners, but their 471 schools comprised 36 per cent of all privately owned compulsory and upper secondary school units. The ten largest alone had 394 units, and the largest, AcadeMedia, had 216 units. We checked the ownership on the database *allabolag.se* and found that the eight largest units were majority owned or controlled by men. Number nine on the list was owned by an NGO, and number ten was a personnel cooperative – these had a woman chairperson. Two years later, consolidation had continued (Friskolornas riksförbund, 2021a), and the second largest school had been bought out from the stock exchange and is now owned by a Luxembourg-based private equity firm.

These statistics show the same tendencies to create large oligopolies as in the elder care market discussed earlier, even if the numbers are not as startling; they also show that, even if many small one-school companies, particularly at the pre-school level, are women-owned or parent cooperatives, ownership or control in the larger companies is dominated by men. However, Sköld (2015) made the point that even at the pre-school level, women were underrepresented as owners in comparison to their share of employees.

To conclude, the privatisation of schools offered many women an opportunity to start a business, but relatively more men have done so, and men also seem to control the businesses that dominate the market.

TAX DEDUCTIONS FOR HOUSEHOLD SERVICES: MORE BUSINESS BUT PRECARIOUS EMPLOYMENT

If the previously discussed reforms seem to be a disappointment for those who wanted more women entrepreneurs, tax deductions for household services appear to be a success story. The number of households deducting half of the labour cost for household services – mainly cleaning – has increased every year since 2007. Women are more likely to buy cleaning services than men, particularly 35–45-year-old women with children, but otherwise the use of tax deductions for household services increases with age – in many instances it is used as home help for seniors, replacing or supplementing municipal care services. Unsurprisingly, it is used more by wealthy people than poorer people (Gavanas, 2013; Sköld & Heggeman, 2012).

Using registry data from 2010–2015, The Swedish Agency for Growth Policy Analysis published a descriptive study in 2018 and an analysis of the reform in 2019 (Tillväxtanalys, 2018, 2019). By the end of the studied period there were about 10,000 RUT-companies. Women made up a higher share of owners (over half) than among the whole population of entrepreneurs. However, women were more likely to have a private firm associated with higher risks than a limited company. About a quarter of both men and women combined a RUT-company with other employment. The average annual sum (50 per cent of the total bill) paid by the Tax Authority in 2015 to a limited RUT-company was SEK 479,000 (about 47,900 euros) but to a private firm only SEK 129,000 (about 12,900 euros) (Tillväxtanalys, 2018). The average company is thus small, especially the private, women-dominated firms.

Every other woman-owned RUT-company was run by a foreign-born woman, but more so by immigrants from other European countries than by immigrating refugees (Tillväxtanalys, 2018). In some instances, immigrants used their national origin as a market niche by marketing a certain ethnicity or language skill as an advantage, and/or marketing their services to a targeted ethnic group (Pettersson & Hedberg, 2013).

Turnover and employment had grown steadily during the 2010–2015 period, but more so for businesses owned by men than by women, and the reform had created 8,500 new jobs at a gross cost of SEK 1.5 million per job, which is comparable to the cost of other job-creating efforts (Tillväxtanalys, 2019). While creating both business opportunities and jobs for women, the seeming success of the reform might still be a mixed blessing if aiming for increased gender equality. In effect, the reform makes it possible for women with enough financial resources to buy services from other women who, as we saw, had a very modest turnover. As Nyberg (2013) argues, tax subsidies are used to increase wealthier working women's leisure time.

Åberg (2013) shows how reforms intended to increase private consumption such as lowered wage taxes or, indeed tax deductions for household services, have increased income gaps in Sweden and also, contrary to previous trends, have led to increased job polarisation, particularly since 2007. The period before 2000 was characterised by the upgrading of jobs, but the period after this has seen a large increase of low-paid jobs in the service sector as well as an increase of highly qualified jobs, while jobs in the middle range are disappearing. Today, more people have money in their pockets and can afford to buy services they previously provided themselves, particularly since some of these services are subsidised by the state.

Nyberg (2013) cites evaluations for the Swedish Tax Authority that show a modest effect on the black market. However, most RUT customers are new consumers of cleaning services – they previously used to clean their own house. According to Gavanas (2013), the hopes of transforming a black cleaning market to a white market with secure job opportunities were only partly met. Most of the black market is still there, while there has been a concurrent growth of a white market, but with precarious employment.

Meanwhile, the black market has become even more marginalised, and there is often a shady line between the two – it is not uncommon that suppliers on the white market use black market subcontractors, disrupting fair competition by pressing wage costs down (Gavanas, 2013; Nyberg, 2013). The black market subcontractors in turn exploit illegal immigrants who are in extremely vulnerable positions since they have no recourse to the social or judicial system. Employees are seldom unionised, and many small cleaning companies do not have collective labour market agreements (Thörnquist, 2014). Thörnquist (2014) holds that the clock has turned back regarding labour market conditions and job security, and those with a weak labour market position are hit first. So, household services offer job opportunities for many women, and many immigrant women, but the jobs are often precarious, both for the employees and business owners, so there is a risk that gender, class and ethnic polarisation on the labour market are here to stay.

THE REPRODUCTION OF INEQUALITIES IN THE NAME OF THE MARKET

Using Acker's (1990) framework of gender processes, we observe the following: First, the policies analysed here positioned women first and foremost as useful for *something else*, some higher purpose than rectifying gender inequalities. They were agents of policy rather than recipients of policy. Women were positioned as useful for economic growth, for job creation, for privatisation of services, for rendering services more effective, for population renewal, for informing civil servants on gender issues and for voluntary service work in the third sector. Women were called to step in where the state stepped out. They were expected to fill in the gaps when the state downsized and privatised public services in traditionally feminine gendered sectors. Women were not, in the first instance, considered as prime targets for starting firms in sectors with high growth and earnings potential such as high tech or life sciences. The *symbolic representation* of women largely reproduced received, subordinate ideas of femininity. This was further reinforced by women-only programmes, and by features such as a beautiful business award, or the expectation that female business ambassadors should give of their time for free.

Second, there were indeed changes in *gender divisions* along several dimensions. However, the government's hopes for the results of reforms in the name of women's entrepreneurship were only partially met, at best, and there were some unintended consequences. More women-owned businesses were indeed created, but men ended up owning the largest ones with the biggest market shares. Women's businesses continued to be small and were positioned in market sectors and market positions with a lower chance of profitability. There was, therefore, no change to the gendered business landscape – the gendered division of labour, as well as the accompanying gendered pattern of remuneration, was reinforced.

The reforms in the organisation of care were intended to increase the possibilities to choose your provider, but the desire to make an active choice was overestimated, which meant that market mechanisms driving both quality and price did not function in this market. There was a proliferation of suppliers of former public services, but it is a matter of debate whether or not quality has improved. In the case of elderly care and cleaning services, the system forced cost cutting and underbidding, resulting in worsened instead of improved labour conditions for employees. In plain language, women continued to work as janitors and in caring professions, but in more precarious jobs. The black cleaning market did not disappear, but it became even more exploitative. We posit that this is a far cry from improving women's position in society.

Further, the policies did not address the issue of class, in our case divisions and inequalities *between* women. The policy on tax deductions for household services took it for granted that gender equality would improve if more women could have a career on the same terms as men by buying household services, and if more women and immigrants could start a business or get a job by providing these same services. The propositions did not problematise that they talked about different groups of women. The results showed a reinforcement of social as well as class and ethnic divisions among women. As Bourne (2010: 23) puts it '… [it supports] women who are climbing to more powerful positions in the corporate world, but it cements other women to the part-time menial floor'. Moreover, it reproduces an ideology that household work is women's work.

The invisible elephant in the room is the category of men. Women's lack of gender equality is presented as a concern for women and something to be rectified by women, on market terms. But leaving this to the invisible hand of the market, to rational choice and self-interest does not seem to work. The 'market' has long appropriated women's labour in order to function. Folbre (2009: 59) cites one of the most famous passages in Adam Smith's *The Wealth of Nations*: 'It is not from the benevolence of the butcher, the brewer or the baker that we expect our dinner but from regard to their self-interest' adding that 'Smith neglected to mention that none of these tradesmen actually puts dinner on the table, ignoring cooks, maids, wives, and mothers in one fell swoop'. In fact, it was Smith's own mother who put dinner on his table (Marçal, 2015). Neo-liberal policies' great belief in the market seems unwarranted. 'Women's work' is overall not better paid in the private sector than it was in the public sector. Indeed, the Swedish public sector provided better working conditions with stable employment contracts and wages. In this case, gendered assumptions of work and gendered valuation of work is the real invisible hand at work.

There is yet another unintended consequence. Wolf (2013) makes the point that even if women were always divided by class, all women had in common that they were discriminated by law, regulations and social customs based on their sex, which made a unified women's movement possible. In fact, it was the upper classes that organised the suffragettes. Today, the upper 20 per cent of American elite working women (in terms of income) are leading lives that are very similar to men's lives. They have similar education, careers and interests, and spend their lives in close interaction with men. Such lives are made possible by the purchase of services from the lower 20 per cent of women, who live lives that are still heavily gender segregated. Wolf talks about the return of the servant classes. The elite working women have more in common with elite working men than they have with other women. The basis for a solidary women's movement is thus quickly eroding. Recent market-based government policy in Sweden risks having the same effect. Sweden might find itself in a situation where the support for state feminist intervention will vanish. This might very well put the Swedish women-friendly welfare system in jeopardy.

In Acker's (1990) terms, we found that even if current neo-liberal political entrepreneurship and welfare state reform presents changes in the *fundamental, ongoing processes of creating and conceptualising social structures*, traditional gender processes appear resilient to such changes. Women's subordination as well as class inequalities are recreated in new forms.

IMPLICATIONS AND AVENUES FOR FUTURE RESEARCH

This chapter demonstrates, by way of example, why a contextual analysis of policy for women's entrepreneurship is paramount. A more limited perspective and a more traditional perspective, i.e. a focus on business performance and growth and factors associated with this (Ahl, 2006), would most likely have studied the programmes carried out, their design, and the number of new businesses created. Such research would most likely have deemed the new policies a success. By widening the research to include contextual factors, such as the gender order, women's labour market position, the division of state and market, etc., a completely different picture emerges. We can only recommend that research on entrepreneurship and policy follows suit.

Our analysis was largely limited to a consideration of gender, but as the results indicate, intersections of race/ethnicity and class will be important to include in future research. As Gill (2014) notes, the discourse of entrepreneurship is contradictory. While it celebrates opportunities for upward class mobility, it simultaneously denies them for women and people of colour. Another limitation is that the available empirical results we used were from different years. A challenge for future research would be to study *all* of the areas touched upon in this chapter in a single study, using registry data from the latest available year.

For policy makers, the research provides valuable information on the gendered results of the privatisation of welfare provision and the role of women's entrepreneurship in this equation. The Swedish government has a goal to gender mainstream all policies. This goal is also present in the EU, and in many member states. Gender mainstreaming means that all proposed policies should be carefully assessed for their consequences for gender equality. Policy makers who take part in this research may think twice before uncritically arguing for women to step in where the state steps out. They might even rethink whether the state should step out in the first place.

CONCLUSIONS

This chapter showed that neo-liberal government reforms in Sweden that were intended to improve women's position in society by exposing part of the public sector to private sector competition had mixed and often negative results. More women-owned businesses were created, but old gender hierarchies were also recreated alongside new ones, often on the grounds of ethnicity. Moreover, the basis for a solidary women's movement risks erosion, putting the Swedish women-friendly state in jeopardy. We contend that there are at least three reasons for this: An unrealistic belief in the market mechanism, disregard of the role of entrenched gender roles and expectations, and exclusion of men's responsibility for household work from the design of the policies. We recommend that policy makers pay attention to these three reasons and amend policies accordingly. We also recommend that entrepreneurship researchers pay more attention to contextual factors, such as, in this case, gender systems and policy changes that might reveal a fuller – and darker – side of entrepreneurship than is usually transmitted in entrepreneurship research.

NOTE

1.   Ahl, Berglund, Pettersson and Tillmar are the founding members of the Embla group, a Swedish virtual excellence centre on studies of women's entrepreneurship. For more information about the group and its publications see www.emblaresearch.se

REFERENCES

Acker, J. (1990). Hierarchies, jobs, bodies: A theory of gendered organizations. *Gender & Society*, *4*(2), 139–158.
Acker, J. (1992). Gendering organizational theory. In A. Mills & P. Tancred (Eds), *Gendering organizational analysis* (pp. 248–260). London: Sage.

Ahl, H. (2004). *The scientific reproduction of gender inequality: A discourse analysis of research texts on women's entrepreneurship.* Copenhagen: CBS Press.

Ahl, H. (2006). Why research on women entrepreneurs needs new directions. *Entrepreneurship Theory and Practice, 30*(5), 595–621.

Ahl, H. & Marlow, S. (2012). Exploring the dynamics of gender, feminism and entrepreneurship: Advancing debate to escape a dead end? *Organization, 19*(5), 543–562.

Ahl, H. & Nelson, T. (2015). How policy positions women entrepreneurs: A comparative analysis of state discourse in Sweden and the United States. *Journal of Business Venturing, 30*(2), 273–291.

Ahl, H., Berglund, K., Pettersson, K. & Tillmar, M. (2016). From feminism to FemInc. ism: On the uneasy relationship between feminism, entrepreneurship and the Nordic welfare state. *International Entrepreneurship and Management Journal, 12*(2), 369–392.

Annink, A., den Dulk, L. & Steijn, B. (2015). Work-family state support for the self-employed across Europe. *Journal of Entrepreneurship and Public Policy, 4,* 187–208.

Arenius, P. & Kovalainen, A. (2006). Similarities and differences across the factors associated with women's self-employment preference in the Nordic countries. *International Small Business Journal, 24,* 31–59.

Bacchi, C. L. (1999). *Women, policy and politics: The construction of policy problems.* London: Sage.

Beach, D. & Sernhede, O. (2011). From learning to labour to learning for marginality: School segregation and marginalization in Swedish suburbs. *British Journal of Sociology of Education, 32*(2), 257–274.

Berglund, K., Ahl, H., Pettersson, K. & Tillmar, M. (2018). Women's entrepreneurship, neoliberalism and economic justice in the postfeminist era: A discourse analysis of policy change in Sweden. *Gender, Work & Organization, 25*(5), 531–556.

Birch, D. (1979). *The job generation process.* Cambridge, MA: The MIT Press.

Blomberg, E., Hedlund, G. & Wottle, M. (2011). Inledning: stat, marknad, familj och individ. In E. Blomberg, G. Hedlund & M. Wottle (Eds), *Kvinnors företagande – mål eller medel?* (pp. 9–35). Stockholm: SNS Förlag.

Blomberg, E., Waldemarson, Y. & Wottle, M. (2011). Jämställt företagande 1990–2010. In E. Blomberg, G. Hedlund & M. Wottle (Eds), *Kvinnors företagande – mål eller medel?* (pp. 76–113). Stockholm: SNS Förlag.

Bock, B. B. (2015). Gender mainstreaming and rural development policy; the trivialisation of rural gender issues. *Gender, Place & Culture, 22*(5), 731–745.

Boje, T. P. & Ejrnaes, A. (2012). Policy and practice. The relationship between family policy regime and women's labour market participation in Europe. *International Journal of Sociology and Social Policy, 32*(9/10), 589–605.

Bourne, K. A. (2010). The paradox of gender equality: An entrepreneurial case study from Sweden. *International Journal of Gender and Entrepreneurship, 2*(1), 10–26.

Brush, C. G., de Bruin, A. & Welter, F. (2014). 1. Advancing theory development in venture creation: Signposts for understanding gender. *Women's Entrepreneurship in the 21st Century: An International Multi-Level Research Analysis,* 11.

Budig, M. J., Misra, J. & Boeckmann, I. (2012). The motherhood penalty in cross-national perspective: The importance of work-family policies and cultural attitudes. *Social Politics, 19*(2), 163–193.

Butler, J. (1990). *Gender trouble: Feminism and the subversion of identity.* London, New York: Routledge.

Calás, M. B. & Smircich, L. (1996). From 'the woman's' point of view: Feminist approaches to organization studies. In S. Clegg, C. Hardy & W. Nord (Eds), *Handbook of Organization Studies* (pp. 218–257). London: Sage.

Calás, M. B., Smircich, L. & Bourne, K. A. (2009). Extending the boundaries: Reframing 'entrepreneurship as social change' through feminist perspectives. *The Academy of Management Review, 34*, 552–569.

Czarniawska-Joerges, B. & Wolff, R. (1991). Leaders, managers, entrepreneurs on and off the organizational stage. *Organization Studies, 12*(4), 529–546.

Dahlstedt, M. & Fejes, A. (2019). *Neoliberalism and market forces in education: Lessons from Sweden*. London: Routledge.

Du Gay, P. (2004). Against enterprise (but not against 'enterprise' for that would be silly). *Organization, 11*(1), 37–57.

EIGE. (2019). Gender Equality Index 2019: Sweden. Retrieved from https://eige.europa.eu/publications/gender-equality-index-2019-sweden

Ekonomifakta. (2020). Vårdcentraler i privat regi. Retrieved from https://www.ekonomifakta.se/Fakta/Valfarden-i-privat-regi/Vard-och-omsorg-i-privat-regi/vardcentraler-i-privat-regi/

Esping-Andersen, G. (1990). *The three worlds of welfare capitalism*. Cambridge: Polity Press.

Esping-Andersen, G. (2009). *The incomplete revolution. Adapting to women's new roles*. Cambridge: Polity Press.

Folbre, N. (1994). *Who pays for the kids? Gender and the structure of constraint*. London: Routledge.

Folbre, N. (2009). *Greed, lust and gender*. Oxford: Oxford University Press.

Forssell, A. & Norén, L. (2006). Konkurrens på likvärdiga villkor på offentliga markander. *Nordiske organisasjonsstudier, 8*(1), 7–29.

Fraser, N. (2009). Feminism, capitalism and the cunning of history. *New Left Review, 56*, 97–117.

Fraser, N. (2014). *Justice interruptus: Critical reflections on the 'postsocialist' condition*. London: Routledge.

Friberg, T. (1993). *Den andra sidan av myntet – om regionalpolitikens enögdhet: en idéskrift ur kvinnligt perspektiv från Glesbygdsmyndigheten*. Östersund: Glesbygdsmyndigheten.

Friskolornas riksförbund. (2017). De största skolhuvudmännen. Retrieved from https://www.friskola.se/app/uploads/imported/Skolhuvudmannen-i-Sverige.pdf

Friskolornas riksförbund. (2018). Friskolornas ägare. Retrieved from https://www.friskola.se/app/uploads/imported/Friskolornas-agare-final.pdf

Friskolornas riksförbund. (2021a). De största friskolehuvudmännen. Retrieved from https://www.friskola.se/vara-fragor/de-storsta-friskolehuvudmannen

Friskolornas riksförbund. (2021b). Fakta om friskolor 2021. Retrieved from https://www.friskola.se/app/uploads/2021/03/faktaomfriskolor_webb.pdf

Gavanas, A. (2013). Rena hem på smutsiga villkor? Hushållstjänster i den globala arbetsfördelningen. In A. Gavanas & C. Calleman (Eds), *Rena hem på smutsiga villkor? Hushållstjänster, migration och globalisering* (pp. 7–26). Göteborg: Makadam.

GEM. (2020). *Global Entrepreneurship Monitor 2019/2020 global report*. Retrieved from https://www.gemconsortium.org/report/gem-2019-2020-global-report

Gill, R. (2014). 'If you're struggling to survive day-to-day': Class optimism and contradiction in entrepreneurial discourse. *Organization, 21*, 50–67.

Gratzer, K., Lönnborg, M. & Olsson, M. (2010). Staligt företagsägande och privatisering i Sverige. *Nordiske organisasjonsstudier, 12*(4), 94–112.

Harvey, D. (2005). *A brief history of neoliberalism.* Oxford: Oxford University Press.

Hedlund, G. (2011). Partnerskap och genus i den regionala röran. In E. Blomberg, G. Hedlund & M. Wottle (Eds), *Kvinnors företagande – mål eller medel?* (pp. 114–138). Stockholm: SNS Förlag.

Hedlund, G. & Lindberg, M. (2012). *New steering methods in regional policy – Transforming the alliance of 'state feminism'.* Paper presented at the Women's Studies International Forum.

Henrekson, M. (2004). *Vägar till ökad jämställdhet i svenskt näringsliv.* Stockholm: SNS förlag.

Hernes, H. (1987). *Welfare state and women power. Essays in state feminism.* Oslo: Norwegian University Press.

Hood, C. (1995). The 'new public management' in the 1980s: Variations on a theme. *Accounting, Organizations and Society, 20*(2–3), 93–109.

Hudson, C. & Rönnblom, M. (2007). Regional development policies and the constructions of gender equality: The Swedish case. *European Journal of Political Research, 46*(1), 47–68.

Kantola, J. & Outshoorn, J. (2007). Changing state feminism. In J. Outshoorn & J. Kantola (Eds), *Changing state feminism* (pp. 1–19). Hampshire and New York: Palgrave Macmillan.

Lancker, W. V. & Ghysels, J. (2012). Who benefits? The social distribution of subsidized childcare in Sweden and Flanders. *Acta Sociologica, 55*(2), 125–142.

Larner, W. (2000) Neo-liberalism: Policy, ideology, governmentality. *Studies in Political Economy, 63*, 5–25.

Lemke, T. (2001). The birth of bio-politics: Michel Foucault's lecture at the Collège de France on neo-liberal governmentality. *Economy and Society, 30*(2), 190–207.

Lewis, J. (1992). Gender and the development of welfare regimes. *Journal of European Social Policy, 2*(3), 159–173.

Lindgren, M. (2001). Kvinnliga entreprenörer i friskolan: Om entreprenörskap och profession i skapandet av identitet. *Nordiske organisasjonsstudier, 3*(1), 32–64.

MacKinnon, C. (1989). *Toward a feminist theory of the state.* Cambridge, MA: Harvard University Press.

Marçal, K. (2015). *Who cooked Adam Smith's dinner?: A story about women and economics.* London: Portobello Books.

Melby, K., Ravn, A.-B. & Carlsson Wetterberg, C. (Eds). (2009). *Gender equality and welfare politics in Scandinavia. The limits of political ambition?* Bristol: The Policy Press.

Motion. (2003/2004: Sk426). Avdrag för hushållsnära tjänster samt för reparation, om- och tillbyggnad. Retrieved from http://www.riksdagen.se/sv/Dokument-Lagar/Forslag/Motioner/Avdrag-for-hushallsnara-tjanst_GR02Sk426/?text=true

Neergaard, H. & Thrane, C. (2011). The Nordic Welfare Model: Barrier or facilitator of women's entrepreneurship in Denmark? *International Journal of Gender and Entrepreneurship, 3*, 88–104.

Nilsson, P. (2010). Constructing p(e)ace-makers for women's enterprise. In F. Bill, B. Bjerke & A. W. Johansson (Eds), *(De)Mobilizing the entrepreneurship discourse* (pp. 15–36). Cheltenham: Edward Elgar.

Nutek. (2007). *Utfall och styrning av statliga insatser för kapitalförsörjning ur ett könsperspektiv [Outcome and governance of state support for capital provision from a gender perspective]* (R 2007:34). Retrieved from Stockholm.

Nyberg, A. (2013). RUT avdraget – subventionering av vit sysselsättning eller av höginkomsttagarnas fritid? *Fronesis*, (42–43), 114–130.

O'Connor, J. (1993). Gender, class and citizenship in the comparative analysis of welfare state regimes: Theoretical and methodological insights. *The British Journal of Sociology*, *44*(3), 501–518.

O'Reilly, J. (2006). Framing comparisons: Gendering perspectives on cross-national comparative research on work and welfare. *Work, Employment & Society*, *20*(4), 731–750.

OECD. (2014). OECD Income Distribution Database: Gini, poverty, income, methods and concepts. Retrieved from http://www.oecd.org/social/income-distribution -database.htm

Orloff, A. S. (1993). Gender and the social rights of citizenship: The comparative analysis of gender relations and welfare states. *American Sociological Review*, *58*(3), 303–328.

Orser, B. & Elliott, C. (2015). *Feminine capital: Unlocking the power of women entrepreneurs*. Stanford, CA: Stanford University Press.

Pettersson, K. (2015). *Två steg fram och ett tillbaka? En genusanalys av policy for kvinnors företagande i Norden* (Info 0596). Retrieved from Stockholm.

Pettersson, K. & Hedberg, C. (2013). Moving out of 'their places'? – Immigrant women care entrepreneurs in Sweden. *International Journal of Entrepreneurship and Small Business*, *19*(3), 345–361.

Pettersson, K., Ahl, H., Berglund, K. & Tillmar, M. (2017). In the name of women? Feminist readings of policies for women's entrepreneurship in Scandinavia. *Scandinavian Journal of Management*, *33*(1), 50–63.

Proposition. (1993/1994: 140). Bygder och regioner i utveckling. Stockholm: Riksdagstryck.

Proposition. (2001/2002: 4). *En politik för tillväxt och livskraft i hela landet [A policy for growth and vitality in the whole country]*. Stockholm.

Proposition. (2006/2007: 94). *Skattelättnader för hushållstjänster, m.m.* Stockholm: Finansdepartementet. Retrieved from http://www.regeringen.se/rattsdokument/ proposition/2007/04/prop.-20060794/

Proposition. (2008/2009: 29). *Lag om valfrihetssystem*. Stockholm: Socialdepartementet. Retrieved from http://www.regeringen.se/rattsdokument/proposition/2008/10/prop .-20080929/

Proposition. (2009/2010: 32). *Fordonsbesiktning*. Stockholm: Sveriges Riksdag.

Sainsbury, D. (Ed.). (1994). *Gendering welfare states*. London: Sage.

Sainsbury, D. (1996). *Gender, equality and welfare states*. Cambridge: Cambridge University Press.

Sainsbury, D. (1999). Gender and social-democratic welfare states. In D. Sainsbury (Ed.), *Gender and welfare state regimes* (pp. 75–115). Oxford: Oxford University Press.

Schumpeter, J. A. (1934/1983). *The theory of economic development* (reprint 1971 edn). New Brunswick, NJ: Transaction Publishers.

Scruggs, L. A. & Allan, J. P. (2008). Social stratification and welfare regimes for the twenty-first century: Revisiting the three worlds of welfare capitalism. *World politics*, *60*, 642–664.

Skolverket. (2014). *Privata aktörer inom förskola och skola* (14:1410). Stockholm: Skolverket.

Sköld, B. (2013). *Strukturerna och företagandet: En longitudinell studie av kvinnors och mäns företagande i spåren av offentlig sektors omvandling [Structures and* business ownership: A longitudinal study of women's and men's business-ownership in the wake of public sector transformation]. Linköping: Linköpings Universitet.

Sköld, B. (2015). *Vad hände? Kvinnors företagande och de strukturella villkoren – en studie i spåren av den offentliga sektorns omvandling.* Linköping: Linköping University.

Sköld, B. & Tillmar, M. (2015). Resilient gender order in entrepreneurship: The case of Swedish welfare industries. *International Journal of Gender and Entrepreneurship,* 7(1), 2–26.

Sköld, L. & Heggeman, H. (2012). RUT vanligast efter 85. Retrieved from http://www.scb.se/sv_/Hitta-statistik/Artiklar/RUT-vanligast-efter-85/

Socialstyrelsen. (2013). *Tillståndet och utvecklingen inom hälso – och sjukvård och socialtjänst. Lägesrapport 2013 (2013-2-2).* Retrieved from Stockholm: http://www.socialstyrelsen.se/Lists/Artikelkatalog/Attachments/18955/2013-02-02.pdf

Solli, R. & Czarniawska, B. (2014). Hur går det för New Public Management i svenska kommuner. *Organisation & Samhälle,* (2), 26–31.

SOU 2008. LOV att välja – Lag Om Valfrihetssystem. In Socialdepartementet (Ed.), 2008:15. Stockholm: Regeringskansliet.

SOU 2008:4. (2008/2015). Omreglering av apoteksmarknaden. Stockholm: Regeringskansliet.

SOU 2020:28. (2020). En mer likvärdig skola – minskad skolsegregation och förbättrad resurstilldelning. Stockholm: Regeringskansliet.

Statistics Sweden. (2010). *Women and men in Sweden.* Örebro: Statistics Sweden.

Statistics Sweden. (2020). *Women and men in Sweden.* Örebro: Statistics Sweden.

Stenmark, L. (2012). *Den regionala utvecklingens logik i policy och praktik: en fall-studie av den regionalpolitiska interventionen Resurscentra för kvinnor [The logic of regional development in policy and practice].* Västerås: Mälardalens högskola.

Sundin, E. (2011). Entrepreneurship and the reorganization of the public sector: A gendered story. *Economic and Industrial Democracy,* 32(4), 631–653.

Sundin, E. (2016). Support to women entrepreneurs – of many kinds and for many reasons. *Scandinavian Journal of Public Administration,* 20(4), 91–113.

Sundin, E. & Rapp, G. (2006). *Städerskorna som försvann, Individen i den offentliga sektorn [The cleaners who disappeared: The individual in the public sector]* (2006: 2). Retrieved from Stockholm.

Sundin, E. & Tillmar, M. (2010). The masculinization of the elderly care sector: Local-level studies of public sector outsourcing. *International Journal of Gender and Entrepreneurship,* 2(1), 49–67.

Svanborg-Sjövall, K. (2014). Privatising the Swedish welfare state. *Economic affairs,* 34(2), 181–192.

Svanlund, J. (2011). I skuggan av den svenska modellen. In E. Blomberg, G. Hedlund & M. Wottle (Eds), *Kvinnors företagande – mål eller medel?* Stockholm: SNS.

Swedish Public Procurement Act 1992:1528. Stockholm: Konkurrensverket [Swedish Competition Authority].

Sørensen, B. M. (2008). 'Behold, I am making all things new': The entrepreneur as savior in the age of creativity. *Scandinavian Journal of Management,* 24(2), 85–93.

Thörnquist, A. (2014). Mångfaldens retorik och arbetets praktik: Konkurrensutsättning och jämställdhet i hemtjänsten. In P. de Los Reyes (Ed.), *Inte bara jämställdhet. Intersektionella perspektiv på hinder och möjligheter i arbetslivet.SOU 214:34* (pp. 115–144). Stockholm: Delegationen för jämställdhet i arbetslivet.

Tillmar, M. (2004). *Är det möjligt? Om villkor för småföretagande inom vård-och omsorgssektorn.* Retrieved from Nutek.

Tillmar, M. (2009). No longer so strange? (Dis)trust in municipality – small business relationships. *Economic and Industrial Democracy*, *30*(3), 1–28.

Tillmar, M., Ahl, H., Berglund, K. & Pettersson, K. (2022). Neo-liberalism translated into preconditions for women entrepreneurs – two contrasting cases. *Journal of Enterprising Communities: People and Places in the Global Economy*, *16*(4), 603–630.

Tillväxtanalys. (2018). *RUT-reformen – en deskriptiv analys av företagen och företagarna. PM 2018-12*. Retrieved from Östersund.

Tillväxtanalys. (2019). *Utvärdering av RUT-avdraget. PM 2019-08*. Retrieved from Östersund: https://www.tillvaxtanalys.se/download/18.62dd45451715a00 666f207d8/1586366207527/PM_2019_08_1_utv%C3%A4rdering%20av%20rut -avdraget.pdf

Tillväxtverket. (2012). *Hur kan företagsstöden bli mer jämställda? Förslag på åtgärder som skapar förutsättningar för en mer jämställd resursfördelning vad avser beviljande av företagsstöd. Rapport 0151 [How can business support become more gender equal?]*. Retrieved from Stockholm.

UNDP. (2020). Human Development Reports 2020. Gender Equality Index. Retrieved from http://hdr.undp.org/en/content/gender-inequality-index-gii

Wahl, A. (1996). Molnet – att föreläsa om feministisk forskning. *Kvinnovetenskaplig tidskrift*, 31–44.

Weedon, C. (1999). *Feminism, theory and the politics of difference*. Oxford: Blackwell.

Welter, F. (2011). Contextualising entrepreneurship: Conceptual challenges and ways forward. *Entrepreneurship Theory & Practice*, *35*(1), 165–184.

Wennström, J. (2020). Marketized education: How regulatory failure undermined the Swedish school system. *Journal of Education Policy*, *35*(5), 665–691.

West, C. & Zimmerman, D. H. (1987). Doing gender. *Gender & Society*, *1*(2), 125–151.

Wolf, A. (2013). *The XX factor: How the rise of working women has created a far less equal world*. New York: Crown.

Åberg, R. (2013). Tjugohundratalets arbetsmarknad – fortsatt uppkvalificering eller jobbpolarisering? *Ekonomisk debatt*, (2), 6–15.

Östh, J., Andersson, E. & Malmberg, B. (2013). School choice and increasing performance difference: A counterfactual approach. *Urban Studies*, *50*(2), 407–425.

5. Mapping ethnic minority women entrepreneurs' support initiatives: experiences from the UK

Helen Lawton Smith and Beldina Owalla

INTRODUCTION

Government departments and agencies, including those which support innovation and entrepreneurship, have clear policy statements on equality of opportunity by protected characteristics such as gender, ethnicity and in some cases ability status. Ethnic minorities and women entrepreneurs have captured the attention of policy makers, with successive governments introducing a range of policy initiatives designed to increase their enterprise levels (Carter et al., 2015; Marlow et al., 2008). This has been a gradual process since 2003, when the UK government introduced the Strategic Framework for Women's Enterprise (SFWE) (Forson, 2006). Subsequently, the UK Equality Act of 2010 and the Public Sector Equality Duty (Advance HE 2019[1]) have made equality, diversity and inclusion (EDI) mainstream in UK policy making.

Part of the context to these initiatives has been the increasing percentage of women entrepreneurs (UENI, 2021), as well as the significant impact that minority businesses make to the UK economy (Legrain and Fitzgerald, 2021; Roberts et al., 2020). For example, Innovate UK (the UK government's innovation agency) – with a role to drive productivity and economic growth by supporting businesses and encouraging diversity within innovation – commissioned a report on women in innovation in 2016, which led to the launching of the 'Women in Innovation' awards to showcase successful women innovators and to inspire others (Lawton Smith and Vorley, 2021).

However, entrepreneurship policies still tend to perceive women entrepreneurs as a homogenous group (Forson, 2006). Similarly, research on entrepreneurial diversity has focused on specific dimensions of diversity. Studies on ethnic entrepreneurs have emphasized the impact of ethnic culture on entrepreneurial motives (Romero and Valdez, 2016), while studies on women's entrepreneurship have focused on the experiences of white middle-class founders (Knight, 2016; Pettersson and Lindberg, 2013). The experiences of ethnic minority women entrepreneurs have, therefore, received limited attention by both scholars and policy makers. Moreover, as evidenced by the recent pandemic, those situated at the intersections of identity categories such as age, race, ethnicity, class, etc., tend to be more vulnerable in times of crises (Martinez Dy and Jayawarna, 2020).

This chapter contributes to filling this knowledge gap by analysing the type of support available to ethnic minority women entrepreneurs in the UK. It maps the support through regional and national initiatives available to this minority group identifying the kinds of activities that existing initiatives are providing, e.g., networking events, training and mentorship.

The chapter draws on evidence from two studies. This first is a 2019 study implemented by the Innovation Caucus[2] on behalf of Innovate UK that adopted an intersectional perspective to understanding the challenges to supporting diversity in business innovation (Vorley et al., 2020). The second is a primary research study which examines the geography of support for Black, Asian and Minority Ethnic (BAME) entrepreneurs and entrepreneurs with disabilities (Lawton Smith, 2020–2021).[3]

To interpret the data we draw on and adapt the entrepreneurial ecosystem model (Stam, 2015) in order to frame our analysis of the support initiatives available to ethnic minority women entrepreneurs.

Our findings demonstrate the fragmented nature of existing support networks and emphasize the need for there to be further *intermediaries* and *networks* within ethnic minority women entrepreneurial ecosystems. The advantage of a systems approach is that it can be used to identify the extent of interconnectedness of different elements, including wider structural factors, within specific kinds of ecosystems and where there are gaps in provision. Our findings reveal other important elements of entrepreneurial ecosystems that do not feature in the general literature. The chief of these is the role of advocacy – on the part of networks in the regions, by national professional support organizations, by relevant All Party Parliamentary Groups (APPG) and by purely web-based initiatives.

The rest of this chapter is organized as follows. In the next section we discuss the context for women's entrepreneurship support initiatives. The entrepreneurial ecosystem model framework is discussed in the following section. The research methodology follows. Succeeding sections present the main findings and analysis, and conclusions. Recommendations for policy and practice are highlighted.

EXPLORING WOMEN'S ENTREPRENEURSHIP SUPPORT INITIATIVES

Context

While the gendered nature of entrepreneurship and innovation is widely acknowledged (Alsos et al., 2013; Jennings and Brush, 2013), entrepreneurship policies still tend to focus on women entrepreneurs' inadequacies or extraordinariness (Ahl and Nelson, 2015; Coleman et al., 2019). A systematic review carried out on women's entrepreneurship policy over a 30-year period (1983–2015) indicates that policy implications from women's entrepreneurship research are mostly vague, conservative and centred around identifying and addressing skills gaps in women entrepreneurs; resulting in the isolation and individualization of problems faced (Foss et al., 2019).

In the UK, ethnic minorities and women entrepreneurs have for a long time captured the attention of policy makers, with successive governments introducing a range of policy initiatives designed to increase their enterprise levels (Carter et al., 2015; Marlow et al., 2008). However, a coherent national strategic approach to the development of women's enterprise policy was missing from the UK policy landscape until the launch of the Strategic Framework for Women's Enterprise (SFWE) in 2003 (Forson, 2006). This umbrella document formed the basis for all initiatives aimed at supporting women's entrepreneurship, and had four action priorities: business support provision, access to finance, childcare and caring responsibilities, and transition from benefits to self-employment (Forson, 2006).

The majority of these policy initiatives treated these two minority groups as distinct, as can be seen in the simultaneous establishment of the Ethnic Minority Business Task Force and the Women's Enterprise Task Force (2007–2009) (Carter et al., 2015). Women's entrepreneurship was valued for the potential impact on the economy, while ethnic minority businesses were valued for their role in promoting social cohesion and multiculturalism (Carter et al., 2015). Furthermore, most initiatives perceived women entrepreneurs as a homogenous group, and assumed that ethnic minority women entrepreneurs would automatically benefit from all gender-based policies (Forson, 2006).

Similarly, research on entrepreneurial diversity has focused on specific dimensions of diversity in isolation. On the one hand, studies on ethnic entrepreneurs have historically emphasized ethnic culture as the main motivation for these communities' engagement (or lack thereof) in entrepreneurship (Romero and Valdez, 2016). Research on women's entrepreneurship on the other hand has homogenized women entrepreneurs by focusing primarily on the challenges faced by white middle-class women (Pettersson and Lindberg,

2013). As a result, the experiences of ethnic minority women entrepreneurs have been largely underestimated by both academics and policy makers (Knight, 2016).

Greater attention to the heterogeneity of women entrepreneurs is therefore necessary, given that the entrepreneurial process is influenced by the privileges and disadvantages created by intersecting identity categories such as gender, race, age, ethnicity and class (Martinez Dy, 2019; Wingfield and Taylor, 2016). Besides, as evidenced in the recent COVID-19 pandemic, the impact of these differences can be amplified during times of crises, especially for those positioned at the intersections (Martinez Dy and Jayawarna, 2020). A more integrated approach that recognizes the myriad of economic and social relationships in which ethnic minority businesses are embedded is vital (Edwards et al., 2016; Owalla et al., 2021; Ram and Jones, 2008). The working lives and experiences of ethnic minority women entrepreneurs are influenced by their race, ethnicity and class (Forson, 2006).

ENTREPRENEURIAL ECOSYSTEMS, EQUALITY, DIVERSITY AND INCLUSION

Even though self-employment and entrepreneurship are important aspects of the labour market experience for minority groups in the UK (Department for Business, Energy and Industrial Strategy (BEIS), 2018; Jones and Latreille, 2011; Office for National Statistics (ONS), 2018), public policies within this area are characterized by a number of unresolved tensions such as the presence of perceived or actual discrimination; the quantity and quality of diverse enterprises; and the potential market failure in the support provided to these communities (Carter et al., 2015).

Research suggests that when it comes to many aspects of entrepreneurial ecosystems, women entrepreneurs are at a disadvantage (Brush et al., 2019). Entrepreneurial ecosystems can be defined as a set of interdependent actors and factors that are mutually reinforcing in such a way as to facilitate entrepreneurial activity (Stam, 2015). The ecosystem elements include the social (formal and informal institutions) and physical conditions impacting human interactions, as well as the systemic conditions (i.e. networks, leadership, finance, talent, knowledge and support services). The presence of these elements and the interaction between them play an important role in the success of an ecosystem (Stam, 2015). While this provides a general framework for policy analysis, at issue is the degree to which ecosystems are open to and supportive of all forms of entrepreneurship (Kruger and David, 2020).

In focusing on ethnic minority women entrepreneurs, our study aims to highlight possible gaps and specificities that need to be taken into account when policy interventions are proposed. Key elements specific to inclusive

Table 5.1   *Elements specific to ethnic minority women entrepreneurs*

Ecosystem elements	Ethnic minority women entrepreneur support
Intermediaries – Supply of support services by a variety of intermediaries can substantially lower entry barriers for new entrepreneurial projects and reduce the time to market of innovations.	Ethnic minority specific support networks or networks that have a high level of BAME women members.
Knowledge – From both public and private organizations.	Access to localized or national specialized support or to support which has a high representation of ethnic minority women entrepreneurs.
Access to financing – Preferably provided by investors with entrepreneurial knowledge.	Financial support that has a high understanding of the specific issues faced by ethnic minority women entrepreneurs.
Demand – Strong potential market demand. Good access to customers in domestic and foreign markets.	Not necessarily ethnic minority specific market demand.
Talent – Broad, deep talent pool of employees. Both technical workers and business-oriented workers (sales, marketing, etc.).	Talent availability, particularly locally.
Leadership – A strong group of entrepreneurs who are visible, accessible and committed to the region being a great place to start and grow a company.	Role models, leaders of influential organizations which can shape advocacy on behalf of ethnic minority women entrepreneurs.
Formal Institutions – Good-quality government and friendly regulatory framework for entrepreneurship.	How government and government agencies provide support for specific groups: is it understood to be sympathetic and accessible to ethnic minority women entrepreneurs? Is the language used welcoming?
Connectivity infrastructure – Good road, rail, air and broadband connections giving access to customers, suppliers, collaborators.	Not specific to ethnic minority women entrepreneurs.
Entrepreneurial culture – Positive social attitudes to entrepreneurship and extent to which it is common.	Positive attitudes towards ethnic minority women entrepreneurs at local, regional and national levels.
Networks – Large number of events to which entrepreneurs can connect. A well-connected community of start-ups and entrepreneurs along with engaged and visible investors, advisors, mentors and supporters.	Local networks and events that profile and support ethnic minority women entrepreneurs.

Source: Authors' adaptation of Stam's (2015) model.

(ethnic minority women) entrepreneurial ecosystems and the relevant geography are shown in Table 5.1. Of particular relevance are intermediaries, leadership, formal institutions, entrepreneurial culture and networks.

A key theme in understanding barriers within entrepreneurial ecosystems for ethnic minority women relates to degrees of openness. The assumption that all entrepreneurs have equal access to resources, support and success outcomes within an ecosystem rarely holds in practice (Brooks et al., 2019; Brush et al., 2019). Substantial evidence indicates that women entrepreneurs differ significantly from their male counterparts in terms of participation, access to resources and outcomes within ecosystems (Berger and Kuckertz, 2016; Brush et al., 2019). This applies particularly at the local level, but also applies nationally.

Furthermore, inequalities existing within ecosystems do not occur in isolation, which means that there is a need to address the broader socio-economic factors, including entrepreneurial culture, influencing women entrepreneurs' participation and access to resources within ecosystems (Marlow and McAdam, 2013; O'Brien and Cooney, 2019).

While difficulties in accessing finance are common for all start-ups, the challenge increases when examining women entrepreneurs' access to equity capital (Brush et al., 2019; Klingler-Vidra, 2018), with ethnic minority women entrepreneurs facing the largest disparities. Wright et al. (2015) argue that if women-led businesses had the same access to resources, this would eliminate the pervasive gender gap in business performance. However, in reality women entrepreneurs typically start with lower resources and perceive higher barriers in accessing finance than their male counterparts (Wright et al., 2015). Moreover, a report on venture capital funding in the UK during the period 2009 to 2019, indicates that Black female founders received only 0.02% of the total amount invested (Brodnock, 2020).

A report by the British Business Bank (2020) also finds that more Black (37%) and Asian and Other Ethnic Minority background (36%) female business owners were likely to report zero profits in 2019 compared to White male business owners (16%). Even when societal inequalities and established gender roles, such as having primary caring duties for children and elderly relatives, are taken into account, women entrepreneurs still experience less success. Location also plays a role. There is uneven geography of access to finance irrespective of ethnicity and gender. While the majority of venture capital investments are made in London (72%), this area was found to be the toughest place in the UK to be an entrepreneur, with just 71% of business owners in London reporting a profit in 2019 (British Business Bank, 2020; Diversity VC and OneTech, 2019). Differences between London and other regions are linked to a higher density of start-ups, tougher market competition, higher costs of living and greater disparity between poorer and wealthier neighbourhoods (British Business Bank, 2020). The role of place in influencing access to resources and entrepreneurial opportunities therefore needs to be further examined (Blake and Hanson, 2005). Mapping the landscape for ethnic minority women entrepreneurs' support initiatives in the UK regions will help to shed light on these geographical specificities (Berglund et al., 2016).

Female founders' access to networks and social support is also influenced by perceived discrimination. A study by Davidson et al. (2010) of 40 ethnic minority women entrepreneurs found that the majority had experienced some sort of discrimination either due to their gender, ethnicity, or both. In particular there is discrimination related to formal business and financial support. As a result, many respondents reported difficulties in accessing different types of formal social support, e.g. business and financial support. Informal support by respondents' families was therefore a key source of both emotional and instrumental support (see also Fielden and Davidson, 2012).

It therefore follows that policy initiatives aiming at improving entrepreneurial ecosystems require a more holistic understanding of the individual stakeholders involved, as well as the institutional environment within which ecosystems are embedded (Foss et al., 2019; Henry et al., 2017). Information on the role of media and advocacy as a function of ecosystems is also missing explicitly in these analytical frameworks. This calls for a greater awareness of the complex challenges that intersecting categories of gender, ethnicity, class, nationality, etc., might present for ethnic minority women entrepreneurs in different regions of the UK – often for different reasons. Implementing policies that go beyond simply reducing gender inequality will help to ensure that ecosystems fulfil their true potential (Berger and Kuckertz, 2016). Besides, there is a need to shift from purely boosting women's participation in entrepreneurship to focusing on improving the sustainability of women-led firms (Marlow et al., 2008).

THE GEOGRAPHY OF INITIATIVES SUPPORTING ETHNIC MINORITY WOMEN ENTREPRENEURS

Methodology

This study builds on evidence that formed the report published by Innovate UK in 2020 (Vorley et al., 2020) which identified the barriers, challenges, opportunities and support needed for minority ethnic groups and disabled people (non-gender specific) participating in business innovation. While this report provided insights into motivations and challenges of the entrepreneurs, the purpose of the follow-on research project undertaken by the first author and funded by the Regional Studies Association[4] was to understand and explain where support for innovators in BAME and disabled groups is available in the UK. The focus is on dedicated networks that exist to provide direct support such as mentoring and raising access to finance for these two categories of entrepreneur (non-gender specific although several address specific gender issues).

The study has two main research stages. The first is a mapping exercise designed to identify by region all dedicated networks which specifically support BAME or disabled entrepreneurs or both. The exercise also included identifying all national networks and organizations, as well as government-based initiatives designed to support entrepreneurship and innovation in the two groups. These include the APPGs and specific initiatives such as those led by Innovate UK.

The mapping exercise extended the initial work on identifying networks in the 2019 Innovate UK. Further networks were identified through extensive search processes involving a variety of sources. These included using a snowball technique of recommendations from the already known networks, the Innovate UK project Advisory Board, help from government agencies, and web searches based on keywords.

The second stage involving interviewing a sample of networks about, for example, their activities, the extent to which location is a factor in what they are able to achieve, what links they have with other local and with national organizations and the challenges they face reinforced the findings below but are not discussed here as the interviews were non-gender specific. Nine BAME supporting networks were interviewed and further interviews were conducted with various policy making bodies such as Innovate UK, UKRI, the Cabinet Office Race Disparity Unit and the organizer of the All Party Parliamentary Group for BAME Businesses.

Data

The mapping exercise identified a total of 63 networks. Outside London, there are 35 organizations of which 18 were ethnic minority entrepreneur specific, 14 disability specific and three which covered both groups. The highest concentration of BAME networks is in the West Midlands which has five networks. In London a further 28 organizations were identified. Of these, 16 support ethnic minority entrepreneurs, seven support disabled entrepreneurs and five more offer general business services for both groups, including those for social enterprises. Only a small number of the networks support ethnic minority women-led entrepreneurs. There are also 12+ national networks.

The survey found that a small number of the networks in the study (six) are network organizations which specifically support ethnic minority women entrepreneurs. Two further are non-gender specific but have a focus on female entrepreneurs. In order to gain a more complete picture of the extent of support for ethnic minority women entrepreneurs, a further data collection exercise was conducted to identify other national initiatives aimed at supporting ethnic minority women's enterprises. This brought the total to 14 organizations of various forms (Table 5.3). The table shows in addition to those six women-only

Table 5.2   *Geographical distribution of support initiatives specifically for ethnically diverse entrepreneurs*

Region	Number
Scotland	3
Northern Ireland	0
North East	0
North West	1
Yorkshire & Humberside	1
East Midlands	1
West Midlands	5
East of England	1
South East	2
Wales	2
South West	2
London	16
Total	**34**

Source: Adapted from Lawton Smith (2021).

and two mixed but focused networks which act as intermediaries between the entrepreneurs, sources of support and policy makers; two networks led by ethnically minority women; two national organizations representing ethnic minority entrepreneurs; and two women-only awareness raising initiatives.

The combined sets of data in Table 5.3 show publicly available information on the organization's websites. Included in this table are the names of a growing phenomenon of influential ethnic minority women in leadership positions in organizations that support ethnic minority entrepreneurs.

In the following section, each element of the modified entrepreneurial ecosystems approach shown in Table 5.1 is used to assess the state of support for ethnic minority women entrepreneurs.

WHAT DOES THE EVIDENCE TELL US?

The data collection exercise has identified 14 entrepreneurial networks and activities that are either led by ethnic minority women or have a sole or primary focus on ethnic minority women entrepreneurs. They are spread unevenly across the UK. There are minor concentrations in organizations in London (three) and two in Scotland. Two are online sites. This suggests that the ethnic minority women entrepreneurial ecosystem with regard to *intermediaries* in the UK is under-developed and very geographically fragmented.

Table 5.3   *Initiatives directed at ethnic minority women entrepreneurs*

BAME network organizations

Hatch Female Founders London	https://femalefounders.london/ Run BAME female founders programme. Focus on underrepresented entrepreneurs. This selective 4-month programme is for Black, Asian and Minority Ethnic women who want to explore new revenue streams, cost structures and ways to market. Expert-led sessions on core business areas (including sales, finance, marketing, branding, and leadership). One-to-one technical support, business coaching and expert consulting. Access to networks and a supportive community of female founders.	Practical programmes and support for female founders to succeed at business and life. Female only.
One Tech Capital Enterprise London	Diversity & Inclusion | CE (capitalenterprise.org) Weareonetech.org Aim is to boost access to investment and entrepreneurial support opportunities for tech start-ups founded by women and by those from minority ethnic backgrounds.	Investment and entrepreneurial support. Mixed but focus.
WCAN London	WCAN | Professional & Personal Development for Black Women WCAN is a young social enterprise dedicated to the personal and professional development of black women. Hosts events for black women entrepreneurs.	Event specifically for Black women who have an interest in starting a company or venture capital. www.wcan.uk/bwii Female only.
Black Young Professionals Network (BYP)	byp-network.com 'The BYP network was founded by the need to connect Black professionals and students from all over the world for role model visibility, career opportunities, business support and ultimately to solve our problems.'	Business support including brand promotion, visibility, role models, networking. Mixed but focus.

AMINA – Muslim Women's Resource Centre Scotland	mwrc.org.uk 'Empowerment via Enterprise (EVE) Project offers innovative and interactive enterprise support to Muslim and Minority Ethnic women across the city of Dundee. We aim to help women utilize their skills, experience and ideas to explore and ultimately start their own business.'	Start-up support.	Female only.
Empower women for Change – Scotland	What we do – Empower Women for Change Supports African youth and women entrepreneurs.	Training, workshops, advice sessions, coaching and mentoring.	Female only.
We Are Tech women	Over the past four years We Are Tech Women has helped thousands of women in tech enhance their careers through events, conferences and awards. It has worked with over 40 multi-sector corporate organizations helping them to attract, retain and develop their female tech talent. We Are Tech Women currently has a membership of 15,000 diverse female members, women working across a multitude of industries and tech disciplines.	Advocacy, networking, upskilling.	Female only.
Bright Futures Women's Leadership and Enterprise Programme Scotland	Funded by the Scottish government and The European Social Fund this programme provides support to Asylum seekers, refugees and migrants who wish to develop their leadership and enterprise skills. Its programme brings together women from all walks of life into a shared learning environment where their leadership and entrepreneurial skills are not only recognized and developed but also applied to inspire others.	Enterprise support for ethnic minority women entrepreneurs.	Female only.
Yorkshire Asian Business Association (YABA) Yorkshire	YABA was created to provide a voice for the Yorkshire Asian Business Community. Research has shown that the community makes an enormous contribution to the UK (yabauk.com)	Advocacy, networking bespoke events, mentoring and support services.	Female founder and Project Director for the Northern Asian Powerlist.

ABCC Birmingham	ABCC supports all businesses. It aims to champion their successes, be firm in the face of adversity, and supportive through tough times. ABCC acts as an advocate for Asian businesses and speaks as an influential voice for the views and opinions of its members, aiming to represent their business needs. ABCC has a 'respect for women' pledge.	Advocacy, networking and training marketing support, networking. Signposting to other organizations, e.g. universities and government schemes. Commitment to women entrepreneurs.	Female Director.

National organizations

The National Black Women's Network	http://nbwn.org/about_nbwn.html NBWN is a non-profit organization dedicated to raising the status and position of women in all walks of life. It provides dynamic initiatives, enabling women from diverse backgrounds and occupations to develop strong professional and social contacts; high-quality training and education programmes; leadership and national recognition through the forum of networking. It brings together entrepreneurs, peers, industry experts and specialists for inspiring, professional and valuable networking opportunities to generate leads and expand women's referral and contact base.	Networking, training, advocacy.	Female only.
APPG for BAME business people	Home	APPG BAME (appgbamebusiness.co.uk) 'The All Party Parliamentary Group for BAME Business Owners aims to promote the advancement of businesses owned by Black, Asian and Minority Ethnic people for the overall benefit of the UK economy. We support economic growth and social mobility through inclusive entrepreneurship and leading an evidence-based business case for greater integration of BAME-owned businesses into industrial planning and policy making.'	Advocacy.	Mixed. Female Special Advisor to APPG and was instrumental in its creation.

Awareness raising initiatives

Forward Ladies	50 Must-Follow BAME Female Entrepreneurs, Influencers & Speakers in 2020 – FL (forwardladies.com)	Advocacy.	Female only.
	It is still not clear to many outside of the BAME community how racial biases can manifest themselves in the workplace. One approach to education is to follow outspoken BAME female leaders who are doing great work to level the playing field.		
Real Business	5 Inspirational Black Female UK Entrepreneurs (realbusiness.co.uk)	Advocacy.	Female only.
	This report highlights that firms owned by women of colour have grown at more than double the rate of all women-owned businesses, and that women-owned businesses in general have grown twice as fast in the last year than they had over the previous five. Often going unnoticed, the women who start and run these businesses are making waves in a number of industries as they put their skills, knowledge and motivation into building successful businesses and brands.		

Source: Lawton Smith (2021).

This pattern exists in spite of the growing national recognition of the prevalence of ethnic minority women entrepreneurs in the economy, the increasing number of reports highlighting the importance of ethnic minority and ethnic minority women entrepreneurs to the economy (for example British Business Bank, 2020; Brodnock, 2020; Roberts et al., 2020), and recent growing political interest (see for example Vorley et al., 2020). Taking a broader view, the entrepreneurial ecosystem includes *networks* which are in fact *intermediaries* as they fulfil intermediary functions (led by BAME women), two national organizations, and a series of awareness raising initiatives such as blogs (e.g. Forward Ladies and Real Business). However, overall this is still little activity, and in some locations it is non-existent or virtually non-existent.

Looking at the geography of support for minority entrepreneurs as a whole, networks are scattered throughout the country, with the highest incidence in the West Midlands, which in the 2011 census was shown to have a high proportion of Asian residents (10.8%) and Black residents (3.3%). London had 40.2% of residents identified with either the Asian, Black, Mixed or Other ethnic group (18.5%), of which 13.3% were Asian.[5] London's 15 networks and other support organizations reflect the dominance of London for support activity, in line with its population demography.

Overall, there is a lack of dedicated activity for ethnic minority women entrepreneurs except to a limited extent in Scotland and London. This represents a seriously under-developed localized entrepreneurial ecosystem in most of the UK. However, other organizations either led by women or part of national programmes potentially lower entry barriers for start-ups and help with growth ambitions. Activities include training (including in entrepreneurship skills), workshops, advice sessions, mentoring, e.g. in marketing, and signposting to other relevant organizations. Evidence from the larger study suggests that the last is a particularly important function of entrepreneurial ecosystems. However, the overall fragmentation of support is a major inhibitor of this function (Lawton Smith, 2021).

While most networking organizations provide practical support for starting and growing a business, one is targeted at women in tech (*knowledge*) (One Tech) which also helps to provide access to investment funding. The geography shown in Table 5.2 reinforces a picture of an uneven *access to financing* for BAME entrepreneurs (British Business Bank, 2020). This appears to be a critical weakness in the ethnic minority women entrepreneurial ecosystem. Access to finance is a major problem faced by women and an even bigger problem for ethnic minority women entrepreneurs (Wright et al., 2015).

There is little evidence of increasing the *supply of talent*. However, this could be part of the networking function that is a basic function of 9 of the 12 organizations shown in Table 5.2.

Where there is evidence of a greater significance is the area of leadership. As well as the five women-only networks, at least two others – YABA (Yorkshire) and ABCC (Birmingham) – have minority ethnic women in leadership positions. In all cases the leaders of these networks are role models. In the cases of YABA and ABCC they are leaders of influential organizations and are strong advocates for ethnic minority women entrepreneurs. This is also the case with the national organization: the National Black Women's Network.

Indeed, advocacy is a very important component of the ethnic minority women entrepreneurial ecosystem. This is both through the networks themselves and through the online media where blogs submitted for example by *Forward Ladies* and *Real Business* highlight the success of ethnic minority women entrepreneurs. Publicity is also given to ethnic minority women entrepreneurs with particular attention paid to the *Alone Together* report (British Business Bank, 2020) in the national press and in online articles.

A further indication of entrepreneurial ecosystem change at the national level is in formal institutions. As well as policy advance by Innovate UK on women innovators and BAME entrepreneurs and innovators, the government has established the All Party Parliamentary Group for BAME Business Owners. The secretariat is provided by a BAME women entrepreneur. Indeed, all the organizations in government with business-facing interests have formalized equality, diversity and inclusion commitments. These include BEIS, the Intellectual Property Office[6] and UK Research and Innovation (UKRI) (a non-departmental public body of the Government of the United Kingdom that directs research and innovation funding and is funded through the science budget of BEIS), as well as the influential Cabinet Office which has separate units for disability and race disparity.

An outcome of this project is a website that connects all of the participants in the research.[7] This is thus an example of 'engaged scholarship' (Ram et al., 2012) which involves sustained and continuous interaction between researchers and practitioners in the field. One of the issues raised in the current research is the nature and accessibility of support for BAME and disabled entrepreneurs. The study is actively informing Innovate UK and Cabinet Office policy, specifically on gaps in knowledge about the geography of support for minority entrepreneurs.

Entrepreneurial culture and networks form the last line in Stam's (2015) entrepreneurial ecosystems elements. What this evidence has shown is that there is an emerging entrepreneurial culture among ethnic minority women entrepreneurs as demonstrated by the range of activity within ethnic minority women networks. However, Stam's approach does not recognize clearly the interdependence of the different elements and hence the drivers of change in the system; rather, it emphasizes compartmentalization of activity.

CONCLUSIONS

Previous studies have shown that ethnic minority-led firms make a significant impact on the UK economy (Legrain and Fitzgerald, 2021; Roberts et al., 2020) and are more likely to engage in innovation activities (Owalla et al., in press). It follows that there is demand for an inclusive entrepreneurial ecosystems framework that provides resources for start-ups and scale-ups for ethnic minority women entrepreneurs. However, even though there is growing publicity, policy interest, advocacy and academic research on ethnic minority women entrepreneurs, the findings can be interpreted as showing that a more integrated understanding of the experiences in different parts of the country is needed. Most relevant in the adapted Stam (2015) framework are intermediaries (networks), access to finance, leadership, and formal institutions at the local and national levels. To clarify the distinction some networks in this study are intermediaries as they have multiple activities including advocacy whereas Stam has them as separate categories with networks playing entrepreneurship support roles.

Overall our results draw attention to the lack of dedicated activity for ethnic minority women entrepreneurs, except to a limited extent in Scotland and London. The fragmented nature of existing targeted support initiatives is an impediment to achieving greater diversity and inclusion within entrepreneurial ecosystems (Lawton Smith, 2021). Given that existing ethnic minority women entrepreneurs' support initiatives are scattered and sparse, one of the Lawton Smith (2020–2021) project outcomes is to provide a website[8] that connects research participants. Policy makers and support institutions could adopt this 'glue' function and extend it further by providing more platforms and/or avenues through which support networks, existing and future, can connect and interact.

Our findings also highlight the need to further develop *intermediaries* and *networks* (as well as make explicit the distinction between them) within ethnic minority women entrepreneurial ecosystems. These should support that group in addressing existing barriers to accessing finance and markets (British Business Bank, 2020). This is especially true outside of London.

Furthermore, both academics and policy makers need to gain a better understanding of the broader socio-economic factors that constrain ethnic minority women entrepreneurs to gendered spaces and feminized sectors that are highly competitive and with low growth prospects for their businesses (Carter et al., 2015; Marlow and McAdam, 2013). Once greater understanding is in place, there is a need for a shift in policy to recognize and provide relevant support for this group. The aim should be not only to increase the portfolio of entrepreneurs, but also to better support existing founders (Marlow et al., 2008).

Given the geographical nature of the need this could be viewed as part of the UK government's much vaunted 'levelling up' agenda for regions and groups of people.

ACKNOWLEDGEMENTS

The authors thank Dina Mansour for her contribution to research and John Slater for comments on an earlier version of this chapter.

NOTES

1. Public sector equality duty | Advance HE (advance-he.ac.uk) (accessed 2 July 2021).
2. https://innovationcaucus.co.uk/
3. Making Business Innovation Accessible to Diverse Groups – Birkbeck, University of London (bbk.ac.uk).
4. Helen Lawton Smith wins Regional Studies Association Regional Studies Association Fellowship Grant – Centre for Innovation Management Research (bbk.ac.uk).
5. Regional ethnic diversity – GOV.UK Ethnicity facts and figures (ethnicity-facts-figures.service.gov.uk) (accessed 22 June 2021).
6. Inclusion and diversity report for 2019–2020 – GOV.UK (www.gov.uk)(accessed 22 June 2021).
7. Making Business Innovation Accessible to Diverse Groups – Birkbeck, University of London (bbk.ac.uk) (accessed 22 June 2021).
8. Making Business Innovation Accessible to Diverse Groups – Birkbeck, University of London (bbk.ac.uk).

REFERENCES

Ahl, H. and Nelson, T. (2015). 'How policy positions women entrepreneurs: A comparative analysis of state discourse in Sweden and the United States', *Journal of Business Venturing*, Elsevier, Vol. 30 No. 2, pp. 273–291.

Alsos, G., Ljunggren, E. and Hytti, U. (2013). 'Gender and innovation: State of the art and a research agenda', *International Journal of Gender and Entrepreneurship*, Emerald Group Publishing Limited, Vol. 5 No. 3, pp. 236–256.

BEIS. (2018). UK Innovation Survey 2017: Main Report.

Berger, E. and Kuckertz, A. (2016), 'Female entrepreneurship in startup ecosystems worldwide', *Journal of Business Research*, Vol. 69 No. 11, pp. 5163–5168.

Berglund, K., Gaddefors, J. and Lindgren, M. (2016). 'Provoking identities: Entrepreneurship and emerging identity positions in rural development', *Entrepreneurship and Regional Development*, Vol. 28 No. 1–2, pp. 76–96.

Blake, M. and Hanson, S. (2005). 'Rethinking innovation: Context and gender', *Environment and Planning A: Economy and Space*, SAGE Publications Ltd, Vol. 37 No. 4, pp. 681–701.

British Business Bank. (2020). *Alone together: Entrepreneurship and diversity in the UK* (british-business-bank.co.uk).

Brodnock, E. (2020). *Diversity Beyond Gender: The State of the Nation for Diverse Entrepreneurs*. Extend Ventures.

Brooks, C., Vorley, T. and Gherhes, C. (2019). 'Entrepreneurial ecosystems in Poland: Panacea, paper tiger or Pandora's box?', *Journal of Entrepreneurship and Public Policy*, Emerald Publishing Limited, Vol. 8 No. 3, pp. 319–338.

Brush, C., Edelman, L., Manolova, T. and Welter, F. (2019). 'A gendered look at entrepreneurship ecosystems', *Small Business Economics*, Vol. 53 No. 2, pp. 393–408.

Carter, S., Mwaura, S., Ram, M., Trehan, K. and Jones, T. (2015). 'Barriers to ethnic minority and women's enterprise: Existing evidence, policy tensions and unsettled questions', *International Small Business Journal*, Vol. 33 No. 1, pp. 49–69.

Coleman, S., Henry, C., Orser, B., Foss, L. and Welter, F. (2019). 'Policy support for women entrepreneurs' access to financial capital: Evidence from Canada, Germany, Ireland, Norway, and the United States', *Journal of Small Business Management*, Routledge, Vol. 57 No. S2, pp. 296–322.

Davidson, M., Fielden, S. and Omar, A. (2010). 'Black, Asian and Minority Ethnic female business owners: Discrimination and social support', *International Journal of Entrepreneurial Behavior & Research*, Vol. 16 No. 1, pp. 58–80.

Diversity VC and OneTech. (2019). *Venturing into Diversity and Inclusion 2019: Addressing the Diversity Deficit in VC*.

Edwards, P., Ram, M., Jones, T. and Doldor, S. (2016). 'New migrant businesses and their workers: Developing, but not transforming, the ethnic economy', *Ethnic and Racial Studies*, Routledge, Vol. 39 No. 9, pp. 1587–1617.

Fielden, S. and Davidson, M. (2012). 'BAME women business owners: How intersectionality affects discrimination and social support', *Gender in Management*, Vol. 27 No. 8, pp. 559–581.

Forson, C. (2006). 'The strategic framework for women's enterprise: BME women at the margins', *Equal Opportunities International*, Vol. 25 No. 6, pp. 418–432.

Foss, L., Henry, C., Ahl, H. and Mikalsen, G. (2019). 'Women's entrepreneurship policy research: A 30-year review of the evidence', *Small Business Economics*, Vol. 53 No. 2, pp. 409–429.

Henry, C., Orser, B., Coleman, S. and Foss, L. (2017). 'Women's entrepreneurship policy: A 13-nation cross-country comparison', *International Journal of Gender and Entrepreneurship*, Vol. 9 No. 3, pp. 206–228.

Jennings, J. and Brush, C. (2013). 'Research on women entrepreneurs: Challenges to (and from) the broader entrepreneurship literature?', *The Academy of Management Annals*, Taylor & Francis, Vol. 7 No. 1, pp. 663–715.

Jones, M. and Latreille, P. (2011). 'Disability and self-employment: Evidence for the UK', *Applied Economics*, Taylor & Francis, Vol. 43 No. 27, pp. 4161–4178.

Klingler-Vidra, R. (2018). Global Review of Diversity and Inclusion in Business Innovation. A Report Prepared for Innovate UK by LSE Consulting.

Knight, M. (2016). 'Race-ing, classing and gendering racialized women's participation in entrepreneurship', *Gender, Work & Organization*, Wiley Online Library, Vol. 23 No. 3, pp. 310–327.

Kruger, D. and David, A. (2020). 'Entrepreneurial education for persons with disabilities – A social innovation approach for inclusive ecosystems', *Frontiers in Education*, Vol. 5 No. 3, pp. 1–17.

Lawton Smith, H. (2021). Regional geographies of innovation and entrepreneurship support: An 'engaged scholarship' approach. Presentation to Birkbeck Diversity Research Group, 13 May 2021.

Lawton Smith, H. and Vorley, T. (2021). 'Chapter 1 United Kingdom', in C. Henry (ed.), *OECD-Global WEP Report Entrepreneurship through a Gender Lens*. Paris: OECD. OECD iLibrary Entrepreneurship through a Gender Lens.

Legrain, P. and Fitzgerald, M. (2021). Minority Businesses Matter: The Contribution and Challenges of Ethnic Minority Businesses in the UK.

Marlow, S. and McAdam, M. (2013). 'Gender and entrepreneurship: Advancing debate and challenging myths; exploring the mystery of the under-performing female entrepreneur', *International Journal of Entrepreneurial Behaviour & Research*, Vol. 19, pp. 114–124.

Marlow, S., Carter, S. and Shaw, E. (2008). 'Constructing female entrepreneurship policy in the UK: Is the US a relevant benchmark?', *Environment and Planning C: Government and Policy*, SAGE Publications Sage UK, Vol. 26 No. 2, pp. 335–351.

Martinez Dy, A. (2019). 'Levelling the playing field? Towards a critical-social perspective on digital entrepreneurship', *Futures*, p. 102438.

Martinez Dy, A. and Jayawarna, D. (2020). 'Bios, mythoi and women entrepreneurs: A Wynterian analysis of the intersectional impacts of the COVID-19 pandemic on self-employed women and women-owned businesses', *International Small Business Journal*, SAGE Publications Ltd, Vol. 38 No. 5, pp. 391–403.

O'Brien, E. and Cooney, T. (2019). 'Expanding university entrepreneurial ecosystems to under-represented communities', *Journal of Entrepreneurship and Public Policy*, Vol. 8 No. 3, pp. 384–407.

ONS. (2018). Trends in Self-Employment in the UK: Analysing the Characteristics, Income and Wealth of the Self-Employed.

Owalla, B., Nyanzu, E. and Vorley, T. (in press). 'Intersections of gender, ethnicity, place and innovation: Mapping the diversity of women-led SMEs in the United Kingdom', *International Small Business Journal*, SAGE Publications.

Owalla, B., Vorley, T., Coogan, T., Lawton Smith, H. and Wing, K. (2021). 'Absent or overlooked? Promoting diversity among entrepreneurs with public support needs', *International Journal of Entrepreneurial Venturing*, Vol. 13 No. 3, p. 1.

Pettersson, K. and Lindberg, M. (2013). 'Paradoxical spaces of feminist resistance', edited by Gry Alsos, *International Journal of Gender and Entrepreneurship*, Emerald Publishing, Vol. 5 No. 3, pp. 323–341.

Ram, M. and Jones, T. (2008). 'Ethnic-minority businesses in the UK: A review of research and policy developments', *Environment and Planning C: Government and Policy*, SAGE Publications, Vol. 26 No. 2, pp. 352–374.

Ram, R., Trehan, K., Rouse, J., Woldesenbet, K. and Jones, T. (2012). 'Ethnic minority businesses in the West Midlands: Challenges and developments', *Environment and Planning C*, Vol. 30, pp. 504–519.

Roberts, R., Ram, M., Jones, T., Idris, B., Hart, M., Ri, A. and Prashar, N. (2020). *Unlocking Opportunity: The Value of Ethnic Minority Firms to UK Economic Activity and Enterprise*.

Romero, M. and Valdez, Z. (2016)., 'Introduction to the special issue: Intersectionality and entrepreneurship', *Ethnic and Racial Studies*, Taylor & Francis, Vol. 39 No. 9, pp. 1553–1565.

Stam, E. (2015). 'Entrepreneurial ecosystems and regional policy: A sympathetic critique', *European Planning Studies*, Vol. 23, pp. 1759–1769.

UENI. (2021). UENI's 2020 Report on Gender and Small Business. UENI's 2020 Report on Gender and Small Business – UENI Blog (accessed 17 June 2021).

Vorley, T., Lawton Smith, H., Coogan, T., Owalla, B. and Wing, K. (2020). *Supporting Diversity and Inclusion*, Policy Brief, Innovate UK. Supporting Diversity and Inclusion in Innovation Report – GOV.UK (www.gov.uk).

Wingfield, A. and Taylor, T. (2016). 'Race, gender, and class in entrepreneurship: Intersectional counterframes and black business owners', *Ethnic and Racial Studies*, Taylor & Francis, Vol. 39 No. 9, pp. 1676–1696.

Wright, M., Roper, S., Hart, M. and Carter, S. (2015). 'Joining the dots: Building the evidence base for SME growth policy', *International Small Business Journal*, Sage Publications, Vol. 33 No. 1, pp. 3–11.

6. Institutional work in Czech and US business assistance programmes and implications for entrepreneurial inclusion

Nancy C. Jurik, Alena Křížková, Marie Pospíšilová and Gray Cavender

INTRODUCTION

In transitional and advanced market economies, small and medium-sized enterprises (SMEs) are identified as an important strategy for increasing economic growth and reducing unemployment (Holienka et al., 2016; Kozubíková et al., 2017; SBA, 2019). Entrepreneurial ventures are also credited with advancing gender equality by helping women escape poverty and balance work and family (Bianco et al., 2017; Rafi, 2020). Although many countries claim increasing numbers of women-owned businesses (WOBs) (Hait, 2021; Lesonsky, 2020; VanderBrug, 2013), these are often associated with lower revenues, less growth, and higher failure rates than men-owned ventures (Robb, 2002; Vossenberg, 2013). Similar "underperformance" problems have been attributed to businesses among poor, immigrant, and minoritized communities (Bernard and Slaughter, 2004; Fairlie and Robb, 2007). Pidduck and Clark (2021: 1–2) introduce the term "transitional entrepreneurs" (TEs) to refer to socially and economically marginalized group members who pursue business ownership to improve their life situation (Foss et al., 2019; Welter et al., 2017). In using the term, they stress that groups included under the TE rubric have differing histories and needs, and work in different contexts.

Business assistance programmes (BAPs) have been touted as one means for helping SMEs, especially those of women business owners (WBOs) and other TEs (e.g., Basaffar et al., 2018; Cho and Honorati, 2013; Jurik, 2005). Notwithstanding the promise of BAPs, critics worry that extending business opportunities more widely requires radical transformation in institutionalized ideals of entrepreneurship (Marlow and McAdam, 2013; Welter, 2011; Welter and Smallbone, 2011). Despite research suggesting that entrepreneurs have diverse needs, many BAPs and business experts adopt a one-size-fits-all approach focused on growth in revenue and job creation, and based upon the business experiences of Western white males (hereafter referred to as male-centric models) (Topimin et al., 2018; Yusuf, 2012). Such models fall short in addressing the often-unique needs of women and other TEs. Accordingly, scholars have called for gender-aware and intersectional (i.e., inclusive) approaches sensitive to the convergent dynamics of gender, race, ethnicity, class, and geographical location in entrepreneurial support programmes (Bianco et al., 2017; Romero and Valdez, 2016).

Institutional theories argue that entrepreneurship is embedded in structural contexts composed of economic, political, and cultural environments that influence entrepreneurial experiences and behaviour (Tlaiss, 2018; Welter and Smallbone, 2011). In this chapter we extend this analysis to BAP staff who are similarly embedded within the organizations in which they work and also in the local, regional, and global contexts surrounding them (Modell, 2020; Neumeyer et al., 2019; Ritchie, 2016). These contexts can offer opportunities for, but also barriers to, inclusive entrepreneurial programming (Jurik, 2020; Knowlton et al., 2015).

An offshoot of institutional theory seeking to understand how organizational work may effect change is the institutional work perspective. Institutional work refers to the ways in which organizational workers engage in habitual and reflexive activities that can reproduce and/or change their internal and external environments (Arenas et al., 2020; Lawrence and Suddaby, 2006; Lawrence et al., 2011; Waylen, 2014). Change efforts are complicated by the socially embedded nature of institutional work. Efforts to expand notions of who can be an entrepreneur and redefine worthwhile business goals can be hampered by normative, political, and economic (aka institutional) contexts (Ahl, 2006; Marlow and Martinez Dy, 2018; Neumeyer et al., 2019). For example, BAP funding may depend on adherence to normative (i.e., male-centric) views of entrepreneurship in their region (Arenas et al., 2020; Jurik, 2005).

The research question that we address in this chapter is: To what extent does the institutional work of BAP staff and business experts foster increased entrepreneurial inclusivity or the reinforcement of male-centric models? What barriers do they identify to programming sensitive to the needs of women and other TEs? We draw on institutional theories of entrepreneurship that stress diversity and intersectionality (e.g., Romero and Valdez, 2016; Waylen, 2014; Welter et al., 2017) to centre analyses of institutional work in entrepreneurial support efforts (Arenas et al., 2020; Katila et al., 2019; Raghubanshi et al., 2021).

Our data come from interviews with BAP staff and business experts in the Czech Republic (CR) (mainly Prague region), a transitional economy, and the

United States (US) (mainly Phoenix region), an advanced market economy. This comparison facilitates examination of the contextual embeddedness of entrepreneurial programming work in two countries with different cultures and at varying stages of development (Longoria, 2018; Smallbone and Welter, 2001; Yousafzai et al., 2018). Our findings reveal the nature and complexity of institutional work challenging barriers to women and other TEs. We find that although some respondents saw no need to alter BAP practices to promote entrepreneurial inclusivity, others developed programme designs to challenge male-centric definitions and practices. Some respondents also identified ways of circumventing pressures to conform to traditional business norms.

In the section below, we provide a literature review, followed by an outline of our analytic framework. We then discuss the CR and US contexts as settings for BAP institutional work. The methodology section describes data gathering, sampling, and analysis procedures. Afterward, we describe the key findings in our research. In the final sections, we summarize the theoretical significance and policy implications of our research.

LITERATURE REVIEW

Business assistance plays a significant role in supporting the development and growth of SMEs, especially for women and other TEs (Ozkazanc-Pan and Muntean, 2018; Watkins et al., 2015; Yusuf, 2012). These entrepreneurs are often labelled as underperforming because they produce less revenue, growth, and employment opportunities. These differences reflect a popular belief that such groups have less skill, knowledge, self-confidence, and are more risk averse than elite, white, Western male-owned businesses (Korpi et al., 2013; Lang et al., 2014; Loscocco et al., 2009; Treanor and Henry, 2010). Some BAPs aim to help women in particular to overcome barriers by offering services including training, lending, networking, and mentoring to improve business knowledge, self-confidence, and capital access (Bullough et al., 2019; Foss et al., 2019; Jurik, 2005; Treanor and Henry, 2010).

However, researchers increasingly question the validity of underper-formance findings because such studies (1) ignore variations in business types, industries, and locations, (2) focus on financial success measures and ignore the non-financial contributions of businesses, and (3) downplay business achievements among women and other marginalized groups (Ahl, 2006; Dean et al., 2019; Henry et al., 2017; Watson, 2020). Scholars advocate moving beyond individual entrepreneur characteristics and attending to the institutional barriers to business opportunities (Hailemariam and Kroon, 2018; Williams and Kedir, 2018; Yousafzai et al., 2018).

Indeed, feminist business scholars challenge male-centric measures of entrepreneurship success (e.g., Ahl, 2006; De Bruin et al., 2007; Marlow and

Martinez Dy, 2018). They argue that instead of male vs. female entrepreneur comparisons, studies attend to the gendered institutional processes that give rise to entrepreneurial disparities (Brush et al., 2009; Welter, 2011). Efforts to promote entrepreneurship must incorporate consideration of the gendered dynamics of business ownership, including the interwoven connections between institutional contexts, business, and family life (Aldrich and Cliff, 2003; Brush et al., 2009).

These insights have prompted calls for gender-aware business support that is mindful of the gendered nature of entrepreneurial opportunities (Brush et al., 2009; Henry et al., 2003). WBOs encounter barriers related to inadequate access to capital, location in labour-intensive competitive business sectors, and disproportionate family care burdens (Ahl and Nelson, 2015; Brush et al., 2009; Dlouhá, 2015; Foss et al., 2019).

Yet, a gender analysis alone is insufficient (Mirchandani, 1999; Wang, 2019). To understand the diversity of relevant experiences, scholars advocate an intersectional approach because business opportunities and barriers are shaped not only by gender relations, but also by other dimensions of individuals' social location such as race, ethnicity, class, family status, and citizenship (Křížková et al., 2018; Romero and Valdez, 2016; Scott and Hussain, 2019). BAPs aiming to assist TEs encounter clients with diverse and intersecting challenges (Ettl and Welter, 2010; Jurik, 2005: 138–140; Rankin, 2002; Valdez, 2016). Adopting an intersectional lens offers important insights for developing BAP services (Scott and Hussain, 2019; Valdez, 2015; Wang, 2019).

Calls for inclusive BAP programming warn against homogenizing TEs, highlighting business deficits or isolating clients from the business and technological mainstreams (Orser et al., 2019; Pandey and Amezcua, 2020; Watkins et al., 2015). Ways that historically disadvantaged groups (e.g., immigrants, women of colour) draw on their social location to build successful businesses and community support groups must not be overlooked (Lang et al., 2014; McNally and Khoury, 2018; Stoyanov and Stoyanova, 2021; Wang, 2019).

BAPs are often pressured by funding sources to prioritize assistance to popular conceptions of high-growth businesses (Brown et al., 2017; Henry et al., 2017; Wang 2019). Such priorities might create barriers for WBOs and other TEs that are concentrated in slower growth, labour intensive, and service sectors (Marlow and McAdam, 2013; Robb, 2002; Yousafzai et al., 2018). Even when women are centred in support programming, variations in business opportunities available to different social groups can lead to exclusion (Bianco et al., 2017; Jurik, 2005; Marlow and Martinez Dy, 2018; Wang and Yu, 2020). These variations converge with other dimensions of social location like geographic locale, government policies, economic conditions, and cultural norms that contextualize goals, experiences, and decisions of entrepreneurs

Dean et al., 2019; Robb, 2002; Romero and Valdez, 2016; Valdez, 2016; Welter et al., 2017).

BAP staff are similarly embedded within the organizations in which they work and in the local, regional, and global contexts surrounding them (Modell, 2020; Neumeyer et al., 2019 Ritchie, 2016). While these contexts can offer opportunities, they can also be barriers to the gender-aware and intersectional approaches to entrepreneurial programming (Jurik, 2020; Knowlton et al., 2015; Scott and Hussain, 2019).

We are interested in how BAPs promote (or fail to promote) entrepreneurial inclusion. Despite the emergence of BAPs targeting women and other TEs, some policies and programmes continue to adopt male-centric success metrics (Ahl and Nelson, 2015; Dean et al., 2019; Jurik, 2020; Pettersson et al., 2017; Reichborn-Kjennerud and Svare, 2014). These orientations assume that true entrepreneurs are profit- and growth-obsessed risk-takers devoid of household responsibilities (Ahl, 2006). It is important to examine BAPs' strategies for promoting entrepreneurial diversity. Even so, BAP practices may be shaped and constrained by institutional contexts (i.e., political, economic, and cultural inequalities) that reinforce entrepreneurship barriers. For example, some BAP staff may hold stereotypical views about WBOs (Braidford et al., 2013; Parisi, 2020; Wang and Yu, 2020). BAPs are accountable to funding sources that may pressure them to meet traditional success metrics (e.g., increasing revenue, jobs created). Conversely, BAP personnel may try to challenge norms and promote entrepreneurial inclusion. In any case, BAPs remain an under-researched aspect of business life (Knowlton et al., 2015; Nanda, 2021; Schallenkamp and Smith, 2008; Wang, 2019).

Transitional economies like the CR's have fewer and younger business services than the US (Dlouhá, 2015; Lukeš, 2017; Smallbone and Welter, 2001). The CR and US present unique histories of gender relations and women's employment, and a contrasting context for comparison of gender and entrepreneurship issues. Despite the importance of entrepreneurship in the CR's economic transformation, SMEs receive little attention and WOBs are rarely studied (Jurik et al., 2016; Křížková et al., 2014; Pospíšilová, 2018). Czech scholars note there is even less research on BAPs, especially programmes targeting women (Křížková et al., 2014; Petlina and Koráb, 2015; Pospíšilová, 2018). Moreover, extant research is correlational rather than offering in-depth interpretive insights into WBO and practitioner perspectives (Bartoš et al., 2015; Dvoulety et al., 2021; Holienka et al., 2016; Kozubíková et al., 2017). While there is research on US SMEs, there are few studies of different types of BAPs, their target populations, their strategies, and their barriers (Jurik, 2005; Knowlton et al., 2015; Wang and Yu, 2020). Comparisons will facilitate contextualized entrepreneurship policy for women (OECD, 2021). We outline the framework for our comparison study of BAP work in the CR and US in the next section.

THEORETICAL FRAMEWORK: INSTITUTIONAL WORK AND COMPARATIVE APPROACH

The observation that BAPs may be constrained by yet transform their institutional context is at the heart of our analytic framework: institutional work. The institutional work concept represents an extension of institutional theory (Lawrence et al., 2011). Institutional theory more generally focuses on the processes and mechanisms whereby structures and practices are routinized and become normative guidelines for behaviour (Scott, 2004). Institutional theory has been criticized for privileging persistence over change, but a focus on institutional work was developed to facilitate attention to ways in which organizational members may effect change (Lawrence et al., 2011). Institutional work focuses on the study of practices of individuals and groups that create, maintain, and disrupt institutions (Lawrence and Suddaby, 2006).

In our analysis, we consider institutional work practices that impact the organizational level as well as broader political, economic, and cultural contexts. According to this perspective, actors (individuals and groups) are embedded in institutional structures, which they may take for granted (Lawrence et al., 2011; Ritchie, 2016; Raghubanshi et al., 2021). However, actors have agency; they are skilful and reflexive. They may cope with, support, resist, and change the institutional arrangements they are part of (Lawrence et al., 2011; also Hampel et al., 2015). Their practices may modify the structures in which they are embedded, but their organization, regional, and national locations may also constrain them (Arenas et al., 2020). The institutional work perspective provides the conceptual ingredients to understand both adherence to the status quo, but also to explain change within an institution setting (Lawrence and Suddaby, 2006).

In terms of change, the institutional work perspective does not emphasize social movement-type mobilizations that produce successful large-scale change or even actions that always successfully produce change at all (Willmott, 2011). Rather, the focus is on the routine practices of individuals or groups. These are mundane or reflexive efforts to fit in and influence the institutions of which they are a part (Arenas et al., 2020).

The institutional work perspective has gained traction over the past two decades. In addition to scholarship that advances the tenets of the perspective (Hampel et al., 2015; Lawrence et al., 2011; Modell, 2020), institutional work has been applied to particular settings. These include: the construction of an entrepreneurial identity (Katila et al., 2019), in industries like the coastal forest industry in British Columbia (Zietsma and Lawrence, 2010), and at corporations (Gawer and Phillips, 2013). Similarly, the concept has inspired a framework for evaluating innovation in subsistence marketplaces (Raghubanshi et al., 2021), sustainable business practices (Arenas et al., 2020), and the cultural norms regulating the behaviours of Afghan women (Ritchie, 2016).

Relevant to our comparative approach, Welter and Smallbone (2011) extend institutional theory to the analysis of how social context shapes entrepreneurial opportunities and behaviour. Institutional contexts including political (policy and regulatory), economic (organization and conditions), and cultural norms shape entrepreneurial opportunities, practices, and business support (Welter and Smallbone, 2011; Yousafzai et al., 2018). Institutional climates for business and family life also vary by country and affect entrepreneur needs for business support differently depending on their social position (Brush et al., 2009; Welter et al., 2017; Welter and Baker, 2020). Thus, intersectional analysis of the combined effects of gender, race, class, and other social group memberships on entrepreneurship must also entail awareness that doing business varies by local and national geographical contexts (Lang et al., 2014; Welter, 2004; Welter and Smallbone, 2011; Yousafzai et al., 2018; Zahra et al., 2014).

For these reasons, comparative studies of institutional work such as business support strategies across countries is important. Further, comparisons of BAPs in transition and advanced market economies like the CR and US respectively are crucial (Henry et al., 2017; Smallbone and Welter, 2001). We analyse the institutional work of BAP respondents examining the degree to which they maintain or challenge male-centric entrepreneurship models so as to include women and other TEs (Gimenez and Calbio, 2018; Jurik, 2020; Lawrence et al., 2011). Moreover, informed by institutional contextual analysis, we also identify ways in which institutional work is embedded in country contexts (Modell, 2020; Raghubanshi et al., 2021). In the next section, we consider differences observed in transitional vs. developed economies and then focus particularly on the contextual comparisons between the CR and US as settings for understanding BAPs institutional work.

CR/US COUNTRY CONTEXTS FOR BUSINESS OWNERSHIP

As an advanced market economy, the US has a continuous history of entrepreneurship. CR business ownership was prohibited during state socialism but increased significantly after the 1989 Velvet Revolution and since then has been transitioning to a full market economy (Dlouhá, 2015; Lukeš, 2017). Although women in transitional countries like the CR are important for economic development, research suggests that they may face more barriers to entrepreneurship and require more support programming than women in advanced capitalist economies (Longoria, 2018; Minniti and Naudé, 2010;

Treanor and Henry, 2010). Consistent with our institutional contextual analysis, we begin this section with a review of issues faced by women and other TE business owners in transitional countries. After that, we turn to specific comparisons of the US and CR contexts.

Transitional and mature market economies exhibit similarities and differences in women's entrepreneurial experiences. WBOs have played a major role in the transition of post-Soviet economies to market economies (Bliss and Garratt, 2001; Longoria, 2018). Gender-segregated labour markets, gender employment discrimination, a lack of flexible employment options, and increases in precarious employment force many women to shift to necessity-based (Longoria, 2018) rather than opportunity-based entrepreneurship (Angulo-Guerrero et al., 2017). Changing economic conditions and support policies affect the ratio of necessity- to opportunity-motivations (Jurik et al., 2020; Treanor and Henry, 2010; Welter and Smallbone, 2011). When owners have limited employment opportunities, dependents, and few resources, self-employment becomes a precarious endeavour (Hašková and Dudová, 2017). Elongated paid family leave policies and the absence of affordable childcare also shape women's decisions to engage in entrepreneurship (Křížková et al., 2018).

Transitional countries have been described as having little support for SMEs and more bureaucratic hurdles, although some case studies suggest this situation has improved (Longoria, 2018; Treanor and Henry, 2010; Zapalska and Wingrove-Haugland, 2018). Transitional and mature market economies share problems of inadequate capital access, underrepresentation of women in high technology and STEM fields, and inequality in unpaid care responsibilities (Dlouhá, 2015; Brush et al., 2009; Lituchy and Reavley, 2004; Wang, 2019). Support programmes sensitive to the needs of TE entrepreneurs including gender-aware policies are lacking (Holienka et al., 2016; Lituchy and Reavley, 2004; OECD, 2021; Wang and Yu, 2020).

More specific CR and US comparisons reveal that the two countries have different histories of business ownership, family policies, and gender norms. During state socialism, men and women alike were required to work. Even once private ownership was allowed in the CR (post 1989), entrepreneurship continued to have negative connotations because of corruption scandals (Lukeš et al., 2014). For the US, business ownership has been a long-standing ideal. As a post-socialist country, the CR has less cultural support for business creation and less available financial support (Nikolova et al., 2012; Szerb and Trumbull, 2014).

According to GEM data, the CR population generally has a higher fear of failure and is less convinced about their entrepreneurial abilities; they also perceive fewer opportunities to start a business compared to the US (GEM 2011, 2020). The percentage of WOBs is increasing in each country, a shift that has been linked to limited flexible employment and childcare opportunities for mothers (Křížková et al., 2011; Weltman, 2021). Approximately 38% of CR businesses and 42% of US businesses are majority-owned by women (Elliott, 2021; MoLSA, 2018). The CR gender gap is higher as women are less convinced about their abilities and opportunities than men (Branchet and Křížková, 2015). The US has more opportunity-driven entrepreneurship (motivational index – opportunity/necessity motive – was 7.2 in the US and 1.23 in the CR) (GEM 2011, 2020).

Yet, WBOs in both countries report continuing barriers including negative gender and ethnic-racial stereotypes that affect access to capital. WBOs face disproportionate care responsibilities and lack affordable pre-school childcare (Brush et al., 2018; Inwood and Stengel, 2020; Jurik et al., 2019; Lituchy and Reavley, 2004; Loscocco et al., 1991; Treanor and Henry, 2010). Both countries have exhibited stereotypical attitudes and discrimination towards immigrants, and ethnic or racial minority populations (Baradaran, 2017; Bell and Strabac, 2020; Heath and Richards, 2019; Jardina, 2019; Thomas et al., 2020; Weinerová, 2014). Such cultural contexts negatively affect the employment and business ownership decisions of women and TEs generally.

The CR is located in the centre of Europe and ranked among the top ten European nations for business start-ups in 2019. The Prague area, where we mostly collected data, has a population of approximately 2.7 million (10 million in total CR). It is the capital and largest city. Although the CR has undergone many modernizations since the end of socialism, many claim that it is still quite bureaucratic (Benáček and Zemplinerová, 1995; European Commission, 2018; Kafkadesk, 2019). Self-reported ethnicity surveys suggest that approximately 67% of the population identifies as Czech, 26% of the population does not identify with any ethnicity, 5% identifies as Moravians, and 1.4% identifies as Slovak. Other groups self-identifying as Ukrainians, Poles, Vietnamese, Germans, Russians, Hungarians, Silesians, and Roma each comprise less than 1% of the population (World Atlas, 2018). However, other estimates suggest that Romani people comprise about 3% (about 300,000) of the population, and other ethnic groups together comprise 5% of the population (CZSO, 2014; Slovo 21, 2014; Úřad vlády ČR, 2019).

After state socialism ended, CR leaders urged women to return home, and policy regimes encouraged extended paid parental leave and reductions in state-supported childcare (Křížková and Vohlídalová, 2009). Women who are part of the national insurance system are allotted 28 weeks of paid maternity leave per child. Women and men are eligible for parental leave that includes paid parental allowances for up to 48 months, and job protection for up to 36 months (Zahradnicek-Haas, 2020). Women take 98% of parental leave (CZSO, 2016). By 2014, the CR eliminated all state-supported childcare for children under three years, effectively forcing women to stay home for longer periods. The lengthy parental leave reinforced employers' negative attitudes towards women in the workplace, and the lack of sufficient flexible part-time employment opportunities encourage women to seek self-employment options (Křížková and Vohlídalová, 2009). However, the difficulty of taking advantage of employee maternity leave benefits may discourage CR women's entrepreneurship during childbearing years (Jurik et al., 2020). After the last economic crisis (between 2010 and 2019), the number of women entrepreneurs aged 40–44 increased by 38% and the increase was even higher for pre-retirement women aged 55–59 (42%) and 60+ (98%) (CZSO, 2020). Women in these vulnerable groups may be more likely to form necessity businesses.

CR public attitudes towards gender roles are more conservative than in the US with almost half of CR survey respondents agreeing that it is a man's job to earn money and a woman's job to look after the home and family. Less than 30% of US respondents agreed with these statements (ISSP, 2012). The US scores higher on The UN Gender Empowerment Measures than does the CR, household labour appears to be more evenly divided in the US, and gender wage gaps are lower than in the CR (World Economic Forum, 2021).

Entrepreneurship is highly valued in the US (Valdez, 2016), including the Phoenix metropolitan area (City of Phoenix, 2017). The area has a population of 4.8 million, and claims a thriving technology industry and some of the largest job increases in the US over the past six years (Office of the AZ Governor, 2020). Arizona ranks in the top half of US states for attracting new businesses. It offers lower tax rates, lower wages, limited regulation, and an affordable cost of living compared to states like New York and California (Bly, 2021; Fernandes, 2020). Arizona has been active in anti-immigrant legislation passing a highly restrictive law in 2010. Several provisions were invalidated by the US Supreme Court, but the resulting climate created a hostile environment for Latinx business owners and workers (Duara, 2016). The US hosts large percentages of racial and ethnic minority populations: Hispanic 18%, Black 13%, Asian 6%, American Indian 2%. In the Phoenix area, Hispanics and American Indians comprise larger population percentages (31% and 3% respectively) (U.S. Census Bureau, 2019a, 2019b). Sixty-four per cent of new WOBs were started by women of colour in 2020 with the largest start-up percentage increase among Latinas (Shepherd, 2020).

Although the US federal and some state and local governments offer paid maternity/parental leave to their employees, there is no national-level paid leave programme. The US does mandate up to 12 weeks of unpaid care leave with job protection, but employers do not always comply (Kelly, 2010). Some employers provide up to six weeks of paid maternity leave, but such jobs are difficult to find, especially for workers lacking formal educational credentials (Jurik et al., 2019). Many US employers offer neither paid leave nor healthcare, and the US Affordable Care Act offers only limited coverage

(Shepherd-Banigan and Bell, 2014). Finally, the US also has no national childcare policy although some childcare supports are available for very low-income women or for middle-class individuals in the form of childcare tax credits (Childcare.gov, n.d.). The lack of universal employee leave/health-care and the absence of state-supported care policies may help to explain the relatively higher level of involvement of US women in self-employment (Ahl and Nelson, 2015).

METHODS, DATA AND ANALYSIS

This project represents a collaboration between researchers at the Czech Academy of Sciences and Arizona State University. The larger project was a qualitative comparative study of WBO needs and BAP services, but we focus this chapter on the BAP data only. We draw on interviews conducted with BAP staff and business experts in the Prague (CR) and Phoenix (Arizona, US) areas. Our sampling plan entailed a combination of convenience, snow-ball, and purposive variations. We first sought to vary our respondents by selecting staff at different types of assistance programmes – lending, training, mentoring, networking, and other support or self-development programmes. We intentionally oversampled BAPs that targeted women and other socially marginalized groups. We also interviewed experts on SMEs and entrepreneur-ial advocacy work in each country who, in turn, suggested others with whom we should speak (see Tables 6.1 and 6.2). Experts also provided information on doing business in each region including bank financing opportunities for SMEs and general business and employment climates. Although our samples were small and not necessarily representative of all BAP staff and experts, we believe that the purposive nature of our sample still offers significant insights about a range of institutional work for entrepreneurship in each country.

We asked BAP staff and experts about their perception of entrepreneur needs, and descriptions of their targeted client populations, service provision efforts, and programme barriers. We interviewed 18 BAP staff and two business experts (n=20) in the US, and 14 BAP staff and three experts on CR immigrant and Roma populations (n=17) in the CR. Seven CR BAP respond-ents and four US BAP respondents came from programmes targeting women in particular. One US and three CR respondents came from programmes not specifically focused on entrepreneurship assistance, but some of their clients were self-employed or seeking business ownership opportunities. In addition to interviews, we participated in workshops within each country (CR 20 November 2019; US 12 April 2019) where we engaged in discussions with experts, staff, and business owners about the conditions for SMEs and WOBs.

The analysis began with BAP target populations and services, particularly strategies for inclusiveness and barriers identified in their institutional work.

Table 6.1 CR BAP and expert respondents' organizations and gender

Case #	Type organization or expert	Target clients/services/activities	R Gender	Funding
1	Networking, conference support	WBOs/networking & counselling	female	Bank loan
2	Freelancer association	General/freelancers/networking organization	male	EU, corp, grants
3	Chamber of Commerce project	WBOs/support, counselling & networking	female	Gvnt
4	Chamber of Commerce projects	WBOs/support, counselling & networking	female	Gvnt
5	Company Developing Business Project	WBOS/design of training programme	female	EU/CZ gvnt
6	Finance bank	General/lending for entrepreneurs	male	EU/CZ gvnt
7	Association for SMEs	General/association & networking SMEs	male	Member fee/corp.
8	Finance/bank	WBOs/Awards programme	female	Private company
9	Ministry office	General policy/funding for Industry and Trade	male	Gvnt
10	Support organization – expert	Socially excluded people, e.g., Roma/support not specifically focused on entrepreneurship	male	Grants, gvnt
11	Support organization – expert	Roma Women/support (not specifically focused on entrepreneurship)	female	Grants, gvnt
12	Support chamber of commerce	Social enterprises/support but not specifically focused on WBOs	male	Gvnt
13	Private consultants re: microfinance feasibility	Microenterprises/research feasibility for Ministry of Labour and Social Affairs	female	Gvnt contract
14	Network/support	WBOs/organization for women entrepreneurs (self-development, networking, etc.)	female	Member fees, corp.
15	Support organization – expert	Vietnamese people/support services (not specific project for entrepreneurs)	female	EU grants
16	Support and finance	General/business incubator (mainly young men)	female	Regional univ. funds
17	Finance agency/bank	WBOs/support services for women entrepreneurs	female	Private funding

Table 6.2   US BAP and expert respondents' organizations and gender

Case#	Type of organization or expert	Target clients/services/activities	R Gender	Funding
1	Univ. Mgt School	International family business/design training-education programmes	female	Univ., grants, private funds
2	Univ. Incubation Centre/Public-Private Partnership	General projects and projects for WBOs, poor, immigrant/networking, counselling, awards	female	Univ., corp., grants
3	University Administrator Entrepreneurship Programmes	Expert – oversees various university-community entrepreneurship partnership projects	female	Univ., corp., grants
4	Business Education Programming	Expert: state and local business climate	female	Univ. and corp.
5	Business Counselling Centre (SBDC)	General/1 on 1 counselling and community networking projects	female	Federal, county, corp.
6	Microlending programme	Latinx/lending to small business & Tech assistance – Latinx focus	female	Interest, city, corp.
7	Business support programme	African American-owned businesses: oversees non-profit side of local business network/support programme	female	City, member fees, corp.
8	Business support programme	Local businesses: oversees non-profit side of local business support – fundraising and business fairs	male	Donations and grants
9	Microlending programme	Latinx/microlending, counselling, and technical assistance	female	Interest, donations, grants
10	Collaborative work space	General but inclusive themed/low-cost business space rental & networking	female	Fees, donations, grants
11	Business Counselling Centre	General/manages business counselling metrics, and fundraising for centre	female	Federal, county, corporate, grants
12	Business support programme founder & advocate	Latinx, immigrant, Black and local businesses/multiple programmes support inc. accelerators for Latinx & Black Bus, networking and PR for local business cause	female	Donations, member fees, grants
13	Business training programme	Latinx & immigrant businesses/lending and technical assistance	male	Grants, donations and fees

Case#	Type of organization or expert	Target clients/services/activities	R Gender	Funding
14	Microlending programme	Low income: online training, counselling, and lending	male	Interest & corp.
15	Training bootcamps	Social enterprises/esp. women's start-ups – short courses	female	Fees, corp.
16	Networking	WBOs/network and some training	female	Fees, corp. donations
17	Microlending programme at university	For business and consumer online lending borrower circles	male	Corp. donations, fees, interest
18	Community Development Organization	Microlending and community development projects	male	City & corp.
19	Training & Networking Org.	Women "in transition"/educ., self-development and business training programme	male	Donations & grants, univ.
20	Microlending programme	Low income esp. Latinx micro and SME loans & tech assistance	male	Interest, fees, donations, grants

We employed qualitative, interpretive analysis techniques (Charmaz, 2006). We explored the perceptions and experiences of our respondents, recognizing that there are multiple and contextualized views about entrepreneur needs, programme practices, and barriers (see McAdam and Marlow, 2007).

Interview transcripts/recordings and observational notes were reviewed by the research team and coded for expected and unanticipated themes surrounding BAP goals, clients, and services. We prepared research memos about findings and links to our research questions. Memos were reviewed and discussed by team members. We reflected on the relationship between our findings and prior research. We identified connections between BAPs and country contexts that will be discussed in our third findings section on barriers. Programme opportunities and disjunctures between client needs (as perceived by BAP staff and experts) and business-related services, and then links to country contexts were identified. For example, we considered how external funding sources, economic conditions, and regulations shaped support and limitations for BAPs. After identifying major themes for each country, we developed country comparisons.

FINDINGS

For women and other TEs, BAPs have been a mechanism to diversify entrepreneurship (Longoria, 2018; Pandey and Amezcua, 2020). Respondents exemplified a range of orientations towards their institutional work. Some assumed a traditional stance towards programming that did not accommodate women or other TEs. Others described their institutional work in ways that suggested attempts to transform traditional entrepreneurship patterns by promoting diversity. Respondents addressed individual, organizational, and external societal opportunities and constraints. Institutional work entailed acquiescence and innovation. We present findings in three thematic areas: (1) business as usual: institutional reproduction; (2) institutional work for inclusive entrepreneurship; (3) challenging institutional barriers to inclusive programming (see Table 6.3).

Business as Usual: Institutional Reproduction

From the institutional work perspective, because actors are embedded in an institutional structure, individuals and groups may maintain the institutions in which they are embedded. Some CR BAP respondents justified existing institutional arrangements (CR-6, CR-9, CR-16). A few respondents denigrated women's businesses because they did not meet traditional growth metrics: *"women's businesses are little more than playing in the sand"* (CR-7).

Table 6.3　　　*Findings: (A) Business as usual: institutional reproduction, (B) Institutional work for inclusive entrepreneurship, and (C) Challenging institutional barriers to inclusive programming*

(A) Business as usual: institutional reproduction	Illustrative quotes
Programme is open to any business owner; no need for changes or programmes to accommodate women. Exemplars of women who made it.	"We deal with everyone that comes" (CR-16) "We have several women (policymakers), mainly White women, who have scaled the mountain and are at the top. They believe every woman can do it" (US-5) "The metric of success is the same for anyone but you just had to not let obstacles exist for you" (US-7)
Gender cultural stereotypes: mothers of small children cannot fully commit to businesses	"The dividing line is not between men and women, but between women with small children ... the moment the woman gives birth, it will be difficult to be fully involved in the business" (CR-3) "My girlfriend is a freelancer, we have a baby. And, of course it is a limitation for her ... she has to do a little more considering the family ... but it is not crucial" (CR-2)
Banking practices: lending to small businesses not profitable	"It is not that they intentionally discriminate, but Czech banks are conservative, so they have a model based on deposits and loans. They evaluate the risk, and small loans have higher transaction costs. If there is a high risk, banks increase the interest rate. And when it is high interest, thee groups are unable to repay. So, banks prefer not to lend at all" (CR-13)
Technology-oriented programmes unwelcoming	"Our IT-oriented programmes are filled with men" (US-4)
(B) Institutional work for inclusive entrepreneurship	**Illustrative quotes**
Inclusive marketing to recruit diverse array of clients	"We network with all sorts of community groups to locate clients. Banks send clients to us also" (US-20)

Moulding programme to suit diverse client needs: microlending, training, mentoring, targeting particular business types, confidence building, welcome co-working space, multilingual programs, work-around regulations	"We organized a programme that focused on food service businesses for low-income and immigrant start-ups. The group met at the public library and we had activities for children at the same time" (US-2) "We are actually meeting the businesswomen, explaining to them like what are modern trends in payment, how to limit their risks to customers, suppliers and the like. We are not trying to just sell them banking products, but rather we are trying to help them simplify their business. Because they have it even harder than guys in that they actually do business, are experts in their fields, and besides they have a family." (CR-8) "We offer our programme in Spanish for our immigrant and Latinx clients. Most of them actually speak English but having it in Spanish really sets a welcome tone" (US-13)
Networking clients	"There is a need for women to meet, share and talk about, talk about it, because then it is possible to establish more cooperation, more contacts, and without that ... I try to connect them." (CR-4) "We hold entrepreneur fairs to show our clients' business success and to get their name out there" (US-13) "[W]e will be doing the Enterprising Woman of the Year award ... it's definitely a way of letting you know about the overall PR and women theme" (CR-4)
BAP advocacy	"Our advocacy group is trying to compile a directory of BAPs to form more of an ecosystem here ... We don't just need another networking group. We need to convey the connectedness of our components ... We also want to advocate that programme funders look at diversity of boards of directors as well as programme clients and move beyond traditional growth metrics" (US-5)
(C) Challenging institutional barriers to inclusive programming	**Illustrative quotes**
Funding shapes & limits programme design (e.g., often short-term, lack operations support monies, and constant application demands)	"We would like to offer more technical assistance in-house; it helps clients repay the loans ... But donors are often unwilling to fund much in the way of operations costs; they want to offer lines of credit for lending." (US-20) "We get a lot of questions about EU subsidies, which is no longer the case. At the beginning, about 3–4 years ago was the Start programme, but the money ran out relatively soon, and then they didn't start again and we do not know what will be in the next programming cycle" (CR-3)

Programme metrics concentrate on financial success of client businesses	*"Our funding depends on meeting our growth metric goals increase in business income and jobs created among our clients. Those goals tend to increase every year"* (US-11)
	"Investors are mostly men and mostly interested in technologies and new trends online. They do not care about someone who is a baker or confectioner or something like that" (CR-4)
Governments prioritize businesses with high-growth potential, often tech & manufacturing	*"We do little work with businesses of the poor. They need other programmes and employment opportunities. We have funding for economic development although again, this is generally focused more on making the Valley (Phoenix) like the Silicon Valley"* (US-3)
	[Our leaders think] "the internet and other IT ventures are a quick way to dot.com wealth" (CR-13)
Lack of childcare and healthcare policies	*"The problem is that women often bring their children when they meet me. While we talk, the child is a constant distraction, and I know that this will be the case in her business also"* (US-9)
	"It would really help SMEs especially women's if we had a national childcare and long-term care support plan and a truly universal health care plan. Business assistance alone is not enough" (US-3) Similar comments from US-1, US-4
	"We have to tell women with small children that it [a business] does not mean that the work will be less, especially at the beginning. So yes, the moment a woman says she has no family support, we have to warn her" (CR-3)
	"We need to get more men involved in childcare. The issue is what women earn versus the cost of private childcare" [for children under 3] (CR-14)

The preceding quote illustrates a difference in country cultural beliefs. Some CR male respondents expressed negative stereotypes of WBOs (see Table 6.3(A)). CR female respondents offered examples wherein men were openly dismissive of WBOs (CR-1, CR-3, CR-4), but two said *"things are improving"* (CR-3, CR-4). CR respondents referenced the US as a model for gender-aware BAPs (CR-1; see Marlow et al., 2008).

However, some US respondents said that programming had declined in terms of funding because Arizona state and local governments were less supportive of WBOs (US-5, US-9). Respondents (US-2, US-5, US-10, US-11) spoke about "unconscious" or "subtle" bias such that women and people of colour did not know why they felt unwelcome in some programmes, but felt excluded nonetheless. One respondent blamed government leaders: *"When I talk about gender diversity in Phoenix, it's, why does this matter? We're tied to this cowboy image, a pull yourself up by your bootstrap mentality"* (US-5).

Exemplary WBO successes were cited as a justification for extant institutional arrangements. A CR government ministerial official said programmes for women were *"unnecessary"* and he cited examples of famous successful WBOs (CR-9). Another respondent said: *"Our programme is gender neutral; there are no barriers to entry"* (CR-2).

The justification that BAP programmes were "open to all" was especially prevalent for IT venture support (CR-16, CR-13, US-2, US-4, US-3). However, women (as well as racial/ethnic minorities) are grossly underrepresented in IT fields (Ozkazanc-Pan and Muntean, 2018). A US respondent said, *"A lot of our technologically-oriented programmes are not welcoming to women and unconsciously wind-up targeting men"* (US-2). A CR respondent at a technological incubation centre acknowledged that his programme had no initiatives to attract women, but was *"surprised"* that it had so few women (CR-16) (see Table 6.3(A)).

Access to financial capital was often mentioned as a problem for women and other TEs in both countries. Consistent with the literature (e.g., Lituchy and Reavley, 2004), CR respondents (CR-1, CR-3) said WBOs need money for wages but often lack tangible assets favoured by lenders. A CR banking expert (CR-6) described a government-subsidized lending programme: *"The amount of loan money is between half a million and fifteen million crowns ($25–$770 thousand USD). It says exactly what the finances can go for ... for tangible assets ... not wages ... So there are few women ... 90 percent men."* Another CR respondent agreed. *"Banks will give business loans, but ... under unfavorable conditions"* (CR-3). A third CR respondent said: *"banks do not discriminate; small loans are simply not profitable"* (CR-13).

US respondents offered similar descriptions. An expert (US-4) said that banks preferred making loans in the millions of dollars. Another respondent (US-12) argued that Arizona was problematic because it had few community-owned banks. Conglomerate banks preferred lending to established businesses in technology, manufacturing, and construction, not to labour-intensive, service-oriented ventures (CR-1, CR-6, US-2, US-5, US-12).

In summary, a business-as-usual orientation was described in both CR and US BAP samples. The lack of significant efforts to rethink business approaches and metrics meant that BAP institutional work often reinforced business-as-usual entrepreneurship models.

Institutional Work for Inclusion

In this section, we discuss how BAPs' institutional work in lending, training, and mentoring promoted more inclusive entrepreneurship models. Targeted clients included TEs who were women, ethnic and racial minorities, immigrants, poor, and/or unemployed. BAPs worked with community organizations to recruit clients (CR-3, CR-4, US-2, US-20). They sought to mould their programmes to recognize the unique needs of TE clients (see Table 6.3(B)). This process entailed sensitivity to clients' intersecting identities. Respondents who worked with Roma populations were cognizant of the combined effects of gender and racial stereotyping (CR-10, CR-11). US respondents discussed how women's race, educational, and social class background framed business options (US-1, US-2, US-3). Programmes serving immigrants factored legal status into programme services (US-13, US-20).

Some organizations helped clients secure business funding. The CR government offered "bridging contributions", small payments for a short duration to create "socially useful jobs", e.g., an employer who hires a worker or an unemployed worker who becomes self-employed (Kadeřábková, 2020; MoLSA, n.d.). Although women and other TEs were eligible, BAP staff complained about small funding amounts and bureaucratic hurdles (CR-1, CR-3, CR-4, CR-14).

The situation is better in the US because of long-standing policies to promote SMEs (Pandey and Amezcua, 2020). The US Small Business Administration (SBA), established in 1953, offers services to entrepreneurs aimed at increasing revenue and job creation (Nanda, 2021; Roth and Morris, 2020). The SBA fostered the creation of Women's Business Development Centers and Small Business Development Centers (SBDCs) around the country. Other SBA programmes guarantee business loans of up to 5 million USD (Pandey and Amezcua, 2020), and provide funding for microloans of $500 to $50,000 USD through 144 intermediary non-profit organizations (Dilger, 2021).

Although the US involvement in microlending is less than that of developing nations, these loans are an important funding source for women and other TEs (Dilger, 2021). There are approximately 260 US microlending programmes (About Microfinance, 2021). Five BAPs in the Phoenix sample

(US-6, US-9, US-13, US-14, US-17) offered microloans directly or through partnering banks or non-profits. However, some respondents (US-3, US-9, US-14, US-20) complained that microloans amounts were too small to help and that new entrepreneurs often needed training and mentoring more than lending. BAPs utilized microlending to help borrowers build their credit history (US-14, US-9, US-17, US-20). Some also offered in-house training and technical assistance to improve repayment rates (US-13, US-14, US-19).

Respondents said that there was little microlending in the CR (CR-1, CR-3, CR-4, CR-10, CR-13, CR-14). One respondent had been to the US to observe microlending programmes. Afterwards, she tried to generate interest in creating programmes in the CR, but she lamented that *"there is no Czech bank that wants to participate"* (CR-1). More common than lending were BAPs focused on training, counselling, and other business services. Some EU-funded programmes focused on immigrants, long-term unemployed persons, women who lost jobs or wanted to become self-employed, and women after maternity leave (CR-4, CR-5, CR-14). In their institutional work, staff stressed motivation and confidence-building activities as part of business training for this clientele (CR-5). They argued that after maternity leave women needed the increased contact with adults that these programmes provided (CR-3, CR-4). US respondents offered a similar observation about women who had been caring for children and had not been in the paid work force (US-1, US-19), but more US respondents emphasized business training and mentoring needs over confidence building (US-5, US-6, US-11, US-12, US-15). Many respondents said that mothers often start businesses to combine paid work with childcare. Three programmes in our sample, one CR (CR-14) and two US (US-2, US-19), set up childcare during training or networking meetings for women clients. Two CR BAPs advocated for cultural changes such as calling for men to play a larger role in care work (CR-3, CR-4).

Several US respondents worked at training programmes for small start-ups (US-2, US-13, US-14, US-15, US-19). Training varied in content and level of intensity from several weeks (US-2, US-13, US-19, US-19) to online (US-14) to bootcamps (US-15) (see Tables 6.1 and 6.2 for full listings of target groups and services). Respondents designed programmes to promote a welcoming environment for diverse clients such as holding training in Spanish (US-13, US-20), or setting events with locations, times, and formats that could accommodate client needs (e.g., mothers, employment schedules) (US-2, US-19, CR-3, CR-4). One programme offered low-cost office space for business owners with an explicit agenda of inclusiveness to challenge male-centric models (US-10). BAPs also promoted positive images of client business via media publicity, business fairs, and awards for business plans and performance (CR-3, CR-4, CR-8, US-2, US-12, US-13, US-15, US-16, US-18, US-19).

Some BAPs that focused on training or lending also offered networking (CR-3, CR-4, CR-12, CR-17, US-2, US-9, US-12, US-13, US-17, US-20). In both countries, there were BAPs for whom networking and conferences were the raison d'être (CR-1, CR-14, US-7, US-13, US-16). However, some respondents (US-5, US-11, CR-1) criticized BAPs focused solely on networking activities. A US respondent said many networking events failed to build contacts outside the BAP: *"At these events, members are just passing out cards to each other for business coaching"* (US-11). A CR respondent (CR-1) expressed a similar concern.

Another aspect of the IW perspective is a focus on small, mundane activities in which actors engage, whether or not they actually effect change (Lawrence and Suddaby, 2006). We found examples of such actions among respondents in both countries. A CR respondent from a BAP for Roma clients encouraged them to start car repair businesses because start-up costs were low and many Roma drove used cars in frequent need of repair (CR-10). Some US staff said they actually changed jobs to have more opportunities to work on entrepreneurial inclusion projects (US-1, US-5). BAP staff in both countries referenced efforts to network with other inclusion-oriented programmes because these connections inspired their own institutional change work (CR-1, CR-3, CR-4, US-2, US-4, US-18). A US respondent said that due to funding metrics focused on growth-oriented businesses, she often helped *"women and other disadvantaged business owners, but in my spare time"* (US-5). Staff in programmes that supported immigrants engaged in regulatory workarounds (Arenas et al., 2020; Henry et al., 2017): to help undocumented clients legally formalize their businesses (US-1, US-6).

Many BAP staff and experts described institutional work activities to transform male-centric models to include women and other TEs. They also exhibited an awareness of the barriers that impeded their efforts.

Challenging Institutional Barriers to Inclusive Programming

BAP respondents were able to describe not only barriers to their efforts, but also insights into further institutional changes needed for inclusion. A major barrier that respondents named was the lack of stable and sufficient programme funding. Often BAP funding was short term despite evidence of successful programme outcomes (CR-3, CR-4, CR-14, US-3). Constant demands for fundraising took time away from client services and programme evaluations (CR-1, US-2, US-10). Funding for some of their most successful programmes ended after a year or two (CR-3, CR-4, CR-11, US-3, US-2, US-9, CR/US workshops). Funding themes shifted frequently, a pattern that made it difficult to build coherent programmes (CR-1, CR-3, CR-4, US-1, US-3, US-11).

Although the US sample described myriad funding opportunities for micro-lending (especially when compared with the CR), US respondents complained that funding for programme operations (e.g., training, technical assistance) was scarce (US-9, US-18, US-20). BAP staff argue that technical support of clients prior to and after lending is associated with successful loan repayment and business longevity (see Jurik, 2005). Microlending staff relied on part-nering organizations for TE services, but said they lacked sufficient quality control and client follow-up to ensure loan repayment (e.g., US-9, US-20).

In general US and CR respondents said that funding assistance for WBOs and other TEs was simply inadequate, and that what funding there was went to high growth, tech-oriented concerns and efforts to attract business from elsewhere, rather than assistance to local SMEs. The Women's Business Center in the Phoenix area closed for two years due to a lack of funding but has since reopened. Respondents argued that the reluctance of governments and commercial banks stems from assumptions that women's businesses are lower-growth, lifestyle enterprises, and more likely to fail (US-2, US-3, US-12, CR-1, CR-3, CR-4) (Brush et al., 2009; Vossenberg, 2013). Some studies (Marlow and McAdam, 2013; Minniti and Naudé, 2010; Watson, 2020) suggest that these assumptions are often incorrect. Still, as scholars (Ahl, 2006; Katila et al., 2019) and our respondents note, discourse about women's entrepreneurship is important and stereotypes about WBOs persist. On this point, a CR staffer discussed the importance of presenting *"women entrepreneurs from various business sectors, not just the ones the media spin"* (CR-14). Similarly, CR and US respondents argued that existing programmes focused too much on start-ups and neglected training and bridge loans needed for established WBOs to grow and attract commercial bank financing (CR-3, CR-4, CR-14, US-3, US-4, US-11).

Traditional programme funding metrics were a barrier to inclusive BAP practices (CR-1, US-2, US-5, CR/US workshops). BAP funding often depends on the revenue growth and job creation for the businesses they assist (Dean et al., 2019; Wang, 2019; Yusuf, 2012). Some respondents mentioned that the preoccupation with traditional metrics created barriers to support for WBOs, and advocated redefining metrics to include recognition that a stable sole proprietorship is a valid economic goal (CR-1, US-2, US-5) (see Henry et al., 2017; Katila et al., 2019). A business counselling centre respondent (US-11) agreed, but said that to insure funding, her BAP had to prioritize traditional metrics: *"If we do not meet them, we lose staff"* (US-11).

Respondents' activities illustrated an important dimension of the IW per-spective: actors are aware of and reflexive about the institutional context in which they are embedded (Lawrence et al., 2011). Respondents engaged in community advocacy for more inclusive entrepreneurial policy. Several US respondents (US-2, US-5, US-9) formed an organization of BAPs to advocate for inclusive policies in Arizona. They recommended an entrepreneurial ecosystem to compile information about support options (see Guerrero et al., 2020; Motoyama et al., 2021). They developed funding criteria that included measures of the diversity for BAP boards of directors, investors, presenters, and funding recipients. They argued that BAPs must offer more connections to mainstream organizations, and discussions of gender issues, racism, and work-family balance would include men as well as women (Empowered PhXX, 2018).

Every programme focusing on WBOs referenced childcare as a barrier to women who did not have adequate funds for private childcare or help from family (see Table 6.3(C)) Yet, only a few respondents, two in the US (US-2, US-19) and one in the CR (CR-14), said that their BAPs provided activities for children. This is especially salient in the CR where childcare increasingly follows a traditional model wherein women are the main caretakers (Annink et al., 2015). A respondent agreed that women are expected to fulfil the *"female role"* even if that impedes business ownership (CR-3). US respondents agreed that the issue of childcare was a major dilemma for women entrepreneurs (US-4, US-10). Along these lines, two US respondents stressed the need for universal health and long-term care policies to support WBOs and low-income business owners (US-3, US-4). Ironically, some US BAP staffers downplayed women's work/family conflicts when appealing to funders out of fear that they would dismiss the seriousness of supporting WOBs (US-2, US-4).

Paid parental leave is a related concern. Although the CR had a relatively generous paid leave, it is designed for employees, not WBOs. WBOs cannot receive paid leave unless they pay into the system well in advance of pregnancy (Jurik et al., 2020). WBOs are actually prohibited from employing others if on maternity leave (Křížková et al., 2014). This pattern may limit CR women's business opportunities. Research on Nordic countries with generous paid leave systems suggests that unless such policies are designed with WBOs in mind, they act as a disincentive for women's business pursuits (Ahl and Nelson, 2015; Neergaard and Thrane, 2011).

In the US, paid maternity leave is not guaranteed by government or private employers. This is particularly true for many low-paid, service sector workers and may force them into precarious self-employment ventures (Gault et al., 2014; Jurik et al., 2019). Leave may be difficult for entrepreneurs, but maternity/parental allowances might provide financial support to hire help during the immediate pre- and post-maternity period (US-1).

Finally, some respondents mentioned inadequate employment opportunities as a barrier that forces women and other TEs into necessity-based employment (US-2, US-3, US-4) (see Holienka et al., 2016; NWBC, 2017). Respondents named necessity-based self-employment as a problem for CR Roma and Vietnamese clients (CR-15, CR-10), for immigrant clients in the US and

CR (US-6, US-9, CR-12), and for mothers who lacked flexible employment options (US-3, US-5, CR-1, CR-3). Some CR Roma women and US Latinx women are relegated to struggling cleaning businesses (CR-10, US-9). Respondents stressed that improved labour-market opportunities would reduce such "precarious survival self-employment" that often failed and worsened clients' situation (CR-7, CR-10, US-3, US-9) (see Hašková and Dudová, 2017).

In summary, BAP staff and experts referenced the need for institutional changes to overcome barriers to entrepreneurial inclusion. Some staff worked with other BAPs and social activist groups to advocate for shifts in their local entrepreneurial ecosystems. These shifts have implications for broader political, economic, and cultural institutional conditions.

CONCLUSIONS AND POLICY IMPLICATIONS

We conducted a comparative study of the institutional work by CR and US BAP staff and business experts to promote more inclusive models of entrepreneurship. We extend institutional theories of the contextual embeddedness of entrepreneurship to the study of how staff and experts maintained or challenged male-centric business models in their activities. Drawing on the institutional work concept allows us to see business assistance from the perspective of those who do it for a living.

Despite commonalities in the CR and US BAP discussions, there were significant differences in provider experiences. Differences relate to the long-standing ethos of small business support in the US and the newer revitalization of business ownership in the CR. The Phoenix area was larger and offered more programme options. Respondents agreed that lending was not sufficiently plentiful in either country, but lending for women and other TEs was rarest in the CR.

Some BAPs, especially CR banks, took a business-as-usual approach. They saw no need to alter their programme designs or otherwise tailor services to WBOs or other TEs. Reflective of gender-role orientation surveys (ISSP, 2012), the stereotyping and dismissal were more overt than in the US. CR respondents noted that funders did not take WBOs seriously. According to US BAPs, these sentiments existed especially in IT groups, but were subtler. Some respondents in both countries said it is enough that women were permitted in their programmes even when few women participated. Such comments illustrate the distinction between gender-neutral and gender-aware approaches, and how male-centric entrepreneurship models were reinforced.

We also spoke with respondents that sought to develop more inclusive assistance models. Inclusive programming meant opening a space for change that was gender-, racially-, and ethnically-aware. Some promoted intersectional understandings of barriers to entrepreneurship and economic well-being. They offered training, networking, and lending or subsidy programmes designed to be sensitive to the unique needs of women and/or other TEs. They sought to challenge the frequent stereotypes of triviality and failure that plague TE businesses by publicizing client successes.

However, policy deficiencies, BAP funding instability, and pressure to meet traditional financial success metrics hindered transformative goals for entrepreneurial inclusivity and socio-economic equality (Foss et al., 2019). Childcare issues were described repeatedly as a challenge. CR and US respondents spoke about problems among WBOs with small children who lacked adequate childcare support.

Despite barriers, respondents reported examples of policy workarounds (e.g., dealing with obstacles in immigration laws), construction of welcoming business spaces, multilingual classes, offering activities for children during training sessions, planning events at times when mothers and employed persons could attend, and using non-traditional collateral for lending. Some US BAP respondents started a network of programme providers to establish an ecosystem in the Phoenix area. They advocated for modifications of business success metrics to be more sensitive to WBOs and other TEs, and argued that programmes should also be evaluated based upon the diversity of leadership, clients, and awards. They called for a balance between programmes that are sensitive to the unique experience of TEs, on the one hand, and special programmes that isolate TEs from the mainstream business world.

Respondents also identified issues with family policy in the two countries, although their policies are quite different. The CR has universal paid parental leave for employed workers, children's allowance, and government subsidized childcare for children over age three (Křížková and Pospíšilová, 2021). The US offered vouchers for low-income families and limited tax credits for childcare for middle-class families, but no coherent national paid leave programme (Childcare.gov, n.d.; Gault et al., 2014). However, CR leave and subsidy policies do not support WBOs (Jurik et al., 2020). Some US respondents argued that national child-, elder-, and health-care policies were needed to assist WBOs.

Of course, a larger and more comprehensive study of each BAP, and more carefully matched samples of programmes, as well as a longitudinal approach would be desirable in future research. Moreover, comparisons of staff with client perceptions of business assistance needs would enhance the understanding of BAP institutional work. Nevertheless, the findings from our present study, particularly respondents' discussions of institutional barriers to inclusive programming, have significant policy implications.

One policy prescription that emerged from interviews was that if governments believe that WBOs and TEs are an important facet in the economic landscape, they should provide access to capital and training at appropriate levels and with the funding predictability that permits rational planning. Along these lines, a second policy prescription would be to continue funding for start-ups but to add more support for ongoing small businesses that have demonstrated some sustainability. Some of the US microlending programmes in our sample tried to make bridge loans to help SMEs expand, but perhaps not in sufficient numbers and without enough quality technical assistance to accompany them.

However, there is an overarching policy implication that is the context for programme and entrepreneur funding deficiencies. As long as traditional measures of financial success and quick-growth potential dominate business support, goals of entrepreneurial diversity and social inclusion will suffer. As noted in prior research (Ahl, 2006; Marlow and Martinez Dy, 2018), traditional economic growth and social equality agendas are not necessarily complementary when designing entrepreneurship policy. Growth metrics need more interrogation to expose the degree to which they replicate male-centric models and exclude TE entrepreneurship. Economic stability cannot always depend on a "blockbuster" mentality, and smaller firms are an essential part of a viable economy (Ribeiro-Soriano, 2017). Although traditional economic goals and metrics are likely to continue, the contributions of small businesses to community, employment, and service innovations as well as the non-economic benefits of inclusive entrepreneurship must be documented and publicly communicated more broadly than is typically the case.

Since our data were gathered, the US SBA has offered two small business relief and an economic stimulus packages during the COVID-19 pandemic (SBA COVID-19, n.d.). Yet, this funding has not been sufficient to keep many SMEs going (Shifflett, 2020). Some sources suggest that WOBs have been more negatively impacted by the pandemic (Manolova et al., 2020; US Chamber of Commerce, 2020). In May of 2021, the SBA introduced a \$2.7 million grant to provide "innovative support" for US Women's Business Development Centers (SBA, 2021).

Although we suggest that BAPs could benefit from more stable and predictable funding, we concur with some respondents that these programmes should be periodically evaluated for their effectiveness in providing business training and facilitating networks that connect TEs with the mainstream business community. As noted by our respondents, such evaluations, however, should be based upon revised BAP success metrics that include measures of programme diversity as well as the non-financial and community benefits associated with TE businesses (Wang, 2019; Yousafzai et al., 2018). In the spirit of gender-aware programming, BAPs should take childcare support for clients more seriously via grant applications and community lobbying efforts. BAPs should use their PR capabilities to publicize childcare issues.

Nationally, both countries need to assess the effects of their family, work, and entrepreneurial policies regarding unpaid family care and parental support (e.g., subsidies during parental leaves to hire paid help, and motivation for higher father involvement in childcare). A more coherent agenda is needed (Henry et al., 2003). In the CR, there are supports but they tend not to help WBOs (Jurik et al., 2020). As part of the first wave of the COVID-19 pandemic, the CR offered an allowance (ošetřovné) for parents to care for sick children up to ten years of age. This allowance was temporarily extended to entrepreneurs and self-employed groups that were never eligible before. Such policy helps to equalize conditions for employees and entrepreneurs and should be considered for permanent implementation.

Since the COVID-19 pandemic, the US has passed temporary assistance monies to families and is considering more paid leave and childcare provisions (US Treasury, n.d.; Snell, 2021). However, the continued lack of a universal healthcare plan is problematic for many US SMEs and employees alike (Bivens, 2020; Davis, 2007).

The last policy point for consideration comes from the respondents in both countries who warned of the precarity of many necessity-driven business ventures (Hašková and Dudová, 2017). They argued that such clients really just needed improved and more flexible employment options. We join others (e.g., Ahl and Nelson, 2015; Marlow et al., 2008; Marlow, 2020; Neergaard and Thrane, 2011) in suggesting that entrepreneurship research and advocacy must be mindful of the link between long-term unemployment and self-employment motivations and question the limitations of entrepreneurship as an answer to joblessness.

Our study is significant for three reasons. First, methodologically, it offers a comparative qualitative analysis of BAP staff and experts in the CR, a country that has recently transitioned to a market economy where business practices are still often viewed negatively (Lukeš et al., 2014), and the US, a country in which entrepreneurship has long been an integral part of the American dream (Valdez, 2015). In particular, in-depth qualitative research on business in the CR is rare. Moreover, BAPs generally and the work that they do is under-researched. Second, and more theoretically, our institutional work framework moves beyond correlational studies and directs attention to the work of staff and experts on the ground level of entrepreneurship service provision. This approach stresses the embeddedness of respondents within their institutional contexts such that our findings identified innovative practices promoting inclusiveness, but also barriers to transforming male-centric entrepreneurship models. Third, by drawing on gender-aware and intersectional perspectives, our analysis was also able to identify challenges faced by BAPs when dealing with the complexities of intersecting client gender, race, class, and citizenship distinctions. Gender-aware programming alone was insufficient in meeting the needs of truly diverse TE populations. In summary, our combination of perspectives offers a useful approach for understanding how male-centric models of entrepreneurship are reinforced, but also challenged in the CR and US through both everyday practices and through organized activism.

ACKNOWLEDGEMENTS

Nancy Jurik wishes to thank the U.S. Fulbright Programme and ASU SkySong's Office of Entrepreneurial Opportunities for funding support for this project. Alena Křížková and Marie Pospíšilová wish to thank the Fulbright Commission in the Czech Republic for support and Czech Science Foundation for support of a project Gendering the Pandemic (reg. nr. 21-13587S). Thank you also to the reviewers for their helpful comments.

REFERENCES

About Microfinance. (2021). A Portal to the World of Microfinance, Financial Inclusion, and Impact Investing. Retrieved from: https://www.aboutmicrofinance .com/latin-america-caribbean/north-america

Ahl, H. (2006). Why research on women entrepreneurs needs new directions. *Entrepreneurship Theory and Practice, 30*(5), 595–621.

Ahl, H., & Nelson, T. (2015). How policy positions women entrepreneurs: A comparative analysis of state discourse in Sweden and the United States. *Journal of Business Venturing, 30*(2), 273–291.

Aldrich, H. E., & Cliff, J. E. (2003). The pervasive effects of family on entrepreneurship: Toward a family embeddedness perspective. *Journal of Business Venturing, 18*(5), 573–596.

Angulo-Guerrero, M. J., Pérez-Moreno, S., & Abad-Guerrero, I. M. (2017). How economic freedom affects opportunity and necessity entrepreneurship in the OECD countries. *Journal of Business Research, 73*, 30–37.

Annink, A., den Dulk, L., & Steijn, B. (2015). Work-family state support for the self-employed across Europe. *Journal of Entrepreneurship and Public Policy, 4*(2), 187–208.

Arenas, D., Strumińska-Kutra, M., & Landoni, P. (2020). Walking the tightrope and stirring things up: Exploring the institutional work of sustainable entrepreneurs. *Business Strategy and the Environment, 29*(8), 3055–3071.

Baradaran, M. (2017). *The color of money: Black banks and the racial wealth gap.* Cambridge, MA: Harvard University Press.

Bartoš, P., Ključnikov, A., Popesko, B., & Macháček, J. (2015). Are men more innovative and aggressive in business? Case study from the Czech Republic. *International Journal of Entrepreneurial Knowledge, 3*(2), 29–39.

Basaffar, A. A., Niehm, L. S., & Bosselman, R. (2018). Saudi Arabian women in entrepreneurship: Challenges, opportunities and potential. *Journal of Developmental Entrepreneurship, 23*(02), 18500013/1850013-20.

Bell, D. A., & Strabac, Z. (2020). Exclusion of Muslims in Eastern Europe and Western Europe. A comparative analysis of anti-Muslim attitudes in France, Norway, Poland

and Czech Republic. *International Journal on Minority and Group Rights*, *28*(1), 117–142. https://doi.org/10.1163/15718115-bja10006

Benáček, V., & Zemplinerová, A. (1995). Problems and environment of small businesses in the Czech Republic. *Small Business Economics*, *7*, 437–450.

Bernard, A. B., & Slaughter, M. J. (2004). *The life cycle of a minority-owned business: Implications for the American economy*. US Department of Commerce, Minority Business Development Agency.

Bianco, M. E., Lombe, M., & Bolis, M. (2017). Challenging gender norms and practices through women's entrepreneurship. *International Journal of Gender and Entrepreneurship*, *9*(4), 338–358.

Bivens, J. (2020). Fundamental health reform like 'Medicare for all' would help the labor market. Economic Policy Institute. (5 March). Retrieved from: https://www.epi.org/publication/medicare-for-all-would-help-the-labor-market/

Bliss, R. T., & Garratt, N. L. (2001). Supporting women entrepreneurs in transitioning economies. *Journal of Small Business Management*, *39*(4), 336–344.

Bly, A. (2021). Phoenix among top 10 metros for new business formation, report says. *Phoenix Business Journal* (3 March). Retrieved from: https://www.bizjournals.com/phoenix/news/2021/03/03/business-formation-report-phoenix-top-10-metro.html

Braidford, P., Stone, I., & Tesfaye, B. (2013). Gender, disadvantage and enterprise support – lessons from women's business centres in North America and Europe. *Journal of Small Business and Enterprise Development*, *20*(1), 143–164.

Branchet, B., & Křížková, A. (2015). Gender and entrepreneurial intentions in a transition economy context: Case of the Czech Republic. *International Journal of Entrepreneurship and Small Business*, *25*(3), 260–281.

Brown, R., Mawson, S., & Mason, C. (2017). Myth-busting and entrepreneurship policy: The case of high growth firms. *Entrepreneurship & Regional Development*, *29*(5–6), 414–443.

Brush, C. G., De Bruin, A., & Welter, F. (2009). A gender-aware framework for women's entrepreneurship. *International Journal of Gender and Entrepreneurship*, *1*(1), 8–24.

Brush, C., Greene, P., Balachandra, L., & Davis, A. (2018). The gender gap in venture capital – progress, problems, and perspectives. *Venture Capital*, *20*(2), 115–136.

Bullough, A., Hechavarría, D. M., Brush, C. G., & Edelman, L. F. (2019). Introduction: Programs, policies and practices: Fostering high-growth women's entrepreneurship. In *High-growth women's entrepreneurship*, pp. 1–12. Cheltenham: Edward Elgar Publishing.

Charmaz, K. (2006). *Constructing grounded theory: A practical guide through qualitative analysis*. Thousand Oaks, CA: Sage.

Childcare.gov. (n.d.). Get Help Paying for Child Care. Retrieved from: https://childcare.gov/consumer-education/get-help-paying-for-child-care

Cho, Y., & Honorati, M. (2013). A meta-analysis of entrepreneurship programs in developing countries. Background paper for the World Bank World Development Review.

City of Phoenix. (2017). Economic development and entrepreneur resources. Retrieved from: https://www.phoenix.gov/econdev/entrepreneur

CZSO (Czech Statistical Office). (2014). Národnostní struktura obyvatel (Nationality structure of the population). Prague: CZSO. Retrieved from: https://www.czso.cz/documents/10180/20551765/170223-14.pdf (accessed 14 July 2021).

CZSO. (2016). Zaostřeno na ženy a muže – (2016). 4. Práce a mzdy. Retrieved from: https://www.czso.cz/csu/czso/4-prace-a-mzdy-iwbtn13wat (accessed 8 June 2018).

CZSO. (2020). Zaostřeno na ženy a muže – 2020 (Focused on women and men – 2020). Retrieved from: https://www.czso.cz/csu/czso/zaostreno-na-zeny-a-muze -2020 (accessed 14 July 2021)

Davis, K. (2007, 17 February). Uninsured in America: Problems and possible solutions. *The BMJ*. Retrieved from: https://www.ncbi.nlm.nih.gov/pmc/articles/ PMC1801027/

De Bruin, A., Brush, C., & Welter, F. (2007). Advancing a framework for coherent research on women's entrepreneurship. *Entrepreneurship Theory and Practice*, *31*(3), 323–339.

Dean, H., Larsen, G., Ford, J., & Akram, M. (2019). Female entrepreneurship and the metanarrative of economic growth: A critical review of underlying assumptions. *International Journal of Management Reviews*, *21*(1), 24–49.

Dilger, R. (2021). Small Business Administration Microloan Program. Washington, DC: Congressional Research Service. Retrieved from: https://fas.org/sgp/crs/misc/ R41057.pdf

Dlouhá, M. (2015). Czech Republic case study. In E. Schulze (Ed.), *Women's entrepreneurship: Closing the gender gap in access to financial and other services and in social entrepreneurship* (pp. 35–39). European Parliament. Retrieved from: http://www.europarl.europa.eu/RegData/etudes/STUD/2015/519230/IPOL _STU(2015)519230_EN.pdf

Duara, N. (2016). Arizona's once-feared immigration law, SB1070, loses most of its power in settlement. *Los Angeles Times* (15 September). Retrieved from: https:/// www.latimes.com/nation/la-na-arizona-law-20160915-snap-story.html

Dvouletý, O., Duháček Šebestová, J., Svobodová, I., Habrmanová, B., & Mullerová, J. (2021). Analysing determinants influencing female entrepreneurship engagement in the Czech Republic: What is the role of caring responsibilities? *World Journal of Entrepreneurship, Management and Sustainable Development*, *18*(1), 3–13.

Elliott, J. (2021). Women in Small Business Statistics in the U.S. Report Based on US. Census Bureau Data and U.S. Bureau of Economic Analysis (17 January). Retrieved from: https://www.fool.com/the-blueprint/women-in-small-business-statistics-in -the-us/

Empowered PhXX Collaborative. (2018). A new vision for Phoenix entrepreneurship: Recommendations to maximize the economic impact of women-owned businesses. Retrieved from: https://www.slideshare.net/ThreeDogMarketing/a-new-vision-for -phoenix-entreprenuership-recommendations-to-maximize-the-economic-impact-of -womenowned-businesses

Ettl, K., & Welter, F. (2010). Gender, context and entrepreneurial learning. *International Journal of Gender and Entrepreneurship*, *2*(2), 108–129.

European Commission. (2018). 2018 Small Business Act Fact Sheet – Czech Republic. European Commission. Retrieved from: https://ec.europa.eu/docsroom/documents/ 32581/attachments/7/translations/en/rendtions/native

Fairlie, R. W., & Robb, A. M. (2007). Why are black-owned businesses less successful than white-owned businesses? The role of families, inheritances, and business human capital. *Journal of Labor Economics*, *25*(2), 289–323.

Fernandes, P. (2020). How to start a business in Arizona. *Business News Daily* (18 May). Retrieved from: https://www.businessnewsdaily.com/9131-doing-business-in -arizona.html

Foss, L., Henry, C., Ahl, H., & Mikalsen, G. H. (2019). Women's entrepreneurship policy research: A 30-year review of the evidence. *Small Business Economics*, *53*(2), 409–429.

Gault, B., Hartmann, H., Hegewisch, A., Milli, J., & Reichlin, L. (2014, March). Paid parental leave in the United States: What the data tell us about access, usage, and economic and health benefits. Report, Institute for Women's Policy Research. Retrieved from: https://iwpr.org/job-quality-income-security/paid-parental-leave -in-the-united-states-what-the-data-tell-us-about-access-usage-and-economic-and -health-benefits/

Gawer, A., & Phillips, N. (2013). Institutional work as logics shift: The case of Intel's transformation to platform leader. *Organization Studies, 34*(8), 1035–1071.

GEM. (2011, 2020) Economy Profiles. Retrieved from https://www.gemconsortium .org/economy-profiles (accessed 15 July 2021).

Gimenez, D., & Calbio, A. (2018). The salient role of institutions in women's entrepreneurship: A critical review and agenda for future research. *International Entrepreneurship and Management Journal, 14*, 857–882.

Guerrero, M., Linan, F., & Caceres-Carrasco, F. (2020). The influence of ecosystems on the entrepreneurship process: A comparison across developed and developing economies. *Small Business Economics, 57*, 1733–1759. Retrieved from: https://doi .org/10,1007/s11187-020-00392-2

Hailemariam, A. T., & Kroon, B. (2018). Redefining success beyond economic growth and wealth generation: The case of Ethiopia. In S. Yousafzai, A. Fayolle, A. Lindgreen, C. Henry, S. Saeed, & S. Sheikh (Eds), *Women's entrepreneurship and the myth of underperformance* (pp. 3–19). Edward Elgar.

Hait, A. (2021). Women business ownership in America on the rise. Retrieved from: https://www.census.gov/library/stories/2021/03/women-business-ownership-in -america-on-rise.html

Hampel, C., Lawrence, T., & Tracey, P. (2015). Institutional work: Taking stock and making it matter. In R. Greenwood, C. Oliver, T. Lawrence, & R. Meyer (Eds), *SAGE handbook of organizational institutionalism* (2nd edn, pp. 558–590). London: Sage.

Hašková, H., & Dudová, R. (2017). Precarious work and care responsibilities in the economic crisis. *European Journal of Industrial Relations, 23*(1), 47–63.

Heath, A., & L. Richards (2019). How do Europeans differ in their attitudes to immigration?: Findings from the European Social Survey 2002/03–2016/17, OECD Social, Employment and Migration Working Papers, No. 222, OECD Publishing, Paris.

Henry, C., Hill, F., & Leitch C. (2003). Developing a coherent enterprise support policy: A new challenge for governments. *Environment and Planning C: Government and Policy, 21*(1), 3–19. doi:10.1068/c0220

Henry, C., Orser, B., Coleman, S., Foss, L., & Welter, F. (2017). Women's entrepreneurship policy: A 13-nation cross-country comparison. *International Journal of Gender and Entrepreneurship, 9*(3), 206–228.

Holienka, M., Jančovičová, Z., & Kovačičová, Z. (2016). Drivers of women entrepreneurship in Visegrad countries: GEM evidence. *Procedia Social and Behavioral Sciences, 220*, 124–133. Retrieved from: https://ecommons.cornell.edu/xmlui/ bitstream/handle/1813/79335/Paid_Parental_Leave_in_the_US.pdf?sequence=1

Inwood, S., & Stengel, E. (2020). Working households: Challenges in balancing young children and the farm enterprise. *Community Development, 51*(5), 499–517.

ISSP Research Group. (2012). *International Social Survey Programme: Family and Changing Gender Roles IV – ISSP 2012 – ZA No. 5900* (Data file version 4.0.0). GESIS Data Archive: Cologne. doi:10.4232/1.12661

Jardina, A. (2019, October). White consciousness and white prejudice: Two compounding forces in contemporary American politics. *The Forum, 17*(3), 447–466.

Jurik, N. C. (2005). *Bootstrap dreams: US microenterprise development in an era of welfare reform.* Ithaca, NY: Cornell University Press.

Jurik, N. C. (2020). Making the case for public support of US women business owners. *University of St. Thomas Journal of Law & Public Policy, XIV*, 178–219.

Jurik, N., Křížková, A., & Pospíšilová (Dlouhá) M. (2016). Czech copreneur orientations to business and family responsibilities: A mixed embeddedness perspective. *International Journal of Gender and Entrepreneurship, 8*(3), 307–326.

Jurik, N., Křížková, A., Pospíšilová, M., & Cavender, G. (2019). Blending, credit, context: Doing business in Czech and US copreneurships. *International Small Business Journal, 37*(4), 317–342.

Jurik, N., Cavender, G., Křížková, A., & Pospíšilová, M. (2020). Structured agency and motherhood among copreneurs in the Czech Republic. In T. Esnard & M. Knight (Eds), *Mothering and entrepreneurship. Global perspectives, identities, and complexities* (pp. 101–134). Demeter Press.

Kadeřábková, M. (2020). Socially effective job: Do you know how to get support? Orange Academy of the Czech Republic (22 June). Retrieved from: https:// orangeacademy.cz/clanky/spolecensky-ucelne-pracovni-misto/

Kafkadesk. (2019). Czech Republic ranked 6th best country in Europe for start-ups (23 February). Retrieved from: https://kafkadesk.org/2019/02/23/czech-republic-ranked -6th-best-country-in-europe-for-startups/

Katila, S., Laine, P. M., & Parkkari, P. (2019). Sociomateriality and affect in institutional work: Constructing the identity of start-up entrepreneurs. *Journal of Management Inquiry, 28*(3), 381–394.

Kelly, E. L. (2010). Failure to update: An institutional perspective on noncompliance with the Family and Medical Leave Act. *Law & Society Review, 44*(1), 33–66.

Knowlton, K., Ozkazanc-Pan, B., Clark Munteach, S., & Motoyama, Y. (2015). Support organizations and remediating the gender gap in entrepreneurial ecosystems. Retrieved from: https://ssrn.com/abstract=2685116 or http://dx.doi.org/10 .2139/ssrn.2685116

Korpi, W., Ferrarini, T., & Englund, S. (2013). Women's opportunities under different family policy constellations: Gender, class, and inequality tradeoffs in western countries re-examined. *Social Politics: International Studies in Gender, State & Society, 20*(1), 1–40.

Kozubíková, L., Lubor, H., & Dimitris, K. (2017). The effect of business environment and entrepreneurs' gender on perception of financial risk in the SMEs sector. *Journal of Competitiveness, 9*(1), 36–50.

Křížková, A., & Pospíšilová, M. (2021). Czech Republic. In *Entrepreneurship policies through a gender lens* (pp. 70–75). OECD Publishing. Retrieved from: https://doi .org/10.1787/71c8f9c9-en

Křížková, A., & Vohlídalová, M. (2009). The labour market and work-life balance in the Czech Republic in historical perspective. In H. Hašková & Z. Uhde (Eds), *Women and social citizenship* (pp. 35–76). Prague: Institute of Sociology, Academy of Sciences of the Czech Republic.

Křížková, A., Jurik, N., & Pospíšilová (Dlouhá), M. (2014). The divisions of labour and responsibilities in business and home among women and men copreneurs in the Czech Republic. In K. Lewis, C. Henry, E. Gatewood & J. Watson (Eds), *Women's entrepreneurship in the 21st century: An international multi-level research analysis* (pp. 258–277), Cheltenham: Edward Elgar.

Křížková, A., Maříková, H., Hašková, H., & Formánková, L. (2011). *Pracovní dráhy žen v české republice* (*Working Paths of Women in the Czech Republic*). Praha: Sociologické nakladatelství (SLON).

Křížková, A., Pospíšilová, M., Jurik, N. & Cavender, G. (2018). Women's entrepreneurial realities in the Czech Republic and the United States: Gender gaps, racial/ethnic disadvantages, and emancipatory potential. In S. Yousafzai et al. (Eds), *Contextual embeddedness of women's entrepreneurship going beyond a gender-neutral approach* (pp. 180–193). London: Routledge.

Lang, R., Fink, M., & Kibler, E. (2014). Understanding place-based entrepreneurship in rural Central Europe: A comparative institutional analysis. *International Small Business Journal, 32*(2), 204–227.

Lawrence, T. B., & Suddaby, R. (2006). Institutions and institutional work. In S. R. Clegg, C. Hardy, W. R. Nord, & T.B. Lawrence (Eds), *The Sage handbook of organization studies* (pp. 215–254). London: Sage.

Lawrence, T., Suddaby, R., & Leca, B. (2011). Institutional work: Refocusing institutional studies of organization. *Journal of Management Inquiry, 20*(1), 52–58.

Lesonsky, R. (2020). The state of women entrepreneurs. Retrieved from: https://www.score.org/blog/state-women-entrepreneurs

Lituchy, T. R., & Reavley, M. A. (2004). Women entrepreneurs: A comparison of international small business owners in Poland and the Czech Republic. *Journal of International Entrepreneurship, 2*(1), 61–87.

Longoria, C. (2018). Women entrepreneurship in developing, developed and transitional economies – differences and similarities. *JWEE*, (3–4), 73–82.

Loscocco, K. A., Robinson, J., Hall, R. H., & Allen, J. K. (1991). Gender and small business success: An inquiry into women's relative disadvantage. *Social Forces, 70*(1), 65–85.

Loscocco, K., Monnat, S. M., Moore, G., & Lauber, K. B. (2009). Enterprising women: A comparison of women's and men's small business networks. *Gender & society, 23*(3), 388–411.

Lukeš, M. (2017). Entrepreneurship development in the Czech Republic. In A. Sauka & A. Chepurenko (Eds), *Entrepreneurship in transition economies* (pp. 209–224). Basel, Switzerland: Springer.

Lukeš, M., Jakl, M., & Zouhar, J. (2014). Global Entrepreneurship Monitor 2013. Podnikatelská aktivita v České republice. Retrieved from: https://www.mpo.cz/cz/podnikani/male-a-stredni-podnikani/studie-a-strategicke-dokumenty/global-entrepreneurship-monitor-2013-podnikatelska-aktivita-v-ceske-republice--149362/

Manolova, T., Brush, C., Edelman, L., & Elam, A. (2020). Pivoting to stay the course: How women entrepreneurs take advantage of opportunities created by the COVID-19 pandemic. *International Small Business Journal, 38*(6), 481–491.

Marlow, S. (2020). Gender and entrepreneurship: Past achievements and future possibilities. *International Journal of Gender and Entrepreneurship, 12*(1), 39–52.

Marlow, S., & Martinez Dy, A. (2018). Annual review article: Is it time to rethink the gender agenda in entrepreneurship research? *International Small Business Journal, 36*(1), 3–22.

Marlow, S., & McAdam, M. (2013). Gender and entrepreneurship: Advancing debate and challenging myths; exploring the mystery of the under-performing female entrepreneur. *International Journal of Entrepreneurial Behavior & Research, 19*, 114–124.

Marlow, S., Carter, S., & Shaw, E. (2008). Constructing female entrepreneurship policy in the UK: Is the US a relevant benchmark? *Environment and Planning C: Government and Policy, 26*, 335–351.

McAdam, M., & Marlow, S. (2007). Building futures or stealing secrets? Entrepreneurial cooperation and conflict within business incubators. *International Small Business Journal, 25*(4), 361–382.

McNally, B., & Khoury, G. (2018). Leveraging micro-level support factors to overcome macro-level challenges: Palestinian and Saudi Arabian female entrepreneurs. In *Contextual embeddedness of women's entrepreneurship* (pp. 60–73). Routledge.

Minniti, M., & Naudé, W. (2010). What do we know about the patterns and determinants of female entrepreneurship across countries? *The European Journal of Development Research, 22*, 277–293.

Mirchandani, K. (1999). Feminist insight on gendered work: New directions in research on women and entrepreneurship. *Gender, Work & Organization, 6*(4), 224–235.

Modell, S. (2020). Accounting for institutional work: A critical review. *European Accounting Review*. Retrieved from: https://doi.org/10.1080/09638180.2020.1820354

MoLSA (Ministry of Labour and Social Affairs). (2018). State Social Support. Retrieved from: https://www.mpsv.cz/en/1603 (accessed 7 May 2021).

MoLSA (Ministry of Labour and Social Affairs). (n.d.). Active labour market policies. Retrieved from: https://www.mpsv.cz/web/en/employment

Motoyama, Y., Muntean, S., Knowlton, K., & Ozkazanc-Pan, B. (2021). Causes of the gender divide within entrepreneurship ecosystems. *Local Economy*. doi:10.1177/0269094221995783. Retrieved from: https://doi-org.ezproxy1.lib.asu.edu/10.1177/0269094221995783

Nanda, H. S. (2021). The impact of integrating an SBDC Program into a college/university career center. Master's Projects. 986. doi:https://doi.org/10.31979/etd.ej6m-rtda.

National Women's Business Council (NWBC). (2017). Necessity as a driver of women's entrepreneurship: Her stories. National Women's Business Council Report (July). Retrieved from: https://www.nwbc.gov/2017/10/11/necessity-as-a-driver-of-womens-entrepreneurship-her-stories/

Neergaard, H., & Thrane, C. (2011). The Nordic Welfare Model: Barrier or facilitator of women's entrepreneurship in Denmark? *International Journal of Gender and Entrepreneurship, 3*(2), 88–104. https://doi.org/10.1108/17566261111140189

Neumeyer, X., Santos, S. C., & Morris, M. H. (2019). Who is left out: Exploring social boundaries in entrepreneurial ecosystems. *The Journal of Technology Transfer, 44*(2), 462–484.

Nikolova, E., Ricka, F., & Simroth, D. (2012). Entrepreneurship in the transition region: An analysis based on the Life in Transition Survey. EBRD Working Papers (141).

OECD. (2021). *Entrepreneurship policies through a gender lens*. OECD Publishing. https://doi.org/10.1787/71c8f9c9-en

Office of the AZ Governor Doug Ducey (2020). New: Arizona's booming job growth ranks second in the nation. News release (28 January). Retrieved from: https://azgovernor.gov/governor/news/2020/01/new-arizonas-booming-job-growth-ranks-second-nation

Orser, B., Riding, A., & Li, Y. (2019). Technology adoption and gender-inclusive entrepreneurship, education and training. *International Journal of Gender and Entrepreneurship, 11*(3), 273–298.

Ozkazanc-Pan, B., & Muntean, S. (2018). Networking towards (in)equality: Women entrepreneurs in technology. *Gender, Work and Organisation, 25*, 379–400.

Pandey, S., & Amezcua, A. (2020). Women's business ownership and entrepreneurship through the lens of US federal policies. *Small Business Economics, 54*, 1123–1152.

Parisi, L. (2020). Canada's new feminist international assistance policy: Business as usual? *Foreign Policy Analysis, 16*(2), 163–180.

Petlina, A., & Koráb, V. (2015). Family business in the Czech Republic: Actual situation. *Trends Economics and Management, 9*(23), 32–42.

Pettersson, K., Ahl, H., Berglund, K., & Tillmar, M. (2017). In the name of women? Feminist readings of policies for women's entrepreneurship in Scandinavia. *Scandinavian Journal of Management, 33*(1), 50–63.

Pidduck, R. J., & Clark, D. R. (2021). Transitional entrepreneurship: Elevating research into marginalized entrepreneurs. *Journal of Small Business Management*, 1–16. Retrieved from: https://doi.org/10.1080/00472778.2021.1928149

Pospíšilová (Dlouhá), M. (2018). Partnery v podniku, domácnosti i životě (Partners in business, home and life), Doctoral dissertation. Prague: Charles University. Retrieved from: https://dspace.cuni.cz/handle/20.500.11956/96093?locale-attribute =en

Rafi, T. (2020) Why women entrepreneurs are critical to economic growth. Forbes Business Council (18 May). Retrieved from: https://www.forbes.com/sites/ forbesbusinesscouncil/2020/05/18/why-women-entrepreneurs-are-critical-to -economic-growth/?sh=3e62289a4523

Raghubanshi, G., Venugopal, S., & Saini, G. K. (2021). Fostering inclusive social innovation in subsistence marketplaces through community-level alliances: An institutional work perspective. *Industrial Marketing Management, 97*, 21–34.

Rankin, K. N. (2002). Social capital, microfinance, and the politics of development. *Feminist Economics, 8*(1), 1–24.

Reichborn-Kjennerud, K., & Svare, H. (2014). Entrepreneurial growth strategies: The female touch. *International Journal of Gender and Entrepreneurship, 6*(2), 181–199.

Ribeir-Soriano, D. (2017). Small business and entrepreneurship: Their role in economic and social development. *Entrepreneurship & Regional Development, 29*, 1–3. doi:10 .1080/08985626.2016.1255438

Ritchie, H. A. (2016). Unwrapping institutional change in fragile settings: Women entrepreneurs driving institutional pathways in Afghanistan. *World Development, 83*, 39–53.

Robb, A. M. (2002). Entrepreneurial performance by women and minorities: The case of new firms. *Journal of Developmental Entrepreneurship, 7*(4), 383–397.

Romero, M., & Valdez, Z. (2016). Introduction to the special issue: Intersectionality and entrepreneurship. *Ethnic and Racial Studies, 39*(9), 1553–1565.

Roth, M. G., & Morris, R. (2020). Here I come to save the day? Reassessing the efficacy of small business development centers in the internet era. *Journal of Entrepreneurship and Public Policy, 9*(3), 319–328.

SBA. (2019). U.S. Small Business Association. Women-owned businesses are important to the U.S. economy (18 March). Retrieved from: https://content.govdelivery .com/accounts/USSBA/bulletins/237a0de

SBA. (2021). Press release: $2.7 million for women's business center resiliency and recovery demonstration grant (17 May). Retrieved from: https://www.sba .gov/article/2021/may/17/27-million-womens-business-center-resiliency-recovery -demonstration-grant

SBA COVID-19. (n.d.). COVID-19 relief options. Retrieved on 22 July 2021 from: https://www.sba.gov/funding-programs/loans/covid-19-relief-options

Schallenkamp, K., & Smith, W. L. (2008). Entrepreneurial skills assessment: The perspective of SBDC directors. *International Journal of Management and Enterprise Development, 5*(1), 18–29.

Scott, J. M., & Hussain, J. (2019). Exploring intersectionality issues in entrepreneurial finance: Policy responses and future research directions. *Strategic Change, 28*(1), 37–45.

Scott, W. Richard. (2004). Institutional theory. In G. Ritzer (Ed.), *Encyclopedia of Social Theory* (pp. 408–414). Thousand Oaks, CA: Sage.

Shepherd, M. (2020) Women-owned businesses: Statistics and overview owned by US women. Retrieved from: https://www.fundera.com/resources/women -owned-business-statistics#:~:text=trillion%20a%20year.-,40%25%20of%20US %20businesses%20are%20women%2Downed.,businesses%20every%20day %20last%20year

Shepherd-Banigan, M., & Bell, J. F. (2014). Paid leave benefits among a national sample of working mothers with infants in the United States. *Maternal and Child Health Journal 18*(1), 286–295.

Shifflett, S. (2020). Hundreds of companies that got stimulus aid have failed (17 November). *The Wall Street Journal.* Retrieved from: https://www.wsj.com/articles/ hundreds-of-companies-that-got-stimulus-aid-have-failed-11605609180

Slovo 21. (2014). Výzkum o postavení romských žen v České Republice (Research on the position of Roma women in the Czech Republic). Prague: Slovo 21.

Smallbone, D., & Welter, F. (2001). The distinctiveness of entrepreneurship in transition economies. *Small Business Economies, 16*(2), 249–262.

Snell, K. (2021). Democrats outline 'care infrastructure' plan, with paid leave and child care. Retrieved from: https://www.npr.org/2021/04/27/991061868/democrats -outline-care-infrastructure-plan-with-paid-leave-and-child-care

Stoyanov, S., & Stoyanova, V. (2021). Learning how to learn and then doing it all over again: The evolving learning modes of migrant entrepreneurs. *International Small Business Journal*, 02662426211016449.

Szerb, L., & Trumbull, W. N. (2014). The development of entrepreneurship in the European transition countries: Is transition complete? *Strategic Change, 23*, 63–80. https://doi.org/10.1002/jsc

Thomas, K., Davis, J. F. Wilson, J., & Sobande, F. (2020). Repetition or reckoning: Confronting racism and racial dynamics in 2020. *Journal of Marketing Management, 36*(13–14), 1153–1168, doi:10.1080/0267257X.2020.1850077

Tlaiss, H. (2018). Gendered expectations and ideologies of patriarchy: Contextualizing Arab women's entrepreneurial leadership. In *Contextual Embeddedness of Women's Entrepreneurship* (pp. 33–45). Routledge.

Topimin, S., Brindley, C., & Foster, C. (2018). Women's business survival and the institutionalization of entrepreneurial support in the Malaysian handicraft industry. In *Contextual Embeddedness of Women's Entrepreneurship* (pp. 206–218). Routledge.

Treanor, L., & Henry, C. (2010). Influences on women's entrepreneurship in Ireland and the Czech Republic. In *Women Entrepreneurs and the Global Environment for Growth. A Research Perspective* (pp. 73–95). Cheltenham, UK and Northampton, MA, USA: Edward Elgar.

Úřad vlády ČR. (2019). Zpráva o stavu romské menšiny v České republice za rok 2019 (Report on the situation of Roma minority in the Czech Republic in 2019). Retrieved from: https://www.vlada.cz/assets/ppov/zalezitosti-romske-komunity/aktuality/ Zprava-o-stavu-romske-mensiny-2019.pdf (accessed on 14 July 2021).

U.S. Census Bureau. (2019a). Quick facts. Retrieved from:_https://www.census.gov/ quickfacts/fact/table/US/PST045219

U.S. Census Bureau. (2019b). Quick facts Maricopa County Arizona. Retrieved from: https://www.census.gov/quickfacts/maricopacountyarizona

US Chamber of Commerce. (2020). Special report on women-owned small businesses during COVID-19. Retrieved from: https://www.uschamber.com/report/special -report-women-owned-small-businesses-during-covid-19

US Treasury. (n.d.). Covid-19 economic relief. Retrieved from: https://home.treasury .gov/policy-issues/coronavirus

Valdez, Z. (2015). *Entrepreneurs and the search for the American dream*. New York: Routledge.

Valdez, Z. (2016). Intersectionality, the household economy, and ethnic entrepreneur- ship. *Ethnic and Racial Studies*, *39*(9), 1618–1636.

VanderBrug, J. (2013). The global rise of female entrepreneurs. *Harvard Business Review*, *4*. Retrieved from: https://hbr.org/2013/09/global-rise-of-female -entrepreneurs

Vossenberg, S. (2013). Women entrepreneurship promotion in developing countries: What explains the gender gap in entrepreneurship and how to close it. *Maastricht School of Management Working Paper Series*, *8*, 1–27.

Wang, H., & Yu, H. (2020). Lack of resources, gender blindness, and competitive skill training programs for women: Research on the Chinese Mongolian women's liveli- hood transformation and resource acquisition for re-employment skills. *International Journal of New Developments in Education*, *2*(7), 40–47.

Wang, Q. (2019). Gender, race/ethnicity, and entrepreneurship: Women entrepreneurs in a US south city. *International Journal of Entrepreneurial Behavior & Research*, *25*(6), 1283–1307.

Watkins, K., Ozkazanc-Pan, B., & Motoyama, Y. (2015). Support organizations and remediating the gender gap in entrepreneurial ecosystems: A case study of St. Louis. SSRN Electronic Journal. doi:10.2139/ssrn.2685116. Retrieved from: https://www .researchgate.net/publications/314458205_support_organizations_and-remediating _the_gender_gap_in_entrepreneurial_ecosystems_a_case_study_of_st_louis

Watson, J. 2020. Exposing/correcting SME underperformance myths. *International Journal of Gender and Entrepreneurship*, *12*(1), 77–88.

Waylen, G. (2014). Informal institutions, institutional change and gender equality. *Political Research Quarterly*, *67*(1), 212–223.

Weinerová, R. (2014) Anti-gypsyism in the Czech Republic: Czechs' perception of Roma in cultural stereotypes. *Acta Ethnographica Hungarica*, *59* (1), 211–221.

Welter, F. (2004). The environment for female entrepreneurship in Germany. *Journal of Small Business and Enterprise Development*, *11*(2), 212–221.

Welter, F. (2011). Contextualizing entrepreneurship – conceptual challenges and ways forward. *Entrepreneurship Theory and Practice*, *35*(1), 165–184.

Welter, F., & Baker, T. (2020). Moving contexts onto new roads: Clues from other disciplines. *Entrepreneurship Theory and Practice*, *112*(1), 27–38.

Welter, F., & Smallbone, D. (2011). Institutional perspectives on entrepreneurial behavior in challenging environments. *Journal of Small Business Management*, *49*(1), 107–125.

Welter, F., Baker, T., Audretsch, D. B., & Gartner, W. B. (2017). Everyday entrepreneurship – a call for entrepreneurship research to embrace entrepreneurial diversity. *Entrepreneurship Theory and Practice, 41*(3), 311–321.

Weltman, B. (2021). The State of Women-Owned Businesses. (March 16). Retrieved from: https://bigideasforsmallbusiness.com/the-state-of-women-owned-businesses/

Williams, C. C., & Kedir, A. (2018). Contesting the underperformance thesis of women entrepreneurs: Firm-level evidence from South Africa. *International Journal of Management and Enterprise Development, 17*(1), 21–35.

Willmott, H. (2011). 'Institutional work' for what? Problems and prospects of institutional theory. *Journal of Management Inquiry, 20*(1), 67–72.

World Atlas. (2018). Ethnic groups in the Czech Republic. Retrieved from: https://www.worldatlas.com/articles/ethnic-groups-in-the-czech-republic.html

World Economic Forum. (2021). Global Gender Gap Report 2021. Retrieved from http://www3.weforum.org/docs/WEF_GGGR_2021.pdf

Yousafzai, S., Fayolle, A., Lindgreen, A., Henry, C., Saeed, S., & Sheikh, S. (Eds). (2018). *Women entrepreneurs and the myth of 'underperformance': A new look at women's entrepreneurship research.* Cheltenham: Edward Elgar Publishing.

Yusuf, J. E. W. (2012). Why do nascent entrepreneurs use external assistance programs? *Journal of Entrepreneurship and Public Policy, 1*(2), 166–182.

Zahra, S. A., Wright, M., & Abdelgawad, S. G. (2014). Contextualization and the advancement of entrepreneurship research. *International Small Business Journal, 32*(5), 479–500.

Zahradnicek-Haas, E. (2020). Maternity leave in the Czech Republic. Retrieved from: https://news.expats.cz/parents-kids/maternity-leave-in-the-czech-republic/

Zapalska, A., & Wingrove-Haugland, E. (2018). The business life-cycle and entrepreneurial ecosystem study of women entrepreneurs in the Polish tourism industry. In *Contextual Embeddedness of Women's Entrepreneurship* (pp. 167–179). Routledge.

Zietsma, C., & Lawrence, T. B. (2010). Institutional work in the transformation of an organizational field: The interplay of boundary work and practice work. *Administrative Science Quarterly, 55*(2), 189–221.

7. Barriers to women's entrepreneurship in Poland and institutional support

Ewa Lisowska and Dariusz Leszczyński

INTRODUCTION

Women's entrepreneurship has been an important phenomenon in Poland since the early 1990s (Leszczyński, 2019) when the country began its transformation from state-planning to a market-oriented economy (Leszczyński, 2015). In 1990–2000, women lost their jobs more often than men because of the restructuring or bankruptcy of the largest state-owned enterprises (e.g., the clothing and footwear industry that employed mainly women). In the absence of alternatives in the labour market, many women decided to establish their own businesses (Lisowska, 2008). The position of women in the labour market has not changed significantly since 2000. There is still some discrimination against women, resulting in limited access to certain professions and managerial positions. These factors push women towards self-employment (Lisowska, 2017).

Since Poland's accession to the European Union in 2004, thanks to many support programmes women's opportunities to start their own businesses have increased (Tarnawa et al., 2020; Lisowska, 2004). However, so far, knowledge about women's entrepreneurship in Poland has been insufficient. Accordingly, in this chapter we examine the barriers that hinder the development of Polish women-owned businesses, analyse the literature on institutional support for women entrepreneurs, and then discuss recommendations for advancing women's entrepreneurship in the country based on the theoretical framework developed. To achieve these research objectives, we ask: How can the specific barriers related to women's entrepreneurship in Poland be overcome?

We review the Polish literature (covering the period 1989–2020) to determine the barriers to women's entrepreneurship and group these into four distinct categories. We then conduct a desk research analysis of the literature on institutional support, spanning from 2000 to 2020, to identify the main topics of institutional support for women's entrepreneurship addressed by Polish researchers. Drawing on a discussion of key barriers to women's entrepreneurship and the empirical findings from our desk research analysis, we develop our theoretical framework. This conceptual model is grounded in Scott's (2014) theoretical model which describes the three pillars underpinning contemporary institutions. Finally, we use our theoretical model as a basis for discussing proposed recommendations regarding institutional support for women's entrepreneurship in Poland.

This chapter contributes to the literature on women's entrepreneurship by presenting a classification of barriers that adversely affect the formation and growth of Polish women-owned firms. Moreover, it adds value to the discourse on institutional support for women entrepreneurs based on the Polish experience. We identify and elaborate on seven recommended policy areas of institutional support. These should be addressed by government and its agencies, as well as educational institutions and non-governmental organisations supporting women entrepreneurs. In our discussion, we emphasise the creation of a more gender-sensitive entrepreneurial culture and business environment in Poland to ensure the advancement of women's entrepreneurship. We also identify some relevant recommendations for future research directions based on the topics explored in this chapter.

WOMEN'S ENTREPRENEURSHIP IN POLAND

Poland is a country with a steadily growing number of women entrepreneurs who are an important source of job creation for their families, local communities and economic growth. Self-employment is a viable way for many women to overcome regional or local unemployment (Elam et al., 2019; Kelley et al., 2013). It is often easier for women to start their own small business than to advance to a senior management position in a large firm. Self-employment empowers women to pursue career aspirations and increase their self-esteem. Business ownership also helps them to overcome many sociocultural stereotypes. These concern the perception of the traditional role of women in Polish society which is related to household duties and raising children (Broniszewska and Ślusarczyk, 2017).

Women set up their own businesses due to: the desire to gain financial and personal independence; autonomy in decision-making; earning money from owning a business; the pursuit of career advancement; willingness to continue running the family business; the desire to make a difference in the world; negative experiences with contract employment; lack of local employment opportunities; and long-term unemployed status in the labour market (Tarnawa et al., 2020, pp. 62–63; Balcerzak-Paradowska et al., 2011, pp. 30–32).

In Poland, the entrepreneurship rate (the percentage of entrepreneurs in the total active labour force) for women is one of the highest compared to other

Table 7.1   *Percentage of female and male entrepreneurs in the total*
                      active labour force in the European Union by country

Country	Women	Men
EU–27	11.4	18.5
Austria	9.6	14.6
Belgium	11.0	18.0
Czech Republic	12.6	20.3
Denmark	5.5	11.2
Finland	9.2	17.3
France	9.3	14.5
Germany	7.0	11.9
Greece	26.5	35.8
Hungary	9.5	14.1
Ireland	8.4	19.7
Italy	16.7	26.7
Netherlands	13.7	20.3
Poland	15.9	24.3
Portugal	12.9	20.7
Slovenia	9.9	14.8
Spain	12.1	19.4
Sweden	5.7	13.7

Note: Data presented are for 2020 or the latest available year.
Source: Authors' own elaboration based on OECD (2021a), *Self-employment rate (indicator)*,
https://doi.org/10.1787/fb58715e-en (accessed 29 December 2021).

European Union countries In 2020, it reached 15.9% compared to an EU-27
average rate of only 11.4 % (see Table 7.1).

Women's businesses operate predominantly as sole proprietorships, are
very small in size (in terms of the number of employees) and are active
in the consumer services sector (retail trade, healthcare, education, hospitality, and catering). Women-owned firms use mainly their own financial
resources (retained business profits, personal and/or family savings), show
lower first-year survival rates than male-founded firms and achieve lower
growth rates compared to male-owned firms. They tend to record lower
innovation rates than male-owned firms and show less commitment to internationalisation processes compared to male-owned businesses (Elam et al.,
2019; Balcerzak-Paradowska et al., 2011; Kasprzak, 2008). Nevertheless,
women-owned firms formulate and implement effective business strategies
such as product or service differentiation, improvement of customer service,

and new product or service offerings (Leszczyński, 2016a; Leszczyński, 2016b).

Studies reveal a correlation between a person's age and their propensity to become a business owner (Bosma et al., 2020, p. 17). In Poland, males in almost all age groups (except the 18–24 category) show a higher level of early-stage entrepreneurial activity compared to their female counterparts (Elam et al., 2019, pp. 76–79). Polish women aged 25–34 and 35–44 are much more likely to engage in entrepreneurship than women aged 18–24 (Kelley et al., 2017, p. 27).

Women with university degrees have more options in the labour market, but some may still prefer entrepreneurship as a career choice. Research findings indicate that higher levels of education have a positive effect on entrepreneurial activity rates among both females and males (Kelley et al., 2017, pp. 24–27). However, at all levels of education, Polish men are more likely than women to engage in entrepreneurial activity (Elam et al., 2019, pp. 76–79).

The 2018/2019 Global Entrepreneurship Monitor (GEM) survey results for Poland reveal that the largest number of female-owned firms in 2019 operated in the wholesale and retail trade sector amounting to 39.3% compared to 28.7% for male-owned businesses. The proportion of women in the government, health, education and social services sector was 29.2% compared to 12.1% for men. In the financial, professional, administrative and consumer services sector, the involvement of both genders in entrepreneurship was nearly identical, with a female share of 15.7% compared to 15.8% for males. In contrast, in the manufacturing and transportation sector, only 5.1% of women are economically active compared to 11.3% of men (Elam et al., 2019, pp. 88–91). The largest gender gap in Poland was recorded in the combined agriculture and mining sector; only 10.1% of women were active in this sector, compared to 24.6% of men. A large gender gap was also observed in the information and computer technologies sector, where only 0.6% of females were operating compared to 7.5% of males (Elam et al., 2019, pp. 88–91).

BARRIERS ADVERSELY AFFECTING POLISH WOMEN ENTREPRENEURS

Polish women entrepreneurs experience many challenges, both at the business start-up stage and during its operation (Grzegorzewska-Mischka, 2010). The risks of starting and running a new business may be greater for women than for men (Leszczyński, 2013a). Polish women entrepreneurs not only have to overcome the problems faced by all entrepreneurs (e.g., economic, educational, or institutional), but they also need to confront some additional obstacles that rarely affect men. These barriers are related to country-specific sociocultural factors (Lisowska, 2004). They may result from operating in a traditionally male-dominated business environment (e.g., manufacturing, transportation and warehousing) or relate to sociocultural pressures associated with the roles played by both genders in society (Kurowska, 2013).

Table 7.2 presents the most important barriers identified in the Polish literature that have negatively affected women entrepreneurs (in starting and running their businesses) since 1989. These obstacles fall into four distinct categories: institutional, economic, educational, and sociocultural barriers.

Institutional barriers refer to macroeconomic obstacles embedded in the existing regulatory environment; established structures and systems that have a negative impact on business owners in Poland (Kuźmicki, 2015). Research indicates that it is much more difficult for women in Poland to start and effectively manage a small business compared to women in countries with an established market economy, such as the United States. This is due to the existence of many country-specific institutional barriers (Rumiński, 2017). The main institutional obstacles to women's entrepreneurship in Poland are: overload of administrative regulations, the instability of the law, complexity of the legal system, inefficiency of the courts, and ineffective government support programmes for women (OECD, 2020; Konfederacja Lewiatan, 2014).

Economic barriers are related to factors in the business environment and access to external capital when starting a business. Barriers such as high tax burdens for small firms, very high non-wage labour costs, insufficient start-up capital, limited access to external sources of financing, difficulties in attracting new customers and unfair competition in the market are among those most frequently mentioned (Kryk, 2014; Balcerzak-Paradowska et al., 2011). Most of these obstacles are universal to small firms and they affect all business owners, regardless of gender (Lisowska, 2017; Lisowska, 2004).

Educational barriers refer to the lack of basic business knowledge on how to start, manage and successfully grow a business. They also relate to access to professional training and its high cost to acquire practical small business management skills, especially in terms of human capital management and financial literacy (Leszczyński, 2019; Balcerzak-Paradowska et al., 2011). Other barriers concern difficulty accessing qualified advisors and lack of advisory centres offered by public institutions (Borowska, 2013; Balcerzak-Paradowska et al., 2011). Educational barriers affect women entrepreneurs from small towns and rural areas to the greatest extent, as well as those with lower levels of education (Lisowska, 2004).

Sociocultural barriers are stereotypes prevailing in Polish society, and which are embedded in social norms and cultural values (Lisowska, 2004; Lisowska, 2002). Women entrepreneurs often report that they experience many difficulties in reconciling professional work with family responsibilities. This sociocultural barrier is related to the limited access to institutional forms of childcare in Poland (Lisowska, 2014).

Table 7.2   Most important barriers experienced and reported by women entrepreneurs in Poland

Institutional barriers	Economic barriers	Educational barriers	Sociocultural barriers
Overload of administrative regulations and government "red-tape"	High tax burdens for small firms	Access to business-related knowledge and information (*)	Traditional socialisation process favouring male entrepreneurship (*)
Unclear and frequently changing legislation	Very high non-wage labour costs	High cost of specialised vocational training offered in the market	Lack of self-confidence in women's own strengths, skills and abilities (*)
Lack of flexibility in labour law	Insufficient start-up capital	Limited opportunities to vocational training (*)	Higher risk-aversion (*)
Inefficiency of the courts	Limited access to external sources of financing	Difficult access to qualified advisors (*)	Difficulty reconciling work and family responsibilities (*)
Ineffective government support for small firms	Difficulties in attracting new customers	Lack of advisory centres offered by public institutions (*)	High cost and limited access to childcare services (*)
Lack of long-term government policy for small business development	Unfair competition on the market		Lack of historical tradition of educating women in entrepreneurship (*)
Lack of government support system for women's entrepreneurship	Existence of shadow (underground) economy		Women's strong fear of making radical changes in their lives (*)
Limited access to technological innovation			High levels of stress associated with running one's own business and fear of failure (*)
High costs and complicated procedures to protect intellectual property			Stereotypical disrespect for women's entrepreneurship in society (*)

Institutional barriers	Economic barriers	Educational barriers	Sociocultural barriers
			Low social acceptance of women's entrepreneurship in rural areas and small towns (*)
			Stereotypical attitudes towards women entrepreneurs in male-dominated industries (*)

Note: Asterisks (*) indicate specific barriers identified in the surveyed literature that are more cumbersome for women entrepreneurs than for men entrepreneurs in Poland.

Source: Authors' own elaboration based on Klimek (2020, p. 181); Konfederacja Lewiatan (2020, pp. 20–37); Tarnawa et al. (2020, pp. 98–101); Leszczyński (2019, pp. 92–103); Gano and Łuczka (2017, pp. 108–109); Lisowska (2017, p. 79); Mazur et al. (2017, pp. 15–56); Rumiński (2017, pp. 153–155); Konfederacja Lewiatan (2014, pp. 5–11); Kryk (2014, pp. 91–93); Lisowska (2014, pp. 297–310); Borowska (2013, pp. 156–159); Grant Thornton (2013, pp. 6–17); Balcerzak-Paradowska et al. (2011, pp. 38–42); Mażewska (2010, p. 87); Rollnik-Sadowska (2010, pp. 134–138); Lisowska (2008, pp. 181–183); Lisowska (2004, pp. 57–67); Lisowska (2002, pp. 35–41).

Sociocultural obstacles are also related to the biased perception of women's work as being less important than men's. In a conservative Polish society, it is acceptable for a woman to work or own a business if she does not neglect her family responsibilities (Balcerzak-Paradowska et al., 2011). Consequently, many women, compared to men, often lack self-confidence and belief in their own abilities, as well as entrepreneurial skills (Lisowska, 2004). In addition, many women also show a stronger aversion to risk-taking than men (Leszczyński, 2016b).

INSTITUTIONAL SUPPORT: RECOMMENDATIONS FOR POLAND

Literature Review on Institutional Support

In Poland, there are currently no public policy initiatives and support programmes provided at the national level that specifically address the needs of women entrepreneurs. This is in accordance with the gender-neutral stance adopted by Polish policymakers (OECD, 2021b). Most entrepreneurship policies implemented in Poland are aimed at the general population, and there is still a lack of support programmes tailored to the needs of specific social groups such as self-employed women (OECD, 2020; OECD/EU, 2018). It is, therefore, assumed that women can benefit from the available public policies and support programmes (e.g., Polish Agency of Entrepreneurship Development) targeted at all categories of business owners classified under the umbrella term small and medium-sized enterprises (Tarnawa et al., 2020).

The existing gap in public institutional support for women entrepreneurs is met by several non-governmental organisations which provide tailored seminars and training workshops on practical business skills combined with mentoring, coaching and networking opportunities (Lisowska, 2017; Klimek and Klimek, 2016). International research on the state and progress of entrepreneurship in different countries recommends the implementation of support programmes specifically targeted at women entrepreneurs. This assistance should address areas such as developing entrepreneurial skills, building coaching and mentoring relationships, providing networking opportunities, and offering professional business advice (OECD, 2021b; OECD, 2020).

Since Poland's accession to the European Union in 2004, institutional support for women entrepreneurs has remained one of the main research topics in the literature on women's entrepreneurship (Lubacha-Sember, 2016). However, to date, the scientific literature on this research problem in Poland is sparse in comparison with the existing volume of studies published in mature market economies (OECD, 2021b; Lisowska, 2014).

The latest research report published by the OECD (2021b, pp. 93–94) discussed the design, implementation, scope and effectiveness of entrepreneurship policies targeted at women entrepreneurs, as well as their implications and limitations for the countries studied. In the case of Poland, the report emphasised the lack of policies and support programmes specifically aimed at Polish women business owners.

Another important research report by the OECD (2020, pp. 23–36) was devoted to assessing current and planned entrepreneurship policies and programmes in Poland, targeting specific groups (e.g., women, immigrants, youth, seniors and the unemployed). This study shows that national policies on entrepreneurship are reasonably well-developed, but only a few of the existing support programmes are tailored to the needs of women entrepreneurs. These are usually provided at the regional level by non-governmental organisations or through regional support initiatives in the provinces. The report's recommendations address promoting entrepreneurial role models among Polish women entrepreneurs.

In addition, a small number of important studies conducted locally in Poland have provided useful recommendations for institutional support aimed at the future progress of women's entrepreneurship. For example, Siemieniak and Łuczka (2016, pp. 65–126) discuss the results of their study, which examined the areas and tools used to support women entrepreneurs, and formulated recommendations for policies to foster the development of women's entrepreneurship. The authors classified various programmes and instruments of support into the following categories: advisory and training; financial; institutional; promotional, and sociocultural. Sociocultural and institutional support instruments are particularly relevant for women business owners. In their study, Siemieniak and Łuczka (2016) indicate that the support programmes and instruments offered to women entrepreneurs in Poland are insufficient and poorly adapted to their needs as reported by the respondents. As the authors emphasise, these needs vary according to the age of the entrepreneur and should be considered in the support planning process.

In turn, Balcerzak-Paradowska et al. (2011, pp. 7–17 and 135–141) have produced a highly influential national research report in cooperation with the Polish Agency for Enterprise Development. The main objectives of this publication were to broaden the knowledge on women's entrepreneurship, to formulate important recommendations on support instruments for women and to overcome various barriers that discourage women from owning a business (see Table 7.3).

Table 7.3 summarises the results of our literature review on selected contemporary scholarly works devoted to institutional support for women entrepreneurs, published between 2002 and 2021. The most frequently addressed policy areas were: developing tailored support programmes for women;

building entrepreneurial skills and competences; providing career support through mentoring and coaching relationships; promoting female role models and networking opportunities; providing access to finance; reducing institutional, economic, educational and sociocultural barriers; promoting work-life balance; providing access to social protection benefits, and overcoming gender role stereotypes in the society.

The data presented in Table 7.3 indicate that comprehensive support policies and programmes dedicated to the specific needs of women are necessary to ensure the progress of women's entrepreneurship in Poland.

Methodology

To conduct our desk research analysis on institutional support for Polish women entrepreneurs, we used the Google Scholar database, widely recognised in the scientific community as a useful resource of scholarly literature and bibliometric data (Halevi et al., 2017). Data on published works were extracted from the Google Scholar database by means of "Harzing's Publish or Perish" © software (Harzing, 2007). The selected search terms contained a combination of two or more words in Polish, such as "barriers", "success factors", "entrepreneurship", "female entrepreneurship", "women's entrepreneurship" and "women". They were used as keywords to identify and select relevant literature on the topic.

Part one of the bibliographic search took place between January and April 2019, while part two took place between March and July 2021. The research process adopted resulted in a total of 812 bibliographic data on relevant scholarly works published mainly in Polish, but in some cases also in English, between 2000 and 2020.

The final selection of documents for review and analysis was made using the following inclusion criteria: (a) scientific works published between 2000 and 2016 in peer-reviewed journals (or other scholarly publications) with an h-index (Hirsch index) citation count metric of $>=10$; (b) scientific works published between 2017 and 2020 in peer-reviewed journals (or other scholarly publications) included in the review, regardless of their h-index citation count metric; (c) written in Polish or English; and (d) relevance of the published work to the topic under investigation. Publications considered for selection, review and data analysis included: scientific articles, books, book chapters and reports.

To minimise subjective bias in the document review process, we followed the guidelines of the PRISMA method (Cardella et al., 2020), adapted to Polish scholarly literature, in terms of: identifying bibliometric records in the database, screening selected records, assessing the abstract or introduction section

Table 7.3   *Summary of research results from selected publications on institutional support for women entrepreneurs in Poland for the period 2002–2021*

Author(s)/ organisation(s)	Year	Policy area of institutional support addressed
OECD	2021b	Building entrepreneurship skills
		Developing mentoring relationships
		Creating networking opportunities
OECD	2020	Providing tailored support at national, regional and local levels
		Organising training for trainers and support providers
		Improving the quality of entrepreneurship training offers
		Promoting entrepreneurship role models to address gender stereotypes
		Creating strong links between support offers to meet women's needs
		Developing entrepreneurship skills by training, coaching and mentoring
		Providing business advisory services
		Facilitating access to finance (e.g., grants, loan guarantees, microfinance)
		Developing financial instruments (e.g., crowdfunding, risk capital)
		Promoting entrepreneurship culture among women in society
		Fostering role models and networking initiatives
		Support for compliance with administrative and tax legislation
		Providing access to childcare facilities and social protection benefits
OECD/EU	2019	Developing an entrepreneurial culture among women in society
		Facilitating access to finance by creating networks of business angels
		Building a sustainable private investment base for women
		Fostering financial literacy through training and mentoring
		Accessing finance by community building, matchmaking or networking
Halabisky	2018	Promoting a positive attitude through role models and ambassadors
		Developing entrepreneurial skills by training courses and mentoring
		Facilitating access to finance using financial literacy
		Facilitating access to finance through financing instruments
		Building entrepreneurial networks

Author(s)/ organisation(s)	Year	Policy area of institutional support addressed
		Ensuring linkages to mainstream infrastructures
		Promoting work-life balance and access to social protection
Lisowska	2014	Creating working environment to support work-life balance
		Building positive social attitudes for women's entrepreneurship
		Overcoming gender role stereotypes in society
		Developing institutional forms of childcare services
Balcerzak-Paradowska et al.	2011	Reducing administrative and bureaucratic institutional barriers
		Limiting the external finance barriers
		Developing entrepreneurial skills and competences
		Providing tailored career support through coaching and mentoring
		Creating entrepreneurial networks
		Developing positive attitudes for women's entrepreneurship
		Promoting women's entrepreneurship through personalised learning paths
		Fostering work-life balance through social protection benefits
		Creating social programmes to promote family-friendly employment
		Developing childcare services (e.g., nurseries and kindergartens)
		Improving the level and quality of caring at childcare institutions
		Making childcare facilities more flexible for women
		Promoting greater involvement of fathers in childcare
		Creating incentives to support women in becoming business owners
		Overcoming gender role stereotypes in society
Lisowska	2002	Creating favourable environment for women's entrepreneurship
		Developing tailored support programmes for women
		Overcoming economic, educational and sociocultural barriers
		Eliminating gender role stereotypes in society

Source: Authors' own elaboration based on OECD (2021b, pp. 9–12 and 35–164); OECD (2020, pp. 23–36); OECD/EU (2019, pp. 301–302); Halabisky (2018, pp. 3–5 and 16–28); Lisowska (2014, pp. 297–310); Balcerzak-Paradowska et al. (2011, pp. 135–141); and Lisowska (2002, pp. 23–43).

of the scholarly publication for eligibility, and inclusion of published work in the analysis of qualitative data.

In the final stage of document review and selection process, a total of 37 publications from the Polish scientific literature on the topic under investigation, published in 2000–2020, were identified and included in our analysis.

Summary of Results from Desk Research Analysis

Table 7.4 shows the topics of institutional support for women's entrepreneurship addressed in the 37 selected research publications (see Table 7.5 in the Appendix), the occurrence of each topic of institutional support in the analysed publications, and the total number of citations found in research publications addressing the topic.

It appears that the researchers addressed a wide range of topics concerning the provision of assistance to women entrepreneurs aimed at reducing existing barriers to setting up and running a business. The most frequently discussed topics of institutional support for women entrepreneurs in the Polish literature during the period 2000–2020 were: business and management skills, national and EU support programmes, work-life balance and gender stereotypes and biases. Business incubators and business ambassador programmes were the least addressed themes of institutional support for women business owners by Polish researchers.

Theoretical Framework of Institutional Support

Institutions have a strong influence on the creation and growth of new firms in a country's ecosystem (Vekić and Borocki, 2017). According to Scott (2014, pp. 56–59), institutions are socioeconomic entities that "provide stability and meaning to social life" by incorporating "regulative, normative, and cultural-cognitive elements" which accompany interrelated activities and key resources (both material and human). Institutions enforce constraints by setting "legal, moral, and cultural boundaries" by determining what is commonly perceived as acceptable and unacceptable conduct. However, they also provide incentives, guidance and resources for taking action, and convey prohibitions and constraints for economic actors. In Scott's view (2005, pp. 408–414), institutional theory should be regarded as a family of approaches or a set of theories, rather than a single, unified system of assumptions and propositions. Institutional theory examines how such institutions and systems are created, how they are disseminated, and what role they play in giving stability and relevance to various social behaviours.

Scott (2014, pp. 59–74) identified regulative, normative and cultural-cognitive systems that comprise the three integral pillars of institutions. Under the first pillar, regulatory aspects constrain and regulate the behaviour of institutions. In contrast, in the second pillar, normative rules, which comprise

Table 7.4   *Main topics of institutional support discussed in the Polish literature during the period 2000–2020*

Topics of institutional support addressed in the selected research publications [a]	Occurrence of the institutional support topic within the examined research publications [b]	Total number of citations of research publications addressing the topic [c]
Business and management skills	32	841
National and EU support programmes	18	399
Work-life balance	18	439
Gender stereotypes and biases	17	473
Access to finance	16	403
Entrepreneurial culture	13	386
Social protection support	13	227
Environment for women's entrepreneurship	11	214
Support by non-profit organisations	7	172
Growth strategies	6	295
Innovation	6	259
Entrepreneurial networks	5	255
Female role models	4	54
Reform of education system	4	132
Technical infrastructure	4	60
Business ambassador programmes	3	45
Business incubators	1	29
Totals	**178**	**4,683**

Notes: (a) The 37 selected research publications included in the analysis consist of books (10), book chapters (1), reports (6) and papers (20). (b) The occurrence of each topic is calculated only once for each research publication, if applicable. (c) The total number of citations for research publications, included in the analysis, was calculated based on data from Google Scholar database using "Harzing's Publish or Perish" © software (Harzing, 2007) as of 12 July 2021.
Source: Own elaboration based on desk research analysis of 37 selected research publications from Polish literature published during the period 2000–2020 (see Table 7.5 in the Appendix). Data were extracted from Google Scholar database using the "Harzing's Publish or Perish" © software (Harzing, 2007).

both values and norms, provide "a prescriptive, evaluative, and obligatory dimension" to social reality. Finally, under the third pillar, emphasis is placed on the cultural and cognitive elements of institutions. These components refer to shared beliefs that form the basis for the meanings people attribute to objects and actions.

In this chapter, we adopted the regulatory approach of Scott's (2014) theoretical model which describes the three pillars of institutions in order to iden-

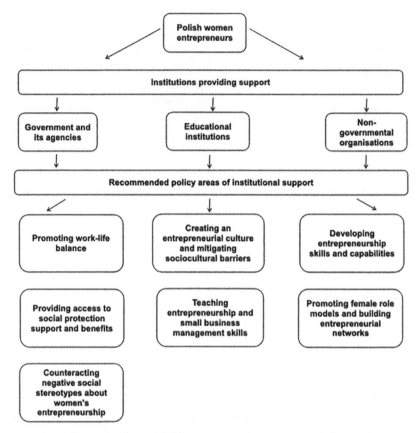

Source: Authors' own elaboration based on Klimek and Klimek (2016, pp. 44–95); Kot et al. (2016, pp. 207–221); Scott (2014, pp. 55–86 and 181–218); Leszczyński (2013b, pp. 73–75); Balcerzak-Paradowska et al. (2011, pp. 38–41 and 135–141); Glinka and Gudkova (2011, pp. 250–302); Rollnik-Sadowska (2010, pp. 118–161); Kupczyk (2009, pp. 68–94); Lemańska-Majdzik (2009, pp. 137–170); Lisowska (2008; pp. 159–193); and Scott (2005, pp. 408–414).

Figure 7.1   *A theoretical framework of institutional support for women entrepreneurs in Poland*

tify the key institutions and their respective roles in providing tailored support for women entrepreneurs in Poland. These include: government, educational institutions and non-governmental organisations (NGOs). Under this theoretical approach, regulatory processes set rules, enforce compliance, and establish reward and punishment systems that influence the behaviour of the identified institutions (Scott, 2014, pp. 59–64). Moreover, the institutional economist

Douglass North (1990) viewed institutions as operating primarily on the basis of the regulatory pillar.

Drawing on the above discussion of key barriers to women's entrepreneurship and the empirical findings from our analysis of the Polish literature (covering the period 2000–2020), we identified seven key areas of institutional support for women entrepreneurs in Poland. These are illustrated in our theoretical framework in Figure 7.1.

The theoretical framework presented in Figure 7.1 lists three key institutions and illustrates their role in providing tailored support for women entrepreneurs in Poland. These include: government and its agencies, public and private educational institutions (at secondary and tertiary levels), and non-governmental organisations supporting women entrepreneurs. In the process of selecting the thematic areas of institutional support, we focused on the sociocultural and educational barriers of our classification (see Table 7.2). These obstacles have a predominantly negative impact on Polish women and are particularly pronounced in the decision-making phase of starting their own firms (Lisowska, 2017; Lisowska, 2002).

The identified institutional support policy areas were assigned to one of three institutions based on their role in the provision of tailored support for women entrepreneurs in Poland. For example, in the case of educational institutions, we emphasised the need to build an entrepreneurial culture among women and to introduce educational programmes designed for women that focus on teaching skills and competences related to entrepreneurship and small business management.

RECOMMENDATIONS FOR POLAND

Government and its agencies at national, regional and local levels should support Polish women entrepreneurs in the areas of promoting work-life balance, providing access to social protection support and benefits and counteracting negative social stereotypes about women's entrepreneurship.

The term work-life balance refers to maintaining a proper balance between work and a person's lifestyle (Agarwal and Lenka, 2015). The need for entrepreneurial women to achieve work-life balance is widely recognised in the literature as it significantly affects their personal and organisational performance (Bird, 2006). Work and family are very important aspects of life for both self-employed women and women employers. For this reason, women entrepreneurs prefer to run their businesses directly from home to properly manage their professional and personal lifestyle (Agarwal and Lenka, 2015).

The ability of Polish women to deal with work-family conflict is a key factor in the development of women's entrepreneurship in the country (Siemieniak and Rembiasz, 2018). Many Polish women entrepreneurs report difficulties in reconciling family and professional responsibilities due to limited access to childcare facilities. These difficulties become more apparent when they are responsible for managing their employees (Lisowska, 2017).

Proposed actions include:

- introducing legislation that enables the provision of financial support and tax benefits to avail of the help of others (e.g., nannies, housekeepers);
- developing affordable nurseries and kindergartens throughout the country;
- promoting a partnership approach within the family.

Workplace policies in European countries have been and continue to be almost entirely concentrated on women as workers (Gatewood et al., 2015). Today, therefore, in most EU Member States, women entrepreneurs have limited access to social protection compared to women with full-time contractual employment (Halabisky, 2018). More recently, policymakers have begun to recognise that social protection policies should be developed to include self-employed and entrepreneurial women who are also employers (Kossek et al., 2010).

In Poland, the government should take more targeted action to ensure that existing family, social and tax policies do not create economic disincentives for women to participate in the labour market in general and in entrepreneurship specifically (Balcerzak-Paradowska et al., 2011). A key starting point for developing social protection policies targeting women entrepreneurs is to examine how women's professional work and their private lives are interrelated, as well as integrated (Kossek et al., 2010). A significant challenge for Polish women entrepreneurs in terms of social protection support is the limited access to childcare facilities (Suwada, 2020).

In recent years, the government in Poland has taken some measures to promote social protection. The most prominent of these are: a 2011 law that enabled greater freedom to open new nurseries and children's clubs; a 2015 regulation that helps to reduce the cost of pre-school education for parents and guardians; a provision in the 2016 tax law that permits tax refunds for childcare expenses; and the launch in 2011 of the "Maluch+" ("Toddler+") programme supporting the development of childcare institutions for children up to the age of three years such as nurseries, children's clubs and day cares (OECD, 2020, pp. 31–32).

The existing social protection measures represent a positive step forward. However, there is still much to be done to improve support for women to significantly increase their involvement in entrepreneurship. For example, more tax breaks could be provided specifically for women entrepreneurs with children, since existing tax laws overwhelmingly benefit women employees

(Balcerzak-Paradowska et al., 2011). Poland still lacks family and social security policies enabling families to take proper care of their children (Suwada, 2020).

Proposed actions include:

- introducing integrated social protection support policies targeted directly at both self-employed women and women employers (Halabisky, 2018);
- amending the legislation on family, social protection and taxation to make it more accessible to women entrepreneurs (OECD, 2020);
- making childcare and educational institutions more flexible (e.g., opening and closing hours, age of admission).

Gender stereotypes and prejudices are regarded as products of adaptation processes that simplify human understanding of the complex nature of the real world which, in turn, enable them to dedicate more time and cognitive resources to perform other tasks in society (Vescio and Weaver, 2013). They pose a serious impediment to the achievement of gender equality and contribute to the phenomenon of gender discrimination in society. Gender stereotypes can hinder the development of the intrinsic talents and capacities of girls and boys, as well as women and men, and their potential educational, personal and career opportunities (Council of Europe, 2021).

Although the participation of women in the labour market and in self-employment has increased significantly over the last few decades, negative gender stereotypes still exist (Halabisky, 2018). They can be a major obstacle to women's career development and their aspiration to have their own business as an alternative career path (Hentschel et al., 2019).

The emergence of entrepreneurship as a "masculine" phenomenon is deeply rooted in history and underpinned by many cultural, social and economic processes, and is also grounded in various sociocultural attitudes, beliefs, values and norms (Hamilton, 2013). From this perspective, women's entrepreneurship viewed as an economic activity is characterised by a lower level of legitimacy compared to male business ownership (Ogbor, 2000). Meeting social pressures from family, competitors and community are major barriers for many women to become entrepreneurs (Türko, 2016). These factors negatively affect the market position of women-owned businesses and their ability to access human, social and financial resources in the market (Brush et al., 2004); they also hinder their survival and long-term growth potential (Marlow and Patton, 2005).

In Poland, many women face barriers associated with their gender due to the stereotypical male and female role assumptions when participating in the labour market, either through employment or business ownership (Balcerzak-Paradowska et al., 2011). Sociocultural factors are a particular obstacle for women entrepreneurs living in rural areas and small towns (Gródek-Szostak et al., 2017). For such women, the intention to start one's own business is often effectively hindered by fear of social acceptance in case of failure, lack of confidence in one's own abilities in starting and running a business, as well as the burden of family responsibilities related to childcare and stereotypes of traditional gender roles (Gródek-Szostak et al., 2017; Lisowska, 2008).

Proposed actions include:

- organising national information campaigns to promote women's entrepreneurship using a variety of traditional and social media;
- holding recurrent social events in small towns and rural areas that encourage women's entrepreneurship;
- collaborating with non-governmental organisations and educational institutions to hold public conferences promoting entrepreneurial values, and combating social prejudices against women entrepreneurs.

Public and private educational institutions should support Polish women entrepreneurs in terms of creating an entrepreneurial culture, mitigating sociocultural barriers, as well as teaching entrepreneurial and small business management skills.

The term "culture" is determined by the symbols, rituals, values, beliefs (attitudes or mindset), role models (heros) and expected behaviours that are shared by people from a particular geographical region and that distinguish them from others living in different geographical regions (Hofstede, 2001, pp. 9–11). In turn, the word "entrepreneurial" describes the specific attributes and activities of entrepreneurs in a society that distinguish them from non-entrepreneurs (Wickham, 2006). Consequently, entrepreneurial culture can be understood as a society that exhibits manifestations of the qualities, values, mindset and behaviours attributed to entrepreneurs, which distinguish them from other persons or social groups in that society (Brownson, 2013, pp. 151–152).

The integral components of entrepreneurial culture, such as attitudes towards risk, attitudes towards entrepreneurs, desire to own a business, entrepreneurial mindset and education are important determinants of job creation and wealth (OECD, 2017). Accordingly, the positive impact of entrepreneurial culture is widely regarded as an important factor in explaining differences in economic success between countries (Leff, 1979).

The 2019 National Expert Survey conducted by the Global Entrepreneurship Monitor (Tarnawa et al., 2020, pp. 70–89) suggests that the education system in Poland does not provide sufficient institutional support for the development of entrepreneurial culture and entrepreneurship education. The experts surveyed rated the Polish education system very low regarding teaching entrepreneurship compared to other countries.

Higher education institutions need to develop attitudes and behaviours that encourage entrepreneurship (e.g., coaching and mentoring programmes for women), and offer more practical courses that teach business skills. Educational institutions should also incorporate positive examples and actions into their curricula and courses (in the form of educational programmes) that aim to counter negative stereotypes about women's entrepreneurship.

Entrepreneurship education is one of the main forms of support that results in increased employment and economic growth, thus leading to a reduction in economic and gender inequalities across countries (Sadera et al., 2019). In Poland, entrepreneurship teaching is particularly well developed in large cities, but not as advanced in educational institutions within small towns and rural areas (OECD, 2020).

It is important to introduce business-related subjects such as entrepreneurship, finance, commercial and civil law, innovation management and the use of information and communication technologies into the national education system at secondary level.

Proposed actions include:

- building positive attitudes towards women's entrepreneurship using real-life case studies, computer role-playing games and modern social media;
- offering coaching and mentoring workshops for girls and women on generating business ideas, recognising opportunities and being prepared to assess and take risks;
- providing career guidance for women to pursue studies in entrepreneurship and small business management;
- inviting women entrepreneurs who can serve as role models to give presentations and meet with students.

Non-governmental organisations should support Polish women entrepreneurs in developing entrepreneurship skills and capabilities, promoting female role models and building entrepreneurial networks.

Polish women are a significant, yet largely untapped, human resource (Lisowska, 2017). This economic underutilisation of women's potential is particularly evident in small towns and rural areas, where the lack of practical entrepreneurial skills and competences is a major obstacle for the development of women's entrepreneurship (Gródek-Szostak et al, 2017; Rollnik-Sadowska,

2010). Therefore, women-led non-governmental organisations can have a significant impact on the promotion of entrepreneurship among women living in rural areas and small towns by providing specific training and advisory services close to where they live or work. Local authorities can also play an important role in this regard (Gródek-Szostak et al, 2017).

Successful, high-profile entrepreneurs who serve as "role models" for many young people (who can easily identify with them) can help transform their imagined opportunities or creative ideas into real business scenarios (Radu and Loué, 2008). To change the historically and culturally embedded stereotypical view of entrepreneurship in Poland, more young women should be encouraged to participate in entrepreneurship. Non-governmental organisations could play an important role in this regard (OECD, 2021b; Lisowska, 2017). With the support of regional or local authorities, NGOs could introduce award programmes in which the achievements of successful women entrepreneurs are highlighted and recognised. Award ceremonies are often important public events that are widely covered by traditional media, as well as popular social media. They help create a positive image of women's entrepreneurship in the country.

Currently, few non-governmental organisations in Poland provide comprehensive support for women (e.g., the Foundation for Female Entrepreneurship, established in 2012), including a range of networking opportunities. Moreover, their programmes are mainly located in large cities (OECD, 2020). However, in small towns and rural areas, local and regional support is still needed to encourage more women to become business owners.

Proposed actions include:

- organising awareness campaigns among women about existing support programmes and initiatives offered by non-governmental organisations;
- organising public events and speaking engagements for successful women entrepreneurs serving as role models;
- establishing regional Women's Business Centres to build and develop women entrepreneurs' networks across the country;
- creating a national e-platform for the exchange of business experience, mentoring and networking opportunities.

CONCLUSIONS AND DIRECTIONS FOR FUTURE RESEARCH

In this chapter, we briefly described the characteristics of Polish women entrepreneurs and their firms, examined the key barriers to setting up and growing businesses operated by women in Poland, explored the literature on institutional support for Polish women entrepreneurs and, finally, discussed proposed recommendations for institutional support aimed at developing women's entrepreneurship in the country. Polish women entrepreneurs face many barriers both when starting new businesses and in the course of operating them. Obstacles that negatively affect women entrepreneurs can be classified into four distinct categories. These include institutional, economic, educational and sociocultural barriers. However, in Poland, women experience many specific barriers that their male counterparts do not. These relate to a range of country-specific sociocultural factors (e.g., difficulty in reconciling work and family responsibilities). In addition, some educational barriers (e.g., difficulty accessing qualified advisors) also tend to negatively affect women entrepreneurs to a greater extent than men. This is particularly pronounced among women from small towns and rural areas, as well as women with lower levels of education. To address the key barriers to entrepreneurship experienced by Polish women since 1989, we developed a theoretical framework of institutional support for women entrepreneurs in the context of Poland. This model was constructed with reference to the regulatory pillar of the theoretical model proposed by Scott (2014), used to describe the multifaceted functions of institutions in a contemporary society. This theoretical approach was applied to identify three key institutions and their specific roles in providing tailored support to the specific needs of women entrepreneurs in Poland. These include: the government and its agencies, educational institutions and specific non-governmental organisations that foster women business owners.

Each of the identified institutions was assigned a specific thematic area of institutional support in relation to their function in Polish society. In the process of selecting the seven areas of support, we made reference to the sociocultural and educational obstacles presented in our classification of barriers. These categories of barriers have a negative impact on starting and running a business primarily for Polish women as opposed to men.

The theoretical framework developed served as a basis for us to formulate relevant recommendations for institutional support tailored to the specific needs of women-owned businesses in Poland. In particular, we recommend that the government and its agencies take practical initiatives that promote work-life balance, ensure access to social support and benefits, as well as counteract negative social stereotypes about women's entrepreneurship. In the case of educational institutions, we propose that institutional support be focused mainly on building an entrepreneurial culture for women, mitigating existing sociocultural barriers and teaching entrepreneurial and small business management skills and competencies. Finally, we encourage non-governmental organisations operating in Poland to provide tailored support to women entrepreneurs in developing entrepreneurial skills and capabilities, as well as promoting female role models and building entrepreneurial networks.

To further expand the knowledge base on women's entrepreneurship in Poland, it would be interesting to find out how women entrepreneurs build, maintain and develop social and professional networking relationships. These results could serve as a guide for Polish policymakers and non-governmental organisations in providing more targeted institutional support for women entrepreneurs in this area.

Researchers could undertake studies to identify the required educational programmes that should be introduced in Poland in public and private educational institutions to build and cultivate an entrepreneurial culture among women. Specific issues to be addressed in such studies include: practical education; vocational training; lifelong learning; acquisition of entrepreneurial traits, mindsets and behaviours. Based on such research, the government and its agencies could develop more effective policies and support programmes to promote entrepreneurship among women in the area of entrepreneurial culture development. Over time, after implementation, these policies and programmes targeted at women can be evaluated for their practical effectiveness and revised if necessary.

Finally, future research agendas should focus on examining existing family, social and entrepreneurship policies and programmes in Poland to assess their effectiveness over time. Any gaps or shortcomings in institutional support policy areas should be identified and appropriately addressed by policymakers to ensure the progress of women's entrepreneurship in the country.

REFERENCES

Agarwal, S. and U. Lenka (2015), 'Study on work-life balance of women entrepreneurs – review and research agenda', *Industrial and Commercial Training*, 47 (7), 356–362.

Balcerzak-Paradowska, B., M. Bednarski, D. Głogosz, P. Kusztelak, A. Ruzik-Sierdzińska, J. Mirosław, M. Krawczyk, A. Tarnawa and D. Węcławska (2011), *Women Entrepreneurship in Poland*, Warsaw: Polish Agency for Enterprise Development (PARP), https://en.parp.gov.pl/index.php/component/publications/publication/838

Bird, J. (2006), 'Work-life balance: doing it right and avoiding the pitfalls', *Employment Relations*, 33 (3), 21–30.

Borowska, A. (2013), 'Determinanty i bariery przedsiębiorczości kobiet w Polsce' ('Determinants and barriers to female entrepreneurship in Poland'), *Ekonomia i Zarządzanie*, 3, 152–162.

Bosma, N., S. Hill, A. Ionescu-Somers, D. Kelley, J. Levie and A. Tarnawa (2020), *Global Entrepreneurship Monitor (GEM): 2019/2020 Global Report*, London: The Global Entrepreneurship Research Association (GERA) and London Business School, https://www.gemconsortium.org/report/gem-2019-2020-global-report

Broniszewska, A. and B. Ślusarczyk (2017), 'Cechy przedsiębiorczych kobiet w wybranych krajach: analiza różnic i podobieństw' ('Characteristics of entrepreneurial women in selected countries: an analysis of differences and similarities'), *Przegląd Organizacji*, 10, 34–45.

Brownson, C.D. (2013), 'Fostering entrepreneurial culture: a conceptualization', *European Journal of Business and Management*, 5 (31), 146–154.

Brush, C., N. Carter, E. Gatewood, P. Greene and M. Hart (2004), *Clearing the Hurdles: Women Building High-Growth Businesses*, Upper Saddle River, NJ: Prentice Hall.

Cardella, G.M., B.R. Hernández-Sánchez and J.C. Sánchez-García (2020), 'Women entrepreneurship: a systematic review to outline the boundaries of scientific literature', *Frontiers in Psychology*, 11, Art. 1557, https://doi.org/10.3389/fpsyg.2020 .01557

Council of Europe (2021), 'Combating gender stereotypes and sexism', Brussels: Gender Equality Commission from the Council of Europe, https://www.coe.int/en/ web/genderequality/gender-stereotypes-and-sexism

Elam, A.B., C.G. Brush, P.G. Greene, B. Baumer, M. Dean and R. Heavlow (2019), *Global Entrepreneurship Monitor (GEM): 2018/2019 Women's Entrepreneurship Report*, London: The Global Entrepreneurship Research Association (GERA), Babson College, Smith College and London Business School, https://www .gemconsortium.org/report/gem-20182019-womens-entrepreneurship-report

Gano, E. and T. Łuczka (2017), 'Badanie postaw przedsiębiorczych młodych kobiet' ('Study on entrepreneurial attitudes of young women'), *Organizacja i Zarządzanie*, 75, 99–113.

Gatewood, E., P. Greene and P. Thulin (2015), *Sweden and the United States: Differing Entrepreneurial Conditions Require Different Policies*, Jubilee Publication of the Swedish Entrepreneurship Forum.

Glinka, B. and S. Gudkova (2011), *Przedsiębiorczość (Entrepreneurship)*, Warszawa: Wolters Kluwer Polska Sp. z o.o.

Grant Thornton (2013), *Bariery rozwoju przedsiębiorstw, czyli co najbardziej hamuje wzrost polskich firm (Barriers to Enterprise Development or What Most Hinders the Growth of Polish Companies)*, https://grantthornton.pl/biurokracja-najbardziej -hamuje-rozwoj-polskich-firm/

Gródek-Szostak, Z., A. Szeląg-Sikora and J. Rorat (2017), 'Znaczenie instytucjonalnego systemu wsparcia przedsiębiorczości i samozatrudnienia wśród kobiet na terenach wiejskich (na przykładzie Punktów Konsultacyjnych Krajowego Systemu Usług)' ('The importance of the institutional support system for entrepreneurship and self-employment among rural women (on the example of the National Service Systems Advisory Points)), *Problemy Drobnych Gospodarstw Rolnych*, 1, 17–27.

Grzegorzewska-Mischka, E. (2010), *Współczesne uwarunkowania rozwoju przedsiębiorczości w Polsce (Contemporary Determinants of Entrepreneurship Development in Poland)*, Warszawa: Szkoła Główna Handlowa w Warszawie.

Halabisky, D. (2018), 'Policy brief on women's entrepreneurship', *OECD SME and Entrepreneurship Papers*, 8, Paris: OECD Publishing, https://doi.org/10.1787/ dd2d79e7-en

Halevi, G., H. Moed and J. Bar-Ilan (2017), 'Suitability of Google Scholar as a source of scientific information and as a source of data for scientific evaluation – Review of the literature', *Journal of Informetrics*, 11 (3), 823–834.

Hamilton, E. (2013), *Entrepreneurship across Generations: Narrative, Gender and Learning in Family Business*, Cheltenham: Edward Elgar Publishing.

Harzing, A.W. (2007), 'Publish or Perish' (Computer software), https://harzing.com/ resources/publish-or-perish

Hentschel, T., M.E. Heilman and C.V. Peus (2019), 'The multiple dimensions of gender stereotypes: a current look at men's and women's characterizations of others and themselves', *Frontiers in Psychology*, 10, Art. 11, 1–19, https://doi.org/10.3389/fpsyg.2019.00011

Hofstede, G.H. (2001), *Culture's Consequences: Comparing Values, Behaviours, Institutions, and Organizations Across Nations*, Second edn, Thousand Oaks, CA: Sage Publications Inc.

Kasprzak, R. (2008), 'Mikroprzedsiębiorstwa kobiet: zarządzanie i rozwój' ('Women's micro-enterprises: management and development'), in Lisowska, E. and R. Kasprzak (eds), *Zarządzanie mikroprzedsiębiorstwem: Podręcznik dla przedsiębiorczej kobiety* (*Micro-enterprise Management: A Handbook for the Entrepreneurial Woman*), Warszawa: Szkoła Główna Handlowa w Warszawie, 206–219.

Kelley, D.J., C.G. Brush, P.G. Greene and Y. Litovsky (2013), *Global Entrepreneurship Monitor (GEM): 2012 Women's Report*, London: The Global Entrepreneurship Research Association (GERA), Babson College and London Business School, https://www.gemconsortium.org/report/gem-2012-womens-report

Kelley, D.J., B.S Baumer, C. Brush, P.G. Greene, M. Mahdavi, M. Majbouri, M. Cole, M. Dean and R. Heavlow (2017), *Global Entrepreneurship Monitor (GEM): Women's Entrepreneurship 2016/2017 Report*, London: The Global Entrepreneurship Research Association (GERA), Babson College and Smith College, https://www.gemconsortium.org/report/gem-20162017-womens-entrepreneurship-report

Klimek, J. and S. Klimek (2016), *Przedsiębiorczość bez tajemnic* (*Entrepreneurship without Secrets*), Second edn, Toruń: Wydawnictwo Adam Marszałek.

Klimek, S. (2020), *Przedsiębiorczość kobiet w Polsce i jej wpływ na rozwój gospodarczy kraju* (*Women's Entrepreneurship in Poland and its Impact on National Economic Development*), Warszawa: Difin.

Konfederacja Lewiatan (2014), *Czarna Lista Barier dla Rozwoju Przedsiębiorczości 2014* (*Black List of Barriers to Enterprise Development 2014*), Warszawa: Konfederacja Lewiatan, http://konfederacjalewiatan.pl/legislacja/wydawnictwa/_files/2014_05/clb2014_2_.pdf

Konfederacja Lewiatan (2020), *2020 Raport Roczny Konfederacji Lewiatan (2020 Annual Report of the Polish Confederation Lewiatan)*, Warszawa: Konfederacja Lewiatan, http://konfederacjalewiatan.pl/o_nas/raporty_roczne

Kossek, E., S. Lewis and L.B. Hammer (2010), 'Work–life initiatives and organizational change: overcoming mixed messages to move from the margin to the mainstream', *Human Relations*, 63 (1), 3–19.

Kot, S., N. Meyer and A. Broniszewska (2016), 'A cross-country comparison of the characteristics of Polish and South African woman entrepreneurs', *Economics & Sociology*, 9 (4), 207–221.

Kryk, B. (2014), 'Dobre praktyki w rozwoju przedsiębiorczości kobiet w Polsce' ('Good practices in the development of women's entrepreneurship in Poland'), *Zeszyty Naukowe Uniwersytetu Szczecińskiego, Studia i Prace Wydziału Nauk Ekonomicznych i Zarządzania*, 37 (1), 89–101.

Kupczyk, T. (2009), *Kobiety w zarządzaniu i czynniki ich sukcesów* (*Women in Management and their Success Factors*), Wrocław: Wyższa Szkoła Handlowa.

Kurowska, A. (2013), 'Uwarunkowania przedsiębioczości kobiet w Polsce związane z macierzyństwem' ('Motherhood-related determinants of women's entrepreneurship in Poland'), *Kobieta i Biznes*, 1/4, 5–13.

Kuźmicki, M. (2015), 'Instytucjonalno-systemowe bariery rozwoju przedsiębiorstw gastronomicznych i noclegowych w województwie lubelskim' ('Institutional and systemic barriers to the development of catering and accommodation enterprises in the Lublin Province'), *Annales Universitatis Mariae Curie-Skłodowska, Sectio H, Oeconomia*, 49 (1), 53–61.

Leff, N.H. (1979), 'Entrepreneurship and economic development: the problem revisited', *Journal of Economic Literature*, 17 (1), 46–64.

Lemańska-Majdzik, A. (2009), *Czynniki sukcesu firm powstałych w wyniku samozatrudnienia* (*Success Factors of Self-employed Businesses*), Częstochowa: Wydział Zarządzania Politechniki Częstochowskiej.

Leszczyński, D. (2013a), 'The investigation into motivations, success factors and barriers among women small business owners: an overview of extant literature', *International Journal of Management and Economics*, 39, 108–125.

Leszczyński, D. (2013b), 'Contemporary challenges of the European tertiary education system', *Przedsiębiorstwo Przyszłości*, 17 (4), 72–83.

Leszczyński, D. (2015), 'Emerging varieties of capitalism in transition countries: literature review', *International Journal of Management and Economics*, 48, 101–124.

Leszczyński, D. (2016a), 'Polish women micro-entrepreneurs from the Mazovia Province: pursued goals, adopted business strategy, and firm characteristics', *International Journal of Contemporary Management*, 15 (4), 135–156.

Leszczyński, D. (2016b), 'Exploration of key success factors that influence business performance: the experiences of women micro-entrepreneurs from Mazovia Voivodeship of Poland', *International Journal of Management and Economics*, 51, 63–89.

Leszczyński, D. (2019), *The Investigation into Key Success Factors in Business: The Case of Women Micro-entrepreneurs from the Mazovia Voivodeship*, Unpublished PhD thesis, Warsaw School of Economics (SGH).

Lisowska, E. (2002), 'Women's entrepreneurship: trends, motivations, and barriers', in *Women's Entrepreneurship in Eastern Europe and CIS Countrie*s, *Series: Entrepreneurship and SMEs*, Geneva: United Nations Publication, United Nations Economic Commission for Europe (UNECE), 23–43.

Lisowska, E. (2004), 'Przedsiębiorczość kobiet w Polsce' ('Female entrepreneurship in Poland'), in *Płeć a Możliwości Ekonomiczne w Polsce: Czy Kobiety Straciły na Transformacji?* (*Gender and Economic Opportunities in Poland: Has Transition left Women Behind?*), Warszawa: Bank Światowy, 29205, 47–69.

Lisowska, E. (2008), 'Analiza położenia kobiet na rynku pracy' ('Analysis of women's position on the labour market'), in Lisowska, E. and R. Kasprzak (eds), *Zarządzanie Mikroprzedsiębiorstwem: Podręcznik dla Przedsiębiorczej Kobiety* (*Micro-enterprise Management: A Handbook for the Entrepreneurial Woman*), First edn, Warszawa: Szkoła Główna Handlowa w Warszawie (SGH), Oficyna Wydawnicza, 159–193.

Lisowska, E. (2014), 'Self-employment and motherhood: the case of Poland', in Lewis, K.V., C. Henry, E.J. Gatewood and J. Watson (eds), *Women's Entrepreneurship in the 21st Century: An International Multi-Level Research Analysis*, Cheltenham: Edward Elgar Publishing Limited, 297–310.

Lisowska, E. (2017), 'Samozatrudnienie kobiet' ('Women's self-employment'), in Skrzek-Lubasińska, M. and R. Sobiecki (eds), *Samozatrudnienie Konieczność czy Wybór Przedsiębiorczych?* (*Self-Employment Necessity or Entrepreneurial Choice?*), First edn, Warszawa: Szkoła Główna Handlowa w Warszawie (SGH), Oficyna Wydawnicza, 67–84.

Lubacha-Sember, J. (2016), 'Główne nurty i kierunki badań nad przedsiębiorczością kobiet' ('The main trends and directions of research on women's entrepreneurship'), *Horyzonty Wychowania*, 15 (34), 343–361.

Marlow, S. and D. Patton (2005), 'All credit to men?', *Entrepreneurship, Finance, and Gender*, 29 (6), 717–735.

Mazur, D., M. Wróbel and R. Żydok (2017), *Główne Ryzyka i Bariery Działalności Gospodarczej w Polsce: Perspektywa Mikroprzedsiębiorców i Małych Przedsiębiorstw* (*Main Risks and Barriers to Business Activity in Poland: A Micro and Small Enterprise Perspective*), Warszawa: Fundacja Republikańska.

Mażewska, M. (2010), 'Przedsiębiorczość kobiet w Polsce: motywacje i bariery' ('Female entrepreneurship in Poland: motivations and barriers'), *Zeszyty Naukowe Uniwersytetu Szczecińskiego, Ekonomiczne Problemy Usług*, 47, 83–91.

North, D. (1990), *Institutions, Institutional Change and Economic Performance* (*Political Economy of Institutions and Decisions*), Cambridge: Cambridge University Press.

OECD (2017), *Entrepreneurship at a Glance 2017*, Paris: OECD Publishing, https://doi.org/10.1787/entrepreneur_aag-2017-en

OECD (2020), *Inclusive Entrepreneurship Policies: Country Assessment Notes Poland*, Paris: OECD Publishing, https://www.oecd.org/cfe/smes/Poland-IE-2020.pdf

OECD (2021a), *Self-employment Rate (Indicator)*, https://doi.org/10.1787/fb58715e -en (accessed on 29 December 2021).

OECD (2021b), *Entrepreneurship Policies through a Gender Lens*, OECD Studies on SMEs and Entrepreneurship, Paris: OECD Publishing, https://doi.org/10.1787/71c8f9c9-en

OECD/EU (2018), *Inclusive Entrepreneurship Policies: Country Assessment Notes Poland*, Paris: OECD Publishing, https://www.oecd.org/cfe/smes/POLAND -Country-Note-2018.pdf

OECD/EU (2019), *The Missing Entrepreneurs 2019: Policies for Inclusive Entrepreneurship*, Paris: OECD Publishing, https://doi.org/10.1787/3ed84801-en

Ogbor, J. (2000), 'Mythicizing and reification in entrepreneurial discourse: ideology critique of entrepreneurial studies', *Journal of Management Studies*, 37 (5), 605–635.

Radu, M. and C. Loué (2008), 'Motivational impact of role models as moderated by "ideal" vs "ought self-guides" identifications', *Journal of Enterprising Culture*, 16 (4), 441–465.

Rollnik-Sadowska, E. (2010), *Przedsiębiorczość kobiet w Polsce* (*Women's Entrepreneurship in Poland*), Warszawa: Diffin S.A.

Rumiński, R. (2017), 'The economic outlook for entrepreneurial women and women-owned enterprises in the U.S. and Poland', *Europa Regionum*, 32 (3), 147–157.

Sadera, J.M., D.A.S. Macaspac and D. Cababaro Bueno (2019), 'Entrepreneurial skills of women in the rural communities', *Institutional Multidisciplinary Research and Development Journal*, 2, 142–148.

Scott, W.R. (2005), 'Institutional theory', in Ritzer G. (ed.), *Encyclopedia of Social Theory*, Thousand Oaks, CA: Sage Publications Inc., 408–414.

Scott, W.R. (2014), *Institutions and Organizations: Ideas, Interests, and Identities*, Fourth edn, Thousand Oaks, CA: Sage Publications Inc.

Siemieniak, P. and T. Łuczka (2016), *Przedsiębiorczość kobiet: Wybrane aspekty ekonomiczne i psychokulturiwe* (*Women's Entrepreneurship: Selected Economic and Psychocultural Aspects*), Poznań: Wydawnictwo Politechniki Poznańskiej.

Siemieniak, P. and M. Rembiasz (2018), 'Work life balance w życiu kobiet – obecnych i potencjalnych przedsiębiorców' ('Work-life balance in the lives of women – current and potential entrepreneurs'), *Organizacja i Zarządzanie*, 76, 229–242.

Suwada, K. (2020), 'Strategie organizacji opieki nad dziećmi w społeczeństwie polskim w perspektywie nierówności społecznych' ('Strategies for organising childcare in Polish society in the perspective of social inequality'), *Przegląd Socjologii Jakościowej*, 16 (2), 152–169, https://doi.org/10.18778/1733-8069.16.2.09

Tarnawa, A., P. Zbierowski, J. Orłowska, A. Skowrońska, R. Zakrzewski and M. Nieć (2020), *Raport z badania Global Entrepreneurship Monitor Polska 2020* (*Global Entrepreneurship Monitor Poland 2020 Research Report*), Warszawa: Polska Agencja Rozwoju Przedsiębiorczości (PARP), Uniwersytet Ekonomiczny w Katowicach and Global Entrepreneurship Research Association (GERA), https://www.parp.gov.pl/storage/publications/pdf/Raport-z-badania-GEM-Polska-2020.pdf

Türko, E.S. (2016), 'Can entrepreneurship education reduce stereotypes against women entrepreneurship?', *International Education Studies*, 9 (11), 53–65.

Vekić, A. and J. Borocki (2017), 'The role of institutions in supporting startup companies', Conference paper, XVII International Scientific Conference on Industrial Systems (IS'17), 4–6 October, Serbia: Novi Sad, University of Novi Sad, Faculty of Technical Sciences, Department for Industrial Engineering and Management, 486–491, http://www.iim.ftn.uns.ac.rs/is17

Vescio, T. and K. Weaver (2013), 'Prejudice and stereotyping', in Oxford Bibliographies in Psychology, https://www.oxfordbibliographies.com/view/document/obo-9780199828340/obo-9780199828340-0097.xml

Wickham, P.A. (2006), *Strategic Entrepreneurship*, Fourth edn, Harlow: Financial Times Prentice Hall.

APPENDIX

Table 7.5   *Brief bibliography of the scholarly works used for desk research analysis (presented in Table 7.4) that were published during 2000–2020*

No.	Author(s)	Year	Language	Category	ISBN, ISSN, DOI or website
1	Klimek S.	2020	Polish	Book	978–83–8085–314–0
2	Siemieniak P. & Rembiasz M.	2018	Polish	Paper	10.21008/j.0239–9415.2018.076.17
3	Gołębiowski G. & Russel P.	2017	Polish	Paper	10.21008/j.0239–9415.2017.075.09
4	Lisowska E.	2017	Polish	Book chapter	978–83–8030–192–4
5	Dźwigoł-Barosz M.	2016	Polish	Paper	1641–3466
6	Klimek J. & Klimek S.	2016	Polish	Book	978–83–8019–376–5
7	Kot S. et al.	2016	English	Paper	10.14254/2071–789X.2016/9–4/13
8	Leszczyński D.	2016	English	Paper	10.1515/ijme–2016–0020
9	Bański J.	2015	Polish	Paper	2353–4362
10	Sikora J.	2014	Polish	Paper	10.22004/ag.econ.210299
11	Ślusarczyk B. & Broniszewska A.	2014	English	Paper	2081–7452
12	Zapalska A. & Brozik D.	2014	English	Paper	1727–7051, 1810–5467
13	Borowska A.	2013	Polish	Paper	10.12846/j.em.2013.03.11
14	Haponiuk M.	2013	Polish	Paper	978–83–63826–32–1
15	Krawczyk-Bryłka B.	2013	Polish	Paper	2084–5189
16	Marks-Bielska R. & Babuchowska K.	2013	Polish	Paper	2081–0644
17	Balcerzak-Paradowska B. et al.	2011	Polish & English	Report	978–83–7633–188–1
18	Glinka B. & Gudkova S.	2011	Polish	Book	978–83–264–1278–3
19	Kotlarska-Michalska A.	2011	Polish	Paper	1507–4943
20	Małyszek E.	2011	Polish	Paper	1733–2486
21	Gryszko M.	2010	Polish	Report	https://odpowiedzialnybiznes .pl/publikacje/zarzadzanie -roznorodnoscia-w-polsce/
22	Rollnik-Sadowska E.	2010	Polish	Book	978–83–7641–279–5
23	Kupczyk T.	2009	Polish	Book	978–83–925470–8–2

No.	Author(s)	Year	Language	Category	ISBN, ISSN, DOI or website
24	Lemańska-Majdzik A.	2009	Polish	Book	978–83–61118–13–8
25	Lisowska E.	2009	Polish	Book	978–83–246–1987–0
26	Lisowska E.	2009	Polish	Report	978–83–94783–8–6
27	Sawicka J.	2009	Polish	Report	978–83–94783–8–6
28	Kunasz M.	2008	Polish	Paper	0867–0005
29	Lisowska E. & Kasprzak R. (eds)	2008	Polish	Book	978–83–7378–402–4
30	Łaguna M.	2006	Polish	Paper	0048–5675
31	Otłowska A. et al.	2006	Polish	Book	83–89666–66–9
32	Zapalska A. et al.	2005	English	Paper	1727–7051, 1810–5467
33	Kalinowska-Nawrotek B.	2004	Polish	Paper	0035–9629
34	Lisowska E.	2004	Polish & English	Report	83–88911–02–3
35	Balcerzak-Paradowska B. (ed.) et al.	2003	Polish	Book	83–87890–33–2
36	Budrowska B. et al.	2003	Polish	Report	https://www.isp.org.pl/pl/publikacje/ szklany-sufit-bariery-i-ograniczenia -karier-polskich-kobiet-raport-z-badan -jakosciowych
37	Lisowska E. et al.	2000	Polish & English	Paper	1230–9427

Source: Authors' own elaboration.

8. Beyond COVID-19: women entrepreneurs and e-commerce policy in the Asia-Pacific

Patrice Braun, Naomi Birdthistle and Antoinette Flynn

INTRODUCTION

The beginning of 2020 catapulted the world into an unprecedented health crisis not experienced since World War II, changing the way we live, work and consume goods. The exogenous COVID-19 shock not only severely impacted people's lives, it also dramatically affected entrepreneurial activity and international trade (Kuckerz & Brändle, 2021), and disproportionally impacted female-led micro and small and medium-size enterprises (MSMEs) in service sectors such as hospitality and retail (OECD, 2020a).

As a result of lockdown measures being imposed by governments worldwide, the pandemic has accelerated the use of information and communication technologies (ICT), in particular the use of electronic commerce (e-commerce) through online transactions. E-commerce can assist MSMEs to reach customers across the globe (Fefer, 2020) and is seen as both an enabler and possible mitigator of the negative effects of COVID-19 on international trade (Hayakawa et al., 2021). Zheng et al. (2009) highlight that e-commerce can promote international trade in many ways, such as decreasing transaction costs, enabling trade quality and efficiency, increasing trade and supplying new trade earnings. With the onset of the pandemic, enterprises have been forced to pivot to new business models in a bid to survive and thrive in the 'new normal' online business environment, accentuating the crucial role of e-commerce.

Both e-commerce and international trade provide great opportunities for nascent women entrepreneurs, as well as opportunities for women to grow their firms (Braun, 2010; Manolova et al., 2020). The digital economy also poses challenges for women entrepreneurs who often have fewer digital skills as well as unequal household responsibilities and, hence, have less free time to engage in e-commerce activities (OECD, 2020a). Indeed, the 'new normal' has spotlighted both the digital divide and women's under-representation in e-commerce and international trade (WTO, 2020a).

Opportunities to remain resilient during a crisis depend on the economic and social environment within which women entrepreneurs operate, as well as the government policies and programmes that enable inclusive recovery (Kuckerz & Brändle, 2021; Manolova et al., 2020). Targeted mitigation policies can enhance gender inclusion and women's capabilities (Australian Government Department of Foreign Affairs, 2021), for example in the areas of e-commerce and international trade. While governments around the world have responded to the crisis by adopting relief measures to help alleviate some of the challenges faced by enterprises in combatting the virus, few COVID-19 mitigation policy responses appear to have considered the gender aspects of entrepreneurship (OECD, 2020a).

Entrepreneurship policy support, including e-commerce and international trade support, is crucial for enterprising women in the Pacific region, the geographic focus of this chapter, as local, regional and international trade create the jobs needed to meet employment targets under the 2030 Sustainable Development Goals (SDGs) (Asian Development Bank, 2018). Entrepreneurship is explicitly embedded in two of the United Nations' SDGs – sustainable economic growth[1] and equitable quality education[2] – both driving forces of economic development (Prieger et al., 2016; Van Stel & Storey, 2004). Interestingly, entrepreneurship is not explicitly targeted within the gender equality goal (SDG 5), which focuses on discrimination, sexual violence, unpaid work, leadership, sexual health and legal rights (United Nations, 2020). This lack of focus on entrepreneurship equality appears to be echoed in the absence of a gender lens in crisis mitigation as well as in e-commerce and international trade policy responses to the pandemic (OECD, 2020a).

This chapter investigates whether pandemic mitigation policy responses in the Pacific region have considered gender aspects of entrepreneurship, e-commerce and international trade. The chapter begins by positioning the research in an entrepreneurial ecosystem framework, with a focus on policy support for female entrepreneurship. It then sketches a picture of the impact of COVID-19 on women, and this is followed by a literature review on women entrepreneurs and the digital divide in a pandemic-driven e-commerce environment. The next section describes the status of women entrepreneurs and international trade, dovetailing into an exploration of region-specific COVID mitigation measures, exploring whether such measures assist women entrepreneurs' recovery from the health crisis. The chapter then widens its scope with a summary of two regional trade policies – one focused on the Pacific and one covering the broader Asia-Pacific region – examining how these policy initiatives impact inclusive entrepreneurship and economic recovery. In the final section, the implications, future directions and limitations of this exploratory study are discussed.

POSITIONING THE RESEARCH

The support structure for entrepreneurship, often theorised as the 'entrepreneurial ecosystem', creates the environment for enterprise emergence and growth (Eversole et al., 2019). The definition of an entrepreneurial ecosystem ranges from interactions and interdependences within the value chain (Adner & Kapoor, 2010) to an emphasis on actors, governance and the general enabling environment for entrepreneurial action (Stam, 2015). Mazzarol (2014) described entrepreneurial ecosystems as a conceptual framework designed to foster economic development via entrepreneurship, innovation and small business growth. Isenberg (2011) identified six domains within the entrepreneurial ecosystem: a conducive culture, availability of appropriate finance, quality human capital, markets, enabling policies and leadership, and a range of institutional supports. Government policy is seen as an important pillar required for a strong entrepreneurial ecosystem, performing a helpful role in stimulating enterprise development and regional innovation (Cooke & Leydesdorff, 2006; World Economic Forum, 2013). Stam (2015) has heralded the entrepreneurial ecosystem as a 'new framework', to transition from entrepreneurship policy towards a policy for an entrepreneurial economy, defining the geographic boundaries of an ecosystem as narrow as a city and as broad as a country or region.

Ecosystem policy is contextual and hence embedded in the social, cultural and political institutions of its environment (Davidsson, 2003; Yousafzai et al., 2015). The institutional environment in turn influences entrepreneurial activity and firms' resulting trajectories (Bruton et al., 2010). There is a growing body of literature on how well entrepreneurial ecosystems policies support women-led enterprises (Braun, 2018; Brush et al., 2019; Foss et al., 2019; Huq & Tan, 2014; Orser et al., 2019). While in theory all entrepreneurs benefit equally from resources within the entrepreneurial ecosystem, Brush et al. (2019) suggest that this is not the case. Indeed, research has shown that entrepreneurial ecosystems do not support female entrepreneurs to the extent that they support male entrepreneurs (Brush et al,. 2019; Eversole et al., 2019). Braun et al. (2021) found that Australian ecosystem policies were both inadequate and gender insensitive, under-supporting the female entrepreneurship pipeline. Without paying heed to gender, entrepreneurial ecosystem policies perpetuate the systemic discrimination of women-led enterprises (Ahl, 2006).

Discussing the state of gendered entrepreneurship policy, researchers agree that women's entrepreneurship policies are not sufficiently underpinned by knowledge and a framework that engage and support enterprising women within entrepreneurial ecosystems, making policies both gender-blind and ineffective (Foss et al., 2019; Henry et al., 2017; OECD, 2021; Stam, 2015; Welter & Smallbone, 2011). This chapter builds on Ahl and Nelson's (2014) call to develop entrepreneurship policy that acknowledges that the business landscape is gendered. It also follows Mason and Brown (2014) who advocate for ecosystem interventions to be holistic and consider the entire entrepreneurial environment to achieve inclusive growth. Adopting the entrepreneurial ecosystem as our framework (Stam, 2015), this chapter offers a gender analysis of COVID mitigation e-commerce and international trade policies in entrepreneurial ecosystems in the Pacific region.

COVID-19'S IMPACT ON WOMEN ENTREPRENEURS

Researchers have referred to the COVID-19 pandemic as an extreme exogenous shock to economic actors (Kuckerz & Brändle, 2021; Manolova et al., 2020), which has led governments to take drastic public health measures. In addition to the human suffering caused by COVID-19, the decline in trade, due to lockdowns and other restrictions, has had severe consequences for enterprises and households alike. The World Trade Organization (WTO) estimated that in 2020 trade would fall between 13 and 32 per cent, likely exceeding the trade slump brought on by the 2008–2009 Global Financial Crisis (GFC) (WTO, 2020a). Estimates of a recovery in 2021 were uncertain, with expected outcomes depending largely on the duration of the pandemic and the effectiveness of government policy responses (ILO, 2020). However, by early 2021, global trade was primed for a strong, if uneven, recovery after the pandemic shock because of major government policy interventions (WTO, 2021).

Less than six months into the pandemic, international organisations were unanimously reporting that women were at the centre of the 2020 health, social and economic crisis (ILO, 2020; ITC, 2020; OECD, 2020a; World Economic Forum [WEF], 2020). Not only were women leading the frontline health response, but they were also bearing a disproportionate share of care responsibilities, such as childcare, home schooling and other unpaid household work (OECD, 2021; Seck et al., 2021). Women – many of whom work in the informal economy[3] – faced greater risk of job and income loss, particularly in developing countries (OECD, 2020b). This included workers in key industry sectors such as tourism, accommodation, agriculture and food services (Manolova et al., 2020).

With economies in full or partial lockdown, many self-employed individuals, especially women, could no longer work, losing substantial revenue and the ability to weather the challenges ahead (ITC, 2020; OECD, 2020b). For those businesses that managed to survive, the need to adopt ICT and e-commerce became even more compelling for survival and competitiveness in international trade, exposing the underlying digital divide (Orser et al., 2019). To mitigate the economic damage, economic fora encouraged policymakers to start planning for the aftermath of the pandemic and lay the foundation for a strong, sustained and socially inclusive recovery (WEF, 2020; WTO, 2020a). Academics argued that COVID-19 presented an opportunity for governments to create gender-aware support policies that paid heed to the digital divide and the rapidly changing digital operating environment (OECD, 2020a), issues which are examined more closely in the next two sections.

WOMEN ENTREPRENEURS AND THE DIGITAL DIVIDE

During the past two decades, the rapid development of ICT and e-commerce has precipitated the information and knowledge revolution. The role of ICT in the global economy – not only in terms of optimised production processes, but also in terms of information management, product consumption, distribution and trade – appeared, a priori, to provide significant economic opportunities for women entrepreneurs (Braun, 2010; Orser et al., 2019). However, when it came to accessing digital technologies and the Internet, there proved to be a glaring digital divide, which refers to the gap between individuals, households, businesses and geographic areas at different socio-economic levels with regard to their opportunity to access ICT and their use of the Internet (Castells, 2002; OECD, 2001; Orser et al., 2019).

At the turn of the century, the digital divide was simply about the uneven distribution of access to the Internet, manifesting in exclusion and inequality because of socio-economic and social-cultural norms (Eastin et al., 2015). This kind of digital divide is now referred to as first-level digital divide (Scheerder et al., 2017). With the arrival of high-speed broadband Internet and telephone connectivity, the focus of the digital divide discourse has shifted to include a wider array of digital skills, or second-level digital divide (ibid.).

Disadvantages experienced by women entrepreneurs were not just attributable to a lack of access to technology and infrastructure, but also to a lack of knowledge economy skills, e.g., comprehensive digital and strategic skills to be able to conduct business in the digital economy[4] (Braun, 2010; Van Deursen et al., 2016). This created a clear gendered order in technology, whereby offline bias was carried online, and women became frequently positioned as end users and men as primary innovators and designers (Marlow & McAdam, 2015). The Internet user gender gap in the Asia-Pacific region has remained at 17 per cent, whereas the global gender gap is 12 per cent (Gooty, 2020). The root causes of the ongoing digital divide include lack of access, unaffordability, lack of digital literacy, concerns for online safety, time poverty, inherent gender biases and socio-cultural norms (OECD, 2019).

In the Fourth Industrial Revolution (4IR) – driven by ground-breaking technologies such as Artificial Intelligence, Internet of Things, Blockchain and Virtual Reality – people who will reap the greatest benefits will be those able to adopt and adapt to the digital environment and have the navigation and digital media skills to navigate the online environment (OECD, 2019). This once again left women entrepreneurs at a disadvantage (Gurumurthy et al., 2019).

With life having shifted exponentially onto digital platforms because of COVID-induced closed markets, lockdowns and social distancing (WTO, 2020b), enterprises were forced to pivot their business models to reduce risk and seize new e-commerce opportunities (Manolova et al., 2020; OECD, 2020b). Suggesting women entrepreneurs could pivot their business models to enjoy more opportunities in the digital era, Manolova et al. (2020) failed to question whether women entrepreneurs had access to both the enabling environment and the tools to join the COVID-induced e-commerce boom. Many women-led enterprises were in fact unable to engage in e-commerce and international trade activities as a result of the digital divide (OECD, 2020a).

For women-led MSMEs and informal enterprises in developing countries, business model adaptation proved next to impossible due to the added lack of ICT literacy, stable infrastructure, e-commerce, and e-payment capabilities, both within their enterprises and their entrepreneurial ecosystems (ITC, 2020). In addition, concerns started to emerge around the inequitable treatment of MSMEs on large international trade platforms, which are supposed to reduce costs through shared procurement and economies of scale. E-commerce is often conducted through platforms. The platform economy is, however, not a level playing field, especially for smaller actors – including women entrepreneurs – who experience high costs and low returns (Gurumurthy et al., 2019). While both the digital divide and women's under-representation in international trade, as outlined below, existed prior to COVID-19, the pandemic has exacerbated these challenges.

WOMEN ENTREPRENEURS AND INTERNATIONAL TRADE

The relationship between trade and gender is well-established in the economics and development literatures (Orser et al., 2010). It is similarly well-established that women-led enterprises face considerable constraints that limit their ability to thrive and grow (e.g., Ahl, 2006; Brush, 1992; Brush, 1997; Marlow, 2002).

While women-led enterprises are not inherently less productive, an inherent gender bias obstructs women-led enterprises from equal access to ecosystem resources such as finance and markets, preventing them from reaching their full international potential (Ahl, 2006; Bosse & Porcher, 2012; Fisher et al.,

1993). Only 15 per cent of exporting firms are led by women entrepreneurs, although women make up almost 40 per cent of all MSMEs worldwide (ITC, 2017), making the internationalisation of MSMEs far from gender neutral.

Gender and trade research also points to the role of government and weak entrepreneurial ecosystems in deterring women from internationalising (Gundlach & Sammartino, 2013), whereby access to ecosystem pillars such as finance, human capital and supports, as identified by Isenberg (2011), continues to negatively impact the trade status of women. To date, researchers have found little empirical evidence that contemporary entrepreneurship policies address gender gaps to increase women's participation in the economic mainstream (Henry et al., 2017). Nor do calls for inclusive trade agreements appear to be heeded to achieve the SDG agenda (Akman et al., 2017). The pandemic and related rise in e-commerce have highlighted the under-representation of women entrepreneurs in international trade, and it remains to be seen whether pandemic mitigation policies will result in more inclusive trade practices (WTO, 2020b). The next two sections review selected Australian and New Zealand COVID-19 relief measures as well as international trade policy responses for the Pacific region and beyond.

COVID-19 POLICY RESPONSES IN THE PACIFIC

This section critiques Australia's and New Zealand's domestic COVID-19 policies, as well as their emergency aid to neighbouring Pacific Island Countries (PICs).

Australia's Pandemic Mitigation Response

In Australia, the immediate economic impact of the COVID-19 crisis disproportionately affected women, with female-dominated industries hardest hit (Stott Despoja, 2020). Australian women worried about keeping their jobs, funding their retirement and carrying a heavier load at home, causing an extreme exacerbation of gender differences, with women feeling the compounding economic, physical and emotional tolls of the pandemic (Carson et al., 2020; Tuohy, 2020).

At the Commonwealth level, Australia's fiscal stimulus package, consisting of expenditure and revenue measures worth A$180.9 billion (9.3 per cent of GDP), was put in place through to FY2023–24. Measures included sizable *JobKeeper* wage subsidies, cash flow support to enterprises, investment incentives and targeted measures for affected regions and industries (IMF, 2020a). Other measures included loan guarantees to cover MSMEs' immediate cash-flow needs. State and Territory governments also announced fiscal stimulus packages, including rent and payroll tax relief for businesses (IMF, 2020a).

None of the measures were gender sensitive in nature. Analysts also expressed concern over Australia's delayed 2020–2021 budget, labelling it a 'male toolkit for economic recession' – e.g., funding for male-dominated industries such as construction – and the lack of measures to boost jobs and childcare for women when they needed it most (Stott Despoja, 2020). Government officials insisted the budget was gender neutral and 'every single measure in the budget was available for women' with no acknowledgement of elements that were not included (Tuohy, 2020).

Much less prominent in the media was the Office for Women's *Second Women's Economic Security Package* to support women through COVID-19 (Australian Government Department of the Prime Minister and Cabinet, 2020). Investing A\$231 million over four years (less than 1 per cent of total budget expenditure), the package aimed to assist women already in employment and education, with a focus on innovation and opportunities in STEM and a refocus on aid funding in the Pacific region (Stott Despoja, 2020). None of these measures was in fact new, but rather a relabelling of funding for the existing *Women@Work* programme and 2018 *Boosting Female Founders (BFF)* initiative,[5] a matched funding scheme to support start-up women entrepreneurs (Australian Government Department of the Prime Minister and Cabinet, 2020). However, the combination of pandemic-related care burdens and the bias women entrepreneurs often face raising private investment capital (Australian Government Department of Industry, Innovation and Science, 2018) may well prevent women-led start-ups from taking advantage of this programme. Together with the reintroduction of childcare fees – which were temporarily frozen during the first months of COVID-19 – Australia's budget measures were more likely to put a handbrake on women's participation in the workforce (Kelsey-Sugg & Zajac, 2021) rather than provide key ecosystem supports for enterprising women battling technological, financial and caregiving disadvantages (OECD, 2020a). As such, there was no evidence that Australia's COVID-19 policy responses acknowledged or addressed women's capabilities in the areas of e-commerce and international trade.

New Zealand's Pandemic Mitigation Response

Like other parts of the world, COVID-19 has impacted women's unemployment in New Zealand far more than men's, with women and marginalised Pacific communities hardest hit (WHO, 2020). New Zealand's labour force is highly segregated by industry and gender, with women more likely to work in lower-paid jobs and part-time work; 71.3 per cent of part-time workers in New Zealand are women (New Zealand Government Ministry for Women, 2020). Some 10,000 of the roughly 11,000 people who lost their job due to

COVID-19 were women, highlighting the need to address industrial patriarchy and create opportunities for women who need them most (Morris, 2020).

New Zealand announced an array of fiscal support packages amounting to a total of NZ$58.5 billion (19.5 per cent of GDP) through 2023–24, including wage subsidies for employers severely affected by COVID-19 and a permanent change in business taxes to help cashflow and loans for SMEs employing less than 50 people (IMF, 2020a). The New Zealand Ministry for Women acknowledged that the dangers and impacts of COVID-19 were exacerbated for women and girls, especially for marginalised indigenous (Maori and Pacific) women, already impacted by existing inequalities as well as financial and caring responsibilities for extended family members (New Zealand Government Ministry for Women, 2020). Nonetheless, New Zealand's COVID mitigation measures were not considered gender responsive and, while an array of start-up business programmes was available, no gender-sensitive ecosystem supports were detected (Morris, 2020). As such, there was no evidence that New Zealand's COVID policy responses acknowledged or provided support for women entrepreneurs in the areas of e-commerce and international trade. Earlier in 2020, the New Zealand Treasury refused to analyse the effects of government policy on women, rejecting a proposal by the Minister for Women to apply a gender lens to government spending to ensure fairer outcomes for women and redress economic imbalances (Alves, 2020).

Australia and New Zealand Pandemic Mitigation Responses for PICs

During the first year of the pandemic, Pacific Island countries such as Papua New Guinea (PNG), Vanuatu, Tonga and Fiji were quick to react to prevent the threat of the pandemic reaching their shores (WTO, 2020a). However, PICs fared less well economically (IMF, 2020a). PICs are typically vulnerable regions as they are subject to climate change and cyclones. They depend heavily on tourism (accounting for up to 20–30 per cent of economic activity), which collapsed due to COVID-19 (IMF, 2020b). PICs also experienced severe disruption to international trade, with decreased demand for resources such as gas and oil (ibid.). The pandemic crisis is likely to have long-lasting effects on these island economies, and especially on women, many of whom depend on tourism for income (ILO, 2020). Women often resort to having to make a living as microbusiness owners or informal employees, with formal MSMEs being pushed into informality (ibid.). These enterprises tend to fall between the cracks of relief policy responses as they are unable to rely on economic support measures, and hence are particularly vulnerable to unanticipated economic shocks (ITC, 2020).

Pacific Island Forum Ministers called for debt relief and donor flexibility, announcing an economic recovery taskforce to support affected sectors. As the

PICs are heavily reliant on their near neighbours, support for economic recovery involved foreign aid from both Australia and New Zealand. New Zealand was quick to respond to the COVID-19 crisis and, by March 2020, had pivoted its foreign aid programme towards rapid financial support for 12 Pacific countries, providing medical equipment as well as economic preparedness support for virtually all Pacific economies facing negative GDP growth in 2020 (King, 2020). New Zealand's involvement in the Economic and Social Commission for Asia and the Pacific (ESCAP) programme, a regional United Nations hub focusing on inclusive and sustainable development, was already operational in Fiji and Samoa, mostly in the form of financial assistance (Gooty, 2020).

Australia's COVID-19 'Development Partnerships for Recovery' economic recovery response focused on keeping the PIC region operational by way of uninterrupted trade, logistics and supply chains. The Southeast Asia and Pacific regions have been the engine for regional growth, underpinning Australia's prosperity for many years (Australian Government Department of Foreign Affairs and Trade, 2020a). Given the considerable implications of COVID-interrupted trade flows, Australia espoused it would support policymaking that promoted economic recovery efforts, private sector resilience, open markets and supply chains, improved livelihoods and inclusive growth (ibid.).

Unlike its domestic recovery policy, and without referencing the SDGs, Australia made special mention of its *Investing in Women* programme to respond to the economic impact of the crisis for women, reduce poverty and support women-led MSMEs. It also extolled the importance of regional Free Trade Agreements (FTAs) to build post COVID-19 strategic confidence to deliver new jobs, international trade and investment opportunities (ibid.). However, e-commerce and specific challenges for women entrepreneurs in the rapidly changing e-business environment were not addressed.

The interdependence of the economies in the Pacific region is highlighted by foreign aid responses to the crisis. Given that interdependence, the next section critiques two regional trade policies and examines how these initiatives approach e-commerce and inclusive entrepreneurship and contribute to post-COVID economic recovery.

TRADE POLICIES IN THE PACIFIC

Similar to entrepreneurship policies, regional trade policies have different effects on men and women, even when the trade policy is intended to be gender neutral, because men and women have unequal access to resources within their entrepreneurial ecosystems (Braun, 2018; Foss et al., 2019; Henry et al., 2017; OECD, 2021; Stam, 2015; Welter & Smallbone, 2011). While trade policies often claim to advance SDGs, mainstreaming gender in trade policy requires assessing the extent to which trade policies are gender responsive and foster economic inclusion (Asian Development Bank, 2018).

Table 8.1   Pacific trade agreements

When established	Agreement focus	Points of note	Gender focus
PACER Plus			
Established in 2017 and includes Australia, New Zealand & 12 independent PICs.	FTA focuses on goods, services and investment.	Lowering tariffs and export rights, especially for Australia and New Zealand.	Limited reference to gender and no explicit gender provisions for women-led MSME.
		No crisis planning or e-commerce chapter.	No agency for PIC women.
APEC			
Established in 1989. Members include *Australia*; Brunei; Canada; Chile; China; Indonesia; Japan; Republic of Korea; Malaysia; Mexico; *New Zealand*; *Papua New Guinea*; Peru; The Philippines; Russia; Singapore; Chinese Taipei; Thailand; United States of America; Vietnam.	Aims to create greater prosperity for APEC economies by promoting balanced, inclusive, sustainable, innovative and secure growth by accelerating regional economic integration.	Non-binding forum encouraging regional economic well-being. Policies include disaster resilience and pandemic planning. E-commerce is a major trade pillar. APEC has a cross-border e-commerce facilitation framework.	Awareness of digital divide and under-representation of women in trade. Awareness of impact of digital age on women's economic inclusion, yet no explicit gender and e-commerce focus.

Table 8.1 summarises two FTAs – Pacific Agreement on Closer Economic Relations Plus (Pacer Plus) and the wider Asia-Pacific Economic Cooperation (APEC) initiative. Gender aspects of these policies are discussed in more detail below.

Pacific Agreement on Closer Economic Relations Plus (PACER Plus)

PACER Plus is skewed towards the interests of Australia and New Zealand, despite rhetoric that the agreement was about the sustainable development needs of the Pacific Islands (AFTINET, 2018). PACER Plus is expected to have significant gender implications for PICs, given the importance of services, tourism, agriculture and fisheries, as well as the large share of (informal) MSMEs in their economies (UNCTAD, 2019). Yet PACER Plus contains limited references to gender and trade interlinkages and has no explicit gender provisions. No ex-ante gender impact assessment of the agreement was carried out (ibid.), neither was gender taken into consideration during lengthy negotiations, resulting in Pacific women's voices being entirely absent from this FTA (George et al., 2018).

Australia claims to have e-commerce chapters in 14 of its 16 FTAs (Australian Government Department of Foreign Affairs and Trade, 2020b), yet PACER Plus does not appear on its list. Besides, e-commerce components being addressed in FTAs tend to pertain to issues such as paperless transactions and customs duties on electronic transmissions (ibid.). There are no particular e-commerce provisions for MSMEs, let alone for women-led MSMEs. Nor are FTAs generally accompanied by comprehensive training. Regional development partners have developed some (unrelated) PICs pilot projects assisting MSMEs in the tourism, cocoa and coconut sectors to develop an online presence and train women in the e-commerce of tourism, handicrafts and vegetables (UNCTAD, 2019). Despite Australia advocating to move this FTA forward, there is little indication it will help women entrepreneurs in Pacific Island nations recover from the impact of COVID-19.

Asia-Pacific Economic Cooperation (APEC)

There are approximately 600 million women in the labour force across the APEC region, which includes the Pacific economies of Australia, New Zealand and Papua New Guinea. With 40 per cent of women engaged in the informal economy, the full potential of women's contribution to the region remains untapped (APEC, 2019). APEC economies faced severe economic repercussions from COVID-19, with a disproportionate impact on women. During the pandemic, APEC Trade Ministers called on member economies to put inclusive policy instruments in place to fast-track recovery, vowing to strengthen APEC's digital agenda, including e-commerce and related services (APEC, 2020a). Acknowledging that the digital age has an unprecedented impact on women's economic inclusion and empowerment, APEC is also promoting digital literacy for MSMEs, emphasising building online business skills as critically important for many sectors in APEC economies (Karr et al., 2020).

Inclusive policy calls notwithstanding, COVID-19 has widened gender gaps in economic opportunities across APEC that will not be closed easily. APEC has a long track record of attempting to mainstream gender into its cooperation and trade policy dating back to its 1999 '*Framework for the Integration of Women in APEC*' which called for gender analysis, the collection and use of sex-disaggregated data and accountability in all processes and activities related to gender, trade and investment liberalisation (APEC, 1999). Despite the development of a series of gender integration tools over the past years, an inclusive APEC region remains elusive.

DISCUSSION

While the COVID-19 virus might be gender neutral, its effects have been anything but. Women have been disproportionally affected, not just by the disease itself, but by the circumstances under which they live and work (ILO, 2020). Worldwide, women bear a greater burden of unpaid care, and women's jobs in service sectors have been among the most vulnerable (OECD, 2020a; OECD, 2021). In the Pacific region women have also disproportionately shouldered the burden of domestic work triggered by lockdowns and lost their livelihoods faster than men (Seck et al., 2021).

Both the digital divide and women's under-representation in international trade existed prior to COVID-19, but the pandemic has clearly exacerbated these challenges. There was, however, little indication that crisis mitigation policies and future economic recovery plans were being formulated in an equitable manner to ameliorate these challenges.

Pacific region policy responses, aimed at mitigating the impact of COVID-19, building resilient enterprises and inclusive economies, were unimaginative from a gender perspective and did little to build an inclusive recovery. Australia offered substantial gender-neutral financial support for MSMEs but failed to address the exacerbated circumstances women-led enterprises were experiencing. While women entrepreneurs in New Zealand were recognised as being more disadvantaged by the pandemic, its policy responses fell short of addressing this disadvantage. As such, policymakers in both countries only superficially acknowledged gender disadvantages and failed to enact meaningful supports for women during the COVID-19 pandemic.

Prima facie, foreign aid policies for the PICs appeared more gender sensitive than domestic mitigation policies, reflecting the substantial dependence on regional trade as well as an awareness of the considerable contribution women make to GDP in their respective economies (George et al., 2018). However, for the many Pacific women working outside the formal economy, crisis mitigation measures were irrelevant. Similarly, Pacific trade policy to assist economic recovery efforts and so-called inclusive growth for the region appeared to be a great deal more beneficial for the developed economies than for smaller island nations in the region. Challenges for (women-led) MSMEs in the rapidly changing international trade environment remained unaddressed and did not reflect a genuine commitment to reduce gender inequalities, exemplified by the fact that no effort was made to include women in the PACER Plus negotiation process (George et al., 2018).

In view of the impact of COVID-19, trade policies should ideally promote digital literacy, e-commerce and international trade opportunities for women entrepreneurs. APEC policies were laudatory in that they were both targeted and proactive in applying a gender lens to both the pandemic and the Fourth Industrial Revolution. Policies acknowledged women entrepreneurs' restricted ability to embrace e-commerce and other digital operations in the changed business environment (APEC, 2020c). Despite APEC prioritising digital upskilling programmes for women entrepreneurs, implementation by member states of APEC mitigation and support measures is voluntary and hence is ineffective in addressing persistent gender gaps.

Despite global organisations encouraging policymakers to embed a gender lens in relief policy responses for an inclusive post-COVID recovery (ILO, 2020; OECD, 2020a), there was little evidence that economic relief packages contributed to women entrepreneurs' economic recovery. With entrepreneurship as a driving force for economic development (Prieger et al., 2016; Van Stel & Storey, 2004) and, more importantly, sustainable economic development (Dhahri & Omri, 2018), it was already imperative for the region to improve the inclusiveness of its entrepreneurial ecosystems to meet female employment targets under the UN's SDG agenda (Asian Development Bank, 2018). The health crisis may well have reversed progress on the SDGs in general, and SDGs 4, 5 and 8 in particular. Indeed, pandemic mitigation policies have somewhat counteracted these SDGs by failing to acknowledge women's economic security needs and undervaluing women's economic contribution to the regional economy (United Nations, 2020).

Gender differences in ICT adoption not only reduce access to resources and capabilities for women-led MSMEs, but also weaken their competitive advantage (Benitez-Amado et al., 2010). This has become particularly visible during the pandemic in terms of women's inability to swiftly pivot their business model and embrace e-commerce and international trade. With the pandemic and emerging 4IR technologies dramatically changing the nature of e-commerce and international trade, Riding et al. (2018) provide sound rationale to embrace strategies that augment the entrepreneurial export propensity of women-led MSMEs.

Well before the 2020 pandemic, researchers applying a gender lens to entrepreneurial ecosystems identified gender gaps caused by several interconnected factors ranging from institutional to financial and social factors (Braun, 2018; Brush et al., 2019; Eversole et al., 2019; Foss et al., 2019; Henry et al., 2017; OECD, 2021). Key policy recommendations to close the gender gap include improving all aspects of the business environment, thereby enabling e-commerce and international trade opportunities for women entrepreneurs. Without the right policies, long-standing obstacles that women encountered in the analogue world are likely to grow exponentially in the digital future

(IT for Change, 2019). Policy interventions can help pave the way to greater gender inclusion in the interrelated areas of e-commerce and international trade. Echoing APEC (2020b) and OECD (2019) policy recommendations, gender-responsive policies that focus on the fundamental role of education, training and access to infrastructure and resources will help bridge the gendered digital divide and women's under-representation in international trade. Such policies need to be intentional about benefiting women (ILO, 2020).

Technology and participation in the digital economy are not isolated artefacts within the entrepreneurial ecosystem (Braun, 2018). Rather, women's participation in the digital economy is predicated on an inclusive ecosystem approach (Gurumurthy et al., 2019). Weak ecosystem supports for women entrepreneurs negatively affect their confidence in FTA and e-commerce development, as well as their access to finance and market-related opportunities (ibid.). In designing recovery and trade policies for the 'new normal', policymakers would do well to consider that entrepreneurial ecosystems are indeed gendered, and that this phenomenon has spilled over into systemic 'e-commerce inequality' (Braun, 2018; Marlow & McAdam, 2015). Policies that adopt a holistic approach to access to resources and supports (Mason & Brown, 2014) are pivotal to revitalising female entrepreneurship in a post-COVID economy, whereby policymakers should consider the entire (digital, entrepreneurship, regulatory, trade, finance, training) environment to unlock the potential of women entrepreneurs and achieve a recovery that is truly inclusive.

CONCLUSIONS

This exploratory chapter has made an initial contribution to knowledge pertaining to the impact of COVID-19 on women in the Pacific region and whether pandemic mitigation, economic recovery and trade policies were designed to be inclusive. To that end, the chapter reviewed the state of the digital divide, the under-representation of women entrepreneurs in international trade, and the prospects for women entrepreneurs as participants in the COVID-induced e-commerce boom. The chapter advances the closely intertwined and mutually reinforcing concepts of e-commerce and international trade. The study also advances the discourses on the gendered digital divide and the need for inclusive entrepreneurial ecosystems. Going forward, regions would benefit from policies that recognise and support the interdependent capabilities of digital literacy, e-commerce and international trade, providing opportunities for women entrepreneurs to enter global markets and grow their firms.

Our exploratory study was confined by its choice of region and selection of policies reviewed, a limitation which can be addressed in future research by broadening the scope to include and compare cross-regional pandemic mitigation and trade policies for their impact on women entrepreneurs. Future research might also include a more in-depth look at how levels of access and use of complex digital technologies impact inclusive development, e-commerce and international trade, and what the potentially transformative nature of digital technologies means for entrepreneurial ecosystems. Regardless of the focus of future research, it is clear women's entrepreneurship policy needs to evolve to comprise inclusive resilience measures that mitigate against exogenous shocks and embrace the changing digital landscape.

NOTES

1. From the Sustainable Development Indicator Framework, the objective of SDG 8 is to 'Promote sustained, inclusive and sustainable economic growth, full and productive employment and decent work for all.' The related target is to '8.3 Promote development-oriented policies that support productive activities, decent job creation, entrepreneurship, creativity and innovation, and encourage the formalization and growth of micro-, small- and medium-sized enterprises, including through access to financial services', and the related indicator is '8.3.1 Proportion of informal employment in total employment, by sector and sex' (UNSTATS, 2020).
2. From the Sustainable Development Indicator Framework, the objective of SDG 4 is to 'Ensure inclusive and equitable quality education and promote lifelong learning opportunities for all.' The related target is '4.4 by 2030, substantially increase the number of youth and adults who have relevant skills, including technical and vocational skills, for employment, decent jobs and entrepreneurship', and the related indicator is '4.4.1 Proportion of youth and adults with information and communications technology (ICT) skills, by type of skill' (UNSTATS, 2020).
3. In 2020, over 2 billion workers earned their livelihoods in the informal economy, constituting 90 per cent of total employment in low-income countries, 67 per cent in middle-income countries, and 18 per cent in high-income countries (ILO, 2020).
4. The ICT-enabled economy is often referred to as the digital economy with 'digital entrepreneurship' comprising economic activities that are carried out on online or via mobile platforms (Leung, 2019).
5. Spread over three years (2020–2023), *BFF* is a matched funding investment scheme seeking to stimulate private sector investment into innovative start-ups led by women entrepreneurs to launch, scale and expand into domestic and global markets. Designed to boost the economy by increasing the diversity of start-up founders, the programme especially targets Indigenous, migrant, refugee and disabled women entrepreneurs. The BFF also provides access to expert mentoring and advice for women entrepreneurs (Australian Government Department of Industry, Innovation and Science, 2018).

REFERENCES

Adner, R & Kapoor, R 2010, 'Value creation in innovation ecosystems: How the structure of technological interdependence affects firm performance in new technology generations', Strategic Management Journal, vol.31, pp.306–333.

AFTINET 2018, *PACER Plus,* Australian Fair Trade & Investment Network Ltd, viewed 9 October 2020, http://www.aftinet.org.au/cms/pacific-islands-trade-agreement/pacific-agreement-closer-economic-relations-pacer

Ahl, H 2006, 'Why research on women entrepreneurs needs new direction', Entrepreneurship Theory and Practice, vol.30, no.5, pp.595–621.

Ahl, H & Nelson, T 2014, 'How policy positions women entrepreneurs: A Comparative analysis of state discourse in Sweden and the United States', Journal of Business Venturing, vol.30, pp.273–291.

Akman, S, Berger, A, Dadush et al. 2017, 'Key policy options for the G20 in 2017 to support an open and inclusive trade and investment system'. G20 Insights. T20 Trade and Investment Task Force, viewed 20 July 2021, https://www.cari.org.ar/pdf/02_Trade_Key-policy-options.pdf

Alves, V 2020, 'Women's groups united against Treasury's gender lens decision', NZHearld.co.nz, 4 June, viewed 21 January 2021, https://www.nzherald.co.nz/nz/womens-groups-united-against-treasurys-gender-lens-decision/237GVJEECAOIFDA6Z5GAPD5YVA/

APEC 1999, 'Framework for Integration of Women, 1999', https://www.apec.org/Publications/1999/12/Framework-for-Integration-of-Women-in-APEC-1999

APEC 2019, Policy Partnership for Women and the Economy, Asia-Pacific Economic Cooperation, viewed 9 October 2020, https://www.apec.org/Groups/SOM-Steering-Committee-on-Economic-and-Technical-Cooperation/Working-Groups/Policy-Partnership-on-Women-and-the-Economy.aspx

APEC 2020a, Statement on COVID-19 by APEC Ministers Responsible for Trade. Asia-Pacific Economic Cooperation, viewed 9 October 2020, https://www.apec.org/Meeting-Papers/Sectoral-Ministerial-Meetings/Trade/2020_trade

APEC 2020b, Women and Girls are at the Center of Economic Recovery Efforts. APEC Women and the Economy Forum, Asia-Pacific Economic Cooperation, viewed 9 October 2020, https://www.apec.org/Press/News-Releases/2020/ 1001_WEF

APEC 2020c, Policy Support Unit Policy Brief No. 38. Women, COVID-19 and the Future of Work in APEC, Asia-Pacific Economic Cooperation, viewed 21 June 2021, https://www.apec.org/Publications/2020/12/Women-COVID-19-and-the-Future-of-Work-in-APEC

Asian Development Bank 2018, Embracing the e-commerce revolution in Asia and the Pacific, Asian Development Bank, viewed 1 September 2020, https://www.adb.org/publications/ecommerce-revolution-asia-pacific

Australian Government Department of Foreign Affairs and Trade 2020a, Partnership for Recovery: Australia's COVID-19 Development Response, Australian Government Department of Foreign Affairs and Trade, viewed 6 October 2020, https://www.dfat.gov.au/publications/aid/partnerships-recovery-australias-covid-19-development-response

Australian Government Department of Foreign Affairs and Trade 2020b, Digital Trade & the Digital Economy, Australian Government Department of Foreign Affairs and Trade, viewed 15 October 2020, https://www.dfat.gov.au/trade/services-and-digital

-trade/Pages/e-commerce-and-digital-trade#ecommerce-chapters-in-australias-free
-trade-agreements

Australian Government Department of Foreign Affairs and Trade 2021, 'Australia's
assistance for gender equality: Partnerships for recovery and gender equality',
viewed 7 December 2021, https://www.dfat.gov.au/development/topics/investment
-priorities/gender-equality-empowering-women-girls/gender-equality

Australian Government Department of Industry, Innovation and Science 2018, Boosting
Female Founders Initiative Discussion Paper, Australian Government Department of
Industry, Innovation and Science, viewed 3 June 2020, https://consult.industry.gov
.au/boosting-female-founders-initiative-design-consultation

Australian Government Department of the Prime Minister and Cabinet 2020, Office for
Women. 2020–21 Budget: Supporting Women, Australian Government Department
of the Prime Minister and Cabinet, viewed 6 October 2020, https://ministers.pmc
.gov.au/payne/2020/2020-21-budget-supporting-women

Benitez-Amado, J, Llorens-Montes, F & Perez-Arostegui, M 2010, 'Information
technology enabled intrapreneurship culture and firm performance', Industrial
Management and Data Systems, vol.110, no.4, pp. 550–566.

Bosse, D & Porcher L 2012, 'The second glass ceiling impedes women entrepreneurs', The Journal of Applied Management and Entrepreneurship, vol.17, no.1,
pp. 152–168.

Braun, P 2010, 'A skilling framework for women entrepreneurs in the knowledge
economy', in C Henry & S Marlow (eds), Innovating Women: Contributions to
Technological Advancement. Contemporary Issues in Entrepreneurship Research,
Volume 1, Emerald Group Publishing Limited, London, pp.35–53.

Braun, P 2018, 'Developing gender-responsive trade ecosystems in the Asia-Pacific',
in S Yousafzai, A Lindgreen, S Saeed & C Henry (eds), Contextual Embeddedness
of Women's Entrepreneurship: Going Beyond a Gender Neutral Approach, Taylor
& Francis Publishing, London, pp.91–105.

Braun, P, Birdthistle, N & Flynn, A 2021, 'Australia', in OECD (ed.), Entrepreneurship
Policies Through a Gender Lens. OECD Studies on SMEs and Entrepreneurship,
OECD Publishing, Paris, pp.40–44, DOI: https://doi.org/10.1787/71c8f9c9-en

Brush, C 1992, 'Research on women business owners: Past trends, a new perspective
and future directions', Entrepreneurship Theory and Practice, vol.16, no.4, pp.5–30.

Brush, C 1997, 'Women owned businesses: Obstacles and Opportunities', Journal of
Developmental Entrepreneurship, vol.2, no.1, pp.1–25.

Brush, C, Edelman, L, Manolova T & Welter, F 2019, 'A gendered look at entrepreneurship ecosystems', Small Business Economics, vol.53, pp.393–408, DOI: https://
doi.org/10.1007/s11187-018-9992-9

Bruton, G, Ahlstrom, D & Li H 2010, 'Institutional theory and entrepreneurship: Where
are we now and where do we need to move in the future?', Entrepreneurship Theory
and Practice, vol.34, no.3, pp.421–440.

Carson, A, Ruppanner, L & Ratcliff, S 2020, The worsening of Australian women's
experiences under COVID-19, La Trobe University, viewed 2 August 2020,
https://arts.unimelb.edu.au/the-policy-lab/projects/women-at-work/the-worsening
-of-australian-womens-experiences-under-covid-19

Castells, M 2002, The Internet Galaxy: Reflections on the Internet, Business, and
Society, Oxford University Press, viewed 2 August 2021, DOI: 10.1093/acprof:oso/
9780199255771.001.0001

Cooke, P & Leydesdorff, L 2006, 'Regional development in the knowledge-based economy: The construction of advantage', Journal of Technology Transfer, vol.31, pp.5–15.

Davidsson, P 2003, 'The domain of entrepreneurship research: Some suggestions', in J Katz & D Shepherd (eds), Cognitive Approaches to Entrepreneurship Research, Elsevier/JAI Press, United Kingdom, Oxford, vol.6, pp.315–372.

Dhahri, S & Omri, A 2018, 'Entrepreneurship contribution to the three pillars of sustainable development: What does the evidence really say?', World Development, vol.106, pp.64–77.

Eastin, MS, Cicchirillo, V, Mabry, A 2015, 'Extending the digital divide conversation: Examining the knowledge gap through media expectancies', Journal of Broadcasting and Electronic Media, vol.59, no.3, pp.416–437.

Eversole, R, Birdthistle, N, Walo, M & Godinho, V 2019, 'Towards a typology of supports for enterprising women: A comparison on rural and urban Australian regions', in A Bullough, D Hechavarria, C Brush & L Edelman (eds), Fostering High-Growth Women's Entrepreneurship: Programs, Policies and Practices, chapter 4, Edward Elgar: Cheltenham: UK, pp.52–77.

Fefer, RE 2020, 'International trade and e-commerce', Congressional Research Service, https://crsreports.congress.gov

Fisher, E, Reuber, R & Dyke, L 1993, 'A theoretical overview and extension of research on sex, gender, and entrepreneurship', Journal of Business Venturing, vol.8, no.2, pp.151–168.

Foss, L, Henry, C, Ahl, H & Mikalsen, G 2019, 'Women's entrepreneurship policy research: A 30-year review of the evidence', Small Business Economics, vol.53, no.1, pp.1–21, DOI: 10.1007/s11187-018-9993-8

George, N, Sami, R, Buadromo, V & The Fuji Women's Right Movement 2018, Gender and Free Trade in the Pacific: Cause for Concern? Viewed 30 September 2020, https://www.dfat.gov.au/sites/default/files/MsNicoleGeorgeandtheFijiWomen%27sRightsMovement.pdf

Gooty, S 2020, Fostering an enabling environment for women entrepreneurs in Asia and the Pacific, Expert Group Meeting: Bangkok, 15 September, United Nations ESCAP.

Gundlach, S & Sammartino A 2013, Australia's Underestimated Resource: Women Doing Business Globally. University of Melbourne in conjunction with Women in Global Business.

Gurumurthy, A, Bhartur, D & Chami, N 2019, Launching platform planet. Development in the intelligence economy, IT for Change, viewed 11 September 2020, https://itforchange.net/launching-platform-planet-development-intelligence-economy

Hayakawa, K, Mukunoki, H & Urata, S 2021, 'Can e-commerce mitigate the negative impact of COVID-19 on international trade?' Japanese Economic Review (Oxford, England), 2021-09-29, pp.1–18.

Henry, C, Orser, B, Coleman, C & Foss, L 2017, 'Women's entrepreneurship policy: A 13 nation cross-country comparison', International Journal of Gender and Entrepreneurship, vol.9, no.3, pp.206–228, viewed 20 July 2021, https://doi.org/10.1108/IJGE-07-2017-0036

Huq, A & Tan C 2014, 'Women in Australian fast growth SMEs: How do they approach growth as a deliberate choice?', paper presented at ICSB Conference, Dublin, 14 June.

ILO 2020, 'COVID-19 crisis and the informal economy: Immediate responses and policy challenges', International Labour Organization, viewed 1 September

2020, https://www.ilo.org/wcmsp5/groups/public/@ed_protect/@protrav/@travail/documents/briefingnote/wcms_743623.pdf

IMF 2020a, Policy responses to COVID-19, Policy Tracker, viewed 18 July 2021, https://www.imf.org/en/Topics/imf-and-covid19/ Policy-Responses-to-COVID-19

IMF 2020b, 'Pacific Islands threatened by COVID-19' International Monetary Fund, viewed 7 October 2020, https://www.imf.org/en/News/Articles/2020/05/27/na-05272020-pacific-islands-threatened-by-covid-19

Isenberg, D 2011, The Entrepreneurship Ecosystem Strategy as a New Paradigm for Economic Policy: Principles for Cultivating Entrepreneurship, The Babson Entrepreneurship Ecosystem Project.

ITC 2017, Closing the Small-business and Gender Gap to Make Trade More Inclusive. In WTO & OECD, Aid for Trade at a Glance. OECD Publishing (pp.219–241), viewed 1 September, 2020, https://doi.org/10.1787/aid_glance-2017-11-en

ITC 2020, SME Competitiveness Outlook 2020: COVID-19: The Great Lockdown and its Impact on Small Business. International Trade Centre, Geneva, viewed 1 September 2020, https://www.intracen.org/uploadedFiles/intracenorg/Content/Publications/ITCSMECO2020.pdf

Karr, J, Loh, K & Wirjo, A 2020, Supporting MSMEs' Digitalization Amid COVID-19, Policy Brief No.35, APEC Policy Support Unit.

Kelsey-Sugg, A & Zajac, B 2021, 'Childcare fees are stopping these families from working. Here's what could help', ABC Radio National, viewed 21 March 2021, https://www.abc.net.au/news/2021-03-10/childcare-fees-stopping-parents-working-solutions/13218714

King, J 2020, Pivoting New Zealand's Aid Programme to Respond to Covid-19, Pacific and Development Group at the New Zealand Ministry of Foreign Affairs and Trade, viewed 8 October 2020, https://devpolicy.org/pivoting-new-zealands-aid-programme-to-respond-to-covid-19-20200508-3/

Kuckerz, A & Brändle, L 2021, 'Creative reconstruction: A structured literature review of the early empirical research on the COVID-19 crisis and entrepreneurship', Management Review Quarterly, https://doi.org/10.1007/s11301-021-00221-0

Leung, WF 2019, Digital Entrepreneurship, Gender and Intersectionality, Dynamics of Virtual Work, Palgrave Macmillan.

Manolova, T, Brush, C, Edelman L & Elam, A 2020, 'Pivoting to stay the course: How women entrepreneurs take advantage of opportunities created by the COVID-19 pandemic', International Small Business Journal: Researching Entrepreneurship, vol.38, no.6, pp.481–491.

Marlow, S 2002, 'Women and self-employment: A part of or apart from theoretical construct?' The International Journal of Entrepreneurship and Innovation, vol.3, no.2, pp.83–91.

Marlow, S & McAdam, M 2015, 'Incubation or induction? Gendered identity work in the context of technology business incubation', Entrepreneurship Theory and Practice, vol.39, no.4, pp.791–816.

Mason, C & Brown, R 2014, 'Entrepreneurial ecosystems and growth-oriented entre-preneurship: Final report to OECD', OECD, viewed 17 September 2020, http://www.oecd.org/cfe/leed/Entrepreneurial-ecosystems.pdf

Mazzarol, T 2014, Growing and sustaining entrepreneurial ecosystems: The role of regulation, infrastructure and financing, White Paper WP02-2014, Small Enterprise Association of Australia and New Zealand (SEAANZ).

Morris, L 2020, 'COVID-19 has hit women hardest – so let's take action', The Spin Off, 6 August 2020, viewed 21 January 2021, https://thespinoff.co.nz/business/06 -08-2020/covid-19-has-hit-women-hardest-so-lets-take-action-now/

New Zealand Government Ministry for Women 2020, COVID-19 and Women, Ministry for Women, viewed 15 September 2020, https://women.govt.nz/news/ covid-19-and-women

OECD 2001, Understanding the Digital Divide, OECD Digital Economy Papers, No.49, OECD Publishing, Paris, https://doi.org/10.1787/236405667766

OECD 2019, The role of education and skills in bridging the digital gender divide. Evidence from APEC economies, OECD, viewed 15 September 2020, https://www .oecd.org/sti/education-and-skills-in-bridging-the-digital-gender-divide-evidence -from-apec.pdf

OECD 2020a, OECD-Webinar-Women-Entrepreneurship-Policy-and-COVID-19_ Summary-Report, OECD, viewed 1 September 2020, https://sites.telfer.uottawa.ca/ were/files/2020/06/OECD-Webinar-Women-Entrepreneurship-Policy-and-COVID -19_Summary-Report.pdf

OECD 2020b, Women at the core of the fight against COVID–19 crisis. Tackling coro-navirus (Covid-19) contributing to a global effort, OECD, viewed 1 September 2020, https://www.oecd.org/coronavirus/policy-responses/women-at-the-core-of-the-fight -against-covid-19-crisis-553a8269/

OECD 2021, Entrepreneurship Policies through a Gender Lens, OECD Studies on SMEs and Entrepreneurship, OECD Publishing, Paris, https://doi.org/10.1787/ 71c8f9c9-en

Orser, B, Riding, A & Li, Y 2019, 'Technology adoption and gender-inclusive entrepreneurship education and training', International Journal of Gender and Entrepreneurship, vol.11, no.3, pp. 273–298.

Orser, B, Spence, M, Riding, A & Carrington, C 2010, 'Gender and export propensity', Entrepreneurship Theory and Practice, vol.3, no.5, pp.933–957.

Prieger, J, Bampoky, C, Blanco, L & Liu, A 2016, 'Economic growth and the optimal level of entrepreneurship', World Development, vol.82, pp.95–109.

Riding, A, Orser B & Li, D 2018, Benchmarking Small and Medium Enterprises as Suppliers to the Government of Canada. Inclusion, Innovation and International Trade, Telfer School of Management, University of Ottawa, Ottawa, viewed 20 July 2021, http://sites.telfer.uottawa.ca/were/

Scheerder, A, Van Deursen, A & Van Dijk, J 2017, 'Determinants of internet skills, uses and outcomes. A systematic review of the second- and third-level digital divide', Telematics and Informatics, vol.34, no.8, pp.1607–1624.

Seck, P, Encarnacion, J, Tinonin, C et al. 2021, 'Gendered impacts of COVID-19 in Asia and the Pacific: Early Evidence on Deepening Socio-Economic Inequalities in Paid and Unpaid Work', Feminist Economics, vol.27, no.1–2, pp.117–132.

Stam, E 2015, 'Entrepreneurial ecosystems and regional policy: A sympathetic cri-tique', European Planning Studies, vol.23, no.9, pp.1759–1769.

Stott Despoja, N 2020, 'After the virus: A plan for women', The Saturday Paper, p.5, viewed 2 August 2021, https://www.thesaturdaypaper.com.au/opinion/topic/2020/ 10/17/after-the-virus-plan-women/160285320010564#hrd

Tuohy, W 2020, 'Triple whammy: Budget overlooked women when they needed it most', The Sunday Age, viewed 11 October 2020, https://www.theage.com.au/ national/victoria/triple-whammy-budget-overlooked-women-when-they-needed-it -most-20201009-p563n0.html

UNCTAD 2019, International trade, transparency and gender equality. The case of the Pacific Agreement on Closer Economic Relations (PACER) Plus, United Nations Conference on Trade and Development (UNCTAD), viewed 9 October 2020, https://unctad.org/system/files/official-document/ditc2019d3_en.pdf

United Nations 2020, The Sustainable Development Goals Report 2020, United Nations, viewed 17 January 2021, https://unstats.un.org/sdgs/report/2020/

Van Deursen, A, Helsper, E & Eynon, R 2016, 'Development and validation of the Internet Skills Scale (ISS)', Information Communication Society, vol.19, no.6, pp.804–823.

Van Stel A & Storey D 2004, 'Link between firm birth and job creation: Is there a Upas Tree effect?' Regional Studies, vol.38, pp.893–909.

Welter, F & Smallbone D 2011, 'Institutional perspectives on entrepreneurial behaviour in challenging environments', Journal of Small Business Management, vol.49, no.1, pp.107–125.

WHO 2020, WHO Coronavirus Disease (COVID-19) Dashboard, World Health Organisation, viewed 21 January 2021, https://covid19.who.int/

World Economic Forum 2013, Entrepreneurial Ecosystems around the Globe and Company Growth Dynamics, Report Summary for the Annual Meeting of the New Champions 2013.

World Economic Forum 2020, Our recovery from the coronavirus crisis must have gender empowerment at its heart, World Economic Forum, viewed 21 July 2021, https://www.weforum.org/agenda/2020/05/industries-gender-women-coronavirus-covid19-economic

WTO 2020a, Trade set to plunge as COVID-19 pandemic upends global economy, World Trade Organization, viewed 1 September 2020, https://www.wto.org/english/news_e/pres20_e/pr855_e.htm

WTO 2020b, E-Commerce, trade and the COVIC-19 pandemic, World Trade Organization, viewed 1 September 2020, https://www.wto.org/english/tratop_e/covid19_e/ ecommerce_report_e.pdf

WTO 2021, World trade primed for strong but uneven recovery after COVID 19 pandemic shock – Press/876, World Trade Organization, viewed 24 July 2021, https://www.wto.org/english/news_e/pres21_e/pr876_e.htm

Yousafzai, S, Saeed, S & Muffatto, M 2015, 'Institutional theory and contextual embeddedness of women's entrepreneurial leadership: Evidence from 92 countries', Journal of Small Business Management, vol.53, no.3, pp. 587–604, DOI: 10.1111/jsbm.12179

Zheng Q., Li S., Han Y., Dong J., Yan L. & Qin J. 2009, 'E-commerce and international trade' in Zheng Q. (ed.), Introduction to E-commerce, Springer, Berlin, Heidelberg, https://doi.org/10.1007/978-3-540-49645-8_11

9. Analysis of Ghana's and South Africa's women's entrepreneurship policies

Mavis S. B. Mensah and Evelyn Derera

INTRODUCTION

Women's entrepreneurship accounts for approximately one quarter of the world's entrepreneurial activities and contributes to economic growth and development through employment creation, income generation, poverty alleviation and innovation (Terjesen et al., 2016; World Bank, 2018). A fundamental assumption of most entrepreneurial ecosystems is that all entrepreneurs have equal access to resources, participation, support and opportunities to succeed (Brush et al., 2019). However, this cannot be said of women, as their economic potential is underutilized and is manifest through a global labour force participation rate of 49.5 per cent, compared to 76.2 per cent for men (World Bank, 2018). Moreover, women's participation in entrepreneurship is generally lower than that of men across the globe with a high concentration in traditional and low-income sectors (Bosma et al., 2020).

A rich body of research has established that underutilization of women's potential is an outcome of their subordination in society through, for example, socio-political, normative and structural biases that breed gender inequality and limit life opportunities for women (Ahl & Marlow, 2017; Henry et al., 2017). Studies also show that women entrepreneurs confront additional challenges such as limited access to resources and skills deficits (Bamfo & Asiedu-Appiah, 2012; Derera et al., 2014; Panda, 2018). Women's entrepreneurship policies are required to address these anomalies and to increase women's entrepreneurial activities for optimal benefit (Foss et al., 2019). Such policies are also important in serving as a guide to decision-making, and performance monitoring and evaluation.

Ghana and South Africa are two factor-driven economies in sub-Saharan Africa where women's entrepreneurship has been touted as critical to women's advancement, household welfare and national economic development

(Langevang et al., 2015; Seshie-Nasser & Oduro, 2018). However, the gendered barriers to women's entrepreneurship have hindered women entrepreneurs from venturing into high-growth sectors, and women-led enterprises do not grow in size compared to the enterprises of their male counterparts (Botha, 2006; Overå, 2003; Overå, 2017).

As an example, in Ghana, enterprises solely owned and operated by women are, on average, 67 per cent smaller in size than those owned by men (Seshie-Nasser & Oduro, 2018). This is in spite of the fact that the total early-stage entrepreneurial activity (TEA) rate among women (38 per cent) exceeds that of men (35 per cent) (Herrington & Kelly, 2012) and 72 per cent of business assets are owned by women (Seshie-Nasser & Oduro, 2018), which is partly due to a predominantly matrilineal inheritance system (Overå, 2003). In contrast, for South Africa, the TEA rate for women is 10.2 per cent compared to 11.4 per cent for men, while the established business ownership rate is also lower for women (2.6 per cent) than for men (4.5 per cent) (Bosma et al., 2020).

Although various efforts by governments and development partners to promote women's entrepreneurship in Ghana and South Africa need to be acknowledged, the gendered barriers to women's entrepreneurship and their negative effects on the growth of women's enterprises in both countries underscore the need for greater policy commitment directed towards achieving effective outcomes. Given the paucity of research on women's entrepreneurship policies in these two countries, this study aims to offer insights into future policy direction. An additional objective is to contribute to the women's entrepreneurship policy research domain by employing an institutional theory framework to analyse Ghana's and South Africa's women's entrepreneurship policies. This responds to Henry et al.'s (2017) call for further cross-country evidence-based research into women's entrepreneurship policies which is critical to foster learning and action. The following research questions guided this study:

1. What kind of women's entrepreneurship policies exist in Ghana and South Africa?
2. To what extent do the women's entrepreneurship policies of each of these countries address the normative, cultural-cognitive and regulatory institutional policy requirements?

In the following section of the chapter, we present a review of related literature on women's entrepreneurship policies, followed by institutional theory in light of women's entrepreneurship policies. We then describe the methodology of the study and present the results and discussions. We end the chapter with conclusions and recommendations.

REVIEW OF PRIOR RESEARCH ON WOMEN'S ENTREPRENEURSHIP POLICIES

Hart (2003) defines entrepreneurship policies as measures taken to stimulate more entrepreneurial behaviour in a region. We thus define women's entrepreneurship policies as government commitments and interventions to promote and develop women's entrepreneurship. Women's entrepreneurship policies can be situated within the broader scope of public policy with related activities often packaged into a public policy instrument/document (Lascoumes & Le Galès, 2007). Prior research attests to the positive impact of women's entrepreneurship policies, such as increasing women's political leadership and access to training, on women's entrepreneurship (Goltz et al., 2015; Meyer & Hamilton, 2020).

In support of the foregoing argument, Goltz et al. (2015) in a study of 53 countries found a significant positive effect of women's political empowerment, in terms of female political representation in parliament, and a country's rule of law on women's entry into entrepreneurship. In another study by Meyer and Hamilton (2020) in South Africa, women entrepreneurs who received entrepreneurial training showed a higher commitment to grow their businesses. Nonetheless, a key prerequisite for achieving lasting gains is that policy should tackle entrenched socio-cultural biases against women and other barriers to women's entrepreneurial activities (Alkhaled & Berglund, 2018; Foss et al., 2019).

Globally, women are marginalized in society (Ahl & Marlow, 2017; Henry et al., 2017). They are regarded as the weaker sex, primarily responsible for taking care of the family and the home without remuneration; subordinate to men and required to seek the consent of their male counterparts in decision-making; designed for certain professions like care work and service provision; and undeserving of equal access to resources and remuneration for work done by both women and men (Alkhaled & Berglund, 2018; Baughn et al., 2006). Women entrepreneurs in developing countries encounter additional constraints in the form of limited access to resources, unstable business environments that affect women more than men and personality-based challenges such as low risk-taking, a lack of self-confidence and excessive self-doubt (Derera et al., 2014; Panda, 2018).

Moreover, in developing countries, most women entrepreneurs, who are also breadwinners, start their businesses out of necessity (Adom & Williams, 2012). Due to low educational levels and limited opportunities in the labour market coupled with marriage and childcare responsibilities, more women engage in economic activities such as retailing and subsistence farming where educational qualifications and strict work schedules do not play a decisive role (Adom & Williams, 2012; Panda, 2018).

Women's disadvantaged status in society has influenced women's entrepreneurship policies in two main ways. Firstly, scholars and policymakers have advanced women's entrepreneurship policies based on the principle that entrepreneurship drives women's empowerment (Alkhaled & Berglund, 2018; Sarfaraz et al., 2014). Empowerment connotes the processes, and associated outcomes, 'by which those who have been denied the ability to make choices acquire such ability' (Kabeer, 2005, p. 13). Empowerment-driven women's entrepreneurship policies have mainly focused on women's micro-credit and savings schemes and skills training programmes (Foss et al., 2019; Henry et al., 2017).

In addition, some developed countries, such as Sweden and Denmark, have adopted childcare support and family leave provisions as additional interventions (Alkhaled & Berglund, 2018). In sum, interventions such as these have empowered women entrepreneurs in countries like South Africa (Botha, 2006), Ghana (Wrigley-Asante, 2012), Sweden and Saudi Arabia (Alkhaled & Berglund, 2018). However, little progress has been made in emancipating women from entrenched discriminatory socio-cultural practices and tendencies (Alkhaled & Berglund, 2018; Foss et al., 2019). To illustrate this point, drawing on United Nations gender development data and data on 41 countries from the Global Entrepreneurship Monitor, Sarfaraz et al. (2014) found that female entrepreneurial activity is not significantly correlated with gender equality.

In contrast to studies that focus on entrepreneurship as a pathway to women's empowerment, other studies regard women's empowerment as a necessary pre-condition for women's active and fruitful engagement in more productive entrepreneurship (Malhotra et al., 2002; Terjesen et al., 2016). Thus, like their male counterparts, women entrepreneurs need a sound, fair and supportive entrepreneurial ecosystem wherein their ventures can thrive and their personal and societal growth and development can flourish (Brush et al., 2019). As advanced in institutional theory, this calls for normative, cultural-cognitive and regulatory women's entrepreneurship policies.

INSTITUTIONAL THEORY AND WOMEN'S ENTREPRENEURSHIP POLICIES

Institutional theory illustrates the important role played by formal and informal rules and norms in economic activities (North, 1990; Scott, 2014). Building on neoclassical theory which assumes efficient markets, institutional theory acknowledges uncertainty and cost in human transactions and the need for appropriate institutions and property rights to promote efficient markets

(North, 2016). According to North (2016), institutions are the formal and informal rules of the game in society that affect the activities of organizations, that is groups of individuals bound by a common purpose to achieve certain objectives. Formal institutions comprise codified rules, laws or constitutions enacted and enforced by governments, while informal institutions consist of customs, norms or a culture that are not legally enforced (Godlewska, 2019). These institutions offer opportunities and incentives for organizations, such as women entrepreneurs, to engage in productive entrepreneurship. In contrast, unsupportive institutions can raise the cost of doing business and can force entrepreneurs to pursue destructive or unproductive entrepreneurship (Eesley et al., 2018; Godlewska, 2019).

Scott's institutional policy framework identifies three broad institutions/pillars namely, normative, cultural-cognitive and regulatory institutions, that must underpin policy to guide the necessary institutional changes for effective outcomes (Baughn et al., 2006; Scott, 2014). Scott (2014) explains that the normative policy pillar aims to tackle negative and discriminatory societal values and norms that have introduced prescriptive, evaluative and obligatory dimensions to social life. This is in line with feminist theories that discriminatory social practices emanating from embedded societal values and norms are the fundamental root cause of the barriers to women's entrepreneurship (Foss et al., 2019; Panda, 2018).

Normative women's entrepreneurship policies, therefore, constitute general interventions such as public education and advocacy aimed at bridging the gender inequality gaps in society and eventual cultural and attitudinal paradigm shifts from unequal power relations, and gendered discriminatory practices towards a more just society (Foss et al., 2019; Wrigley-Asante, 2012). They also comprise values, expectations and standards that aim to increase participation in entrepreneurship (Foss et al., 2019; Terjesen et al., 2016). Empirical research by Baughn et al. (2006), Yousafzai et al. (2015) and Goltz et al. (2015) demonstrates the positive impact of supportive normative women's entrepreneurship policies on women's entrepreneurship.

The second policy pillar, cultural-cognitive institutions, focuses on various forms of empowerment of women entrepreneurs. Terjesen et al. (2016) and Foss et al. (2019) explain that cultural-cognitive women's entrepreneurship policies aim to build entrepreneurship capacity to increase individuals' acceptance of entrepreneurship and entrepreneurial performance. In like fashion, North (2016) argues that the kinds of skills and knowledge individuals and their organizations acquire will shape evolving perceptions of opportunities and hence, choices that will incrementally alter institutions. Generally, empirical studies have established the positive impact of skills training and financial support on women's TEA and the performance of women's enterprises (Maru & Chemjor, 2013; Meyer & Hamilton, 2020). Nonetheless, Foss et al. (2019)

argue that there has been an overemphasis on skills training and funding to the detriment of other equally important policies.

Regulatory institutions, that comprise the third policy pillar, are mandatory provisions in the form of laws, governance and monitoring systems aimed at increasing the quality and outcomes of entrepreneurship (Terjesen et al., 2016). In contrast to cultural-cognitive institutions and normative institutions that are largely informal in nature, regulatory institutions are formal (Eesley et al., 2018; Godlewska, 2019). Researchers strongly recommend regulations and provision for childcare services including those that are publicly subsidized, paid family leave, maternity/paternity support, formalization of women's enterprises and tax reliefs due to their positive impact on women's entrepreneurial activities (Panda, 2018; Ratten & Tajeddini, 2018).

Yousafzai et al.'s survey (2015) of 92 countries on the GEM demonstrates the positive effect of supportive regulatory policies on women's entrepreneurial leadership. Nevertheless, Neergaard and Thrane's (2011) research, on Scandinavian countries' much lauded maternity leave and childcare provisions, highlights the need to approach the design of such policies with caution and to look beyond the general aim of stimulating female employment, as attached conditions, such as a reduced allowance for working during maternity leave, can affect the continuity of women's enterprises.

The three policy pillars interact to influence women's entrepreneurial outcomes with a tendency for informal institutions to have a more profound effect on new business entry when formal and informal institutions are misaligned (Eesley et al., 2018). As an example, research by Gimenez-Jimenez et al. (2020) shows that a dominant culture of masculinity and low levels of individualism weaken the impact of public expenditures on childcare on women's TEA, highlighting the need to address female subordination and male supremacy. Ultimately, governments' commitment to the normative, cultural-cognitive and regulatory women's entrepreneurship policies is indispensable to promote more productive women's entrepreneurship, alleviate poverty and advance personal, household and societal well-being and national economic development (Foss et al., 2019; Seshie-Nasser & Oduro, 2018).

METHODOLOGY

We employed the transformative research paradigm to conduct a qualitative study of Ghana's and South Africa's women's entrepreneurship policies. Creswell (2014) explains that transformative research focuses on the needs of marginalized groups and individuals with the aim of giving them a voice, raising their consciousness or advancing an agenda for change to improve their lives. Our research was premised on the fact that women entrepreneurs constitute a disadvantaged group in relation to their male counterparts (Bosma et al.,

2020; Seshie-Nasser & Oduro, 2018). They confront entrenched socio-cultural challenges, especially gender discrimination and suppression which hamper their ability to venture into more productive economic activities and grow their enterprises (Hampel-Milagrosa, 2011). We, therefore, used the transformative research paradigm to analyse Ghana's and South Africa's women's entrepreneurship policies and to advocate for more policies in support of women's enterprises for their personal and societal development.

In the absence of a single comprehensive women's entrepreneurship policy document in each country, we purposively sampled policy instruments from the websites of government ministries/departments in Ghana and South Africa. The inclusion criteria were that the policy documents focused on promoting female or women's entrepreneurship or they had general provisions that would directly or indirectly support women's entrepreneurship. The search produced 25 policy documents (13 for Ghana and 12 for South Africa).

We designed a document review guide based on the tenets of institutional theory, particularly focusing on those enshrined in Scott's institutional policy framework and supported by the transformative philosophical underpinnings of feminist theories that advocate for appropriate policies to address the barriers to women's entrepreneurship (Boohene, 2009; Foss et al., 2019). The guide consisted of four sections; namely: background information; gender-neutrality in the presentation of the document; a section on women's entrepreneurship policies containing prompts and questions on normative, cultural-cognitive and regulatory policies; and a final section on the comprehensiveness of the policies for women's entrepreneurship. Within the context of this chapter, our analysis relies primarily on data from the first and third sections of the document review guide.

The review of the policy documents and data extraction and analysis were conducted from November 2020 to January 2021. We manually coded data for each country through open and axial coding and adopted a descriptive research approach (Creswell, 2014; Henry et al., 2017) to analyse and interpret the data using an analytical framework of women's entrepreneurship policies.

Data Sources

In this section, we present an overview of the policy instruments analysed. Two of Ghana's policy documents, the Co-ordinated Programme of Economic and Social Development Policies – 2017–2024 (CPESDP) and the Medium-Term National Development Policy Framework – 2018–2021 (MTNDPF) focused on the country's economic and social development policies with some key WEP prescriptions that were further developed in the remaining 11 policy documents, in line with the mandate of relevant government ministries (Table 9.1).

Table 9.1   Ghana's policy documents

No.	Document and issuing authority	Year of publication	Relevant themes
1	The Co-ordinated Programme of Economic and Social Development Policies (CPESDP) (2017–2024) (Office of the President)	2017	National economic and social development policies with provisions on women's entrepreneurship.
2	Medium-Term National Development Policy Framework (MTNDPF) (2018–2021) (National Development Planning Commission)	2017	National economic and social development policies with similar provisions on women's entrepreneurship as the CPESDP.
3	National Agriculture Investment Plan (2018–2021) (Ministry of Food and Agriculture)	2018	Agriculture development policies with provisions on women in agriculture.
4	Medium-Term Expenditure Framework (MTEF) for 2019–2022 (Ministry for Business Development)	Not specified	Entrepreneurship, small enterprise development, internationalization.
5	National Science, Technology and Innovation Policy (2017–2020) (Ministry of Environment, Science, Technology and Innovation – MESTI)	2017	Science, technology and innovation (STI), science and mathematics education, entrepreneurial skills development.
6	National Gender Policy (Ministry of Gender, Children and Social Protection – MoGCSP)	2015	Gender equality, social protection and women empowerment with some provisions on entrepreneurship and small enterprise development.
7	National Social Protection Policy (MoGCSP)	2015	Social protection.
8	Fisheries Management Plan of Ghana Marine Fisheries Sector 2015–2019 (Ministry of Fisheries and Aquaculture Development and the Fisheries Commission)	2015	Fisheries management including post-harvest activities and business opportunities.
9	National Employment Policy, Volume 1, 2014 (Ministry of Employment and Labour Relations)	2014	Employment related issues with mention of women.

No.	Document and issuing authority	Year of publication	Relevant themes
10	Ghana National Climate Change Policy by MESTI	2013	STI, finance, international co-operation, women and climate change.
11	National Energy Policy (Ministry of Energy)	2010	Energy, gender and energy.
12	Ghana Industrial Policy (Ministry of Trade and Industry – MoTI)	Not specified	Production and distribution; technology and innovation, incentives and regulatory regime; gender in industry.
13	Ghana Trade Policy (MoTI)	Not specified	Multilateral trade, domestic trade, distribution, etc.

Source: Authors' Compilation (2020).

South Africa's women's entrepreneurship policies were primarily contained in the White Paper on National Strategy for the Development and Promotion of Small Business in South Africa (hereafter referred to as the White Paper on Small Business Development). The White Paper on Small Business Development is complemented by several national and regional policies to achieve its mandate. There are also numerous national, regional, local and sectoral programmes that support the White Paper's objectives. Given this background, we used the White Paper on Small Business Development as the primary document for analysis while also drawing on other national policies and government departments' strategy documents that support women's entrepreneurship (Table 9.2).

Analytical Framework for Women's Entrepreneurship Policies

In accordance with Scott's institutional policy framework (Henry et al., 2017; Scott, 2014), the analytical framework for women's entrepreneurship policies (Table 9.3) incorporates the three policy pillars and their objectives as well as policy prescriptions that might be expected to address obstacles to women's entrepreneurship. Normative policy requirements, that are both generic and specific in nature, address discriminatory socio-cultural practices. As shown in Table 9.3, typical examples of normative policies are policies on gender equality and policies ensuring that women and females, in general, have an equal voice in society (Panda, 2018; Peprah et al., 2019). The specific normative policies cited relate to enhancing societal values and norms for women's entrepreneurship, and include awareness raising and education on its benefits (Terjesen et al., 2016). Realization of the normative policy pillar will enable women entrepreneurs to operate in a supportive environment that will encourage them to venture into more productive sectors in the spirit of transformational entrepreneurship (Ratten & Tajeddini, 2018; Terjesen et al., 2016).

The core objective of the cultural-cognitive pillar (Table 9.3) is capacity building, that is, empowerment of female entrepreneurs to enable them to define and manage their own life choices and to have equal access to resources for effective and efficient outcomes (Kabeer, 2005; Wrigley-Asante, 2012). Malhotra et al. (2002) and Wrigley-Asante (2012) highlight the need for policies on the social, economic, interpersonal/relational, psychological and leadership empowerment of women (Table 9.3). The third policy pillar in the form of regulatory policies, namely rules, their enforcement and sanctions, seeks to increase the level, quality and outcomes of women's entrepreneurial activities (Panda, 2018; Ratten & Tajeddini, 2018). As shown in Table 9.3, regulatory policy requirements can be organized in the three main categories of social interventions, economic incentives and formalization of female enterprises (Hampel-Milagrosa, 2011; Panda, 2018; Ratten & Tajeddini, 2018).

Table 9.2   *South Africa's policy documents*

No.	Document and issuing authority	Year of Publication	Relevant themes
1	White Paper on National Strategy for Development and Promotion of Small Business in South Africa (Government of South Africa)	1995 (amended in 2004)	Entrepreneurship development; creating an enabling environment for small enterprises; advancement of women's entrepreneurship.
2	South Africa's National Policy Framework for Women's Empowerment and Gender Equality (Government of South Africa)	Not specified	Gender equality; women empowerment; equal voice; women's entrepreneurship.
3	Broad-based Black Economic Empowerment (B-BBEE) Act (Government of South Africa)	2013	Principles of B-BBEE; women's entrepreneurship and procurement support.
4	National Development Plan 2030 – Our Future – make it work (NDP-2030) (Government of South Africa)	Not specified	Poverty alleviation; gender equality; women empowerment; small business sector support; creating an enabling environment for entrepreneurship.
5	Department of Small Business Development – 2020–2025 Strategic Plan (DSBDSP – 2020–2025) (Government of South Africa)	Not specified	Entrepreneurship development; creating an enabling environment for the small business sector; gender equality; women empowerment; economic transformation and job creation for women.
6	White Paper on Agriculture (Government of South Africa)	1995	Creating an environment for agriculture development; empowerment of women in agriculture.
7	National Tourism Sector Strategy (Government of South Africa)	Not specified	Tourism development; women in tourism with a special focus on black women.
8	Strategic Framework on Gender and Women's Economic Empowerment [DTI – Gender and Women Empowerment (GWE) Unit] (Government of South Africa)	2007	Sustainable economic activity and employment for all South Africans; celebrating women entrepreneurs.
9	Department of Rural Development and Land Reform Strategic Plan 2015 – 2020 (Government of South Africa)	Not specified	Land use plan and security of tenure for households, particularly for vulnerable people such as females.

No.	Document and issuing authority	Year of Publication	Relevant themes
10	White Paper on Science, Technology and Innovation (Government of South Africa)	2019	STI; targeted support to women researchers and techno-entrepreneurs; gender equality; innovation awareness among women.
11	Financial Sector Charter (Government of South Africa)	2003	Black Economic Empowerment; Addressing inequalities in the financial sector; providing accessible financial services to black people; black women-empowered enterprises.
12	Women Empowerment and Gender Equality (WEGE) Bill	2013	Equal enjoyment of all rights and freedoms; gender equality; women empowerment; minimum of 50 per cent representation and meaningful participation of women in decision-making structures; public education to promote gender equality and social cohesion.

Source: Authors' Compilation (2020).

Table 9.3   *Analytical framework for women's entrepreneurship policies*

Policy pillar	Objectives	Policy requirements
Normative pillar		
Values and norms '... that introduce a prescriptive, evaluative and obligatory dimension into social life' (Scott, 2014, p. 64)	To increase awareness and acceptance of the benefits of entrepreneurship (Terjesen et al., 2016).	Giving women an equal voice; gender equity; entrepreneurship awareness creation. Examples: Addressing gender biases in cultural and social norms (Foss et al., 2019; Wrigley-Asante, 2012). Vocal support for women's rights; better educational opportunities; women in government and corporations (Panda, 2018). Appointing government advocates for entrepreneurship; promoting entrepreneurship through media, community events and conferences (Terjesen et al., 2016).
Cultural-cognitive pillar		
An individual's '... internalized symbolic representations of the world' (Scott, 2014, p. 67)	To build entrepreneurship capacity and to increase the quality and outcome of entrepreneurial activities (Terjesen et al., 2016).	Women's empowerment: Social empowerment including human resource development/capacity building, entrepreneurial training and other business development services (Malhotra et al., 2002; Peprah et al., 2019). Economic empowerment including access to and control over physical and financial resources (Malhotra et al., 2002; Wrigley-Asante, 2012). Interpersonal/relational empowerment including social capital development (Malhotra et al., 2002; Sallah & Caesar, 2020). Psychological/emotional empowerment, e.g. building their self-esteem and risk-taking propensity (Kuada, 2009; Panda, 2018). Leadership empowerment (Malhotra et al., 2002; Panda, 2018).

Policy pillar	Objectives	Policy requirements
Regulatory pillar		
'The capacity to establish rules, inspect others' conformity to them, and, as necessary, manipulate sanctions — rewards or punishments — in an attempt to influence future behavior' (Scott, 2014, p. 59)	To increase the levels, quality and outcomes of entrepreneurial activities (Terjesen et al., 2016).	Social interventions including childcare support, paid family leave, maternity/paternity support provisions (Panda, 2018; Ratten & Tajeddini, 2018). Economic incentives such as special tax relief and tax exemptions (Peprah et al., 2019; Ratten & Tajeddini, 2018). Formalization of enterprises through business registration and formation of associations (Hampel-Milagrosa, 2011)

Source: Authors' Compilation (2020).

National policies are indispensable to define a country's commitment and direction in addressing the constraints to women's entrepreneurship. Accordingly, we addressed the study's research questions by examining Ghana's and South Africa's women's entrepreneurship policies using the analytical framework for women's entrepreneurship policies.

RESULTS AND DISCUSSIONS

In this section, we present the results and discussions of Ghana's women's entrepreneurship policies first, followed by those of South Africa.

Ghana's Women's Entrepreneurship Policies

In line with the first research question, we analysed Ghana's 13 policy instruments to understand the kinds of women's entrepreneurship policies they embraced. The analysis revealed normative, cultural-cognitive and regulatory policy prescriptions for women's entrepreneurship (see Exhibit 9.1 for excerpts from the policy prescriptions). Nine of the 13 documents contained normative policies while 12 and four policy instruments covered cultural-cognitive policies and regulatory policies, respectively. Thus, there were more policy instruments with cultural-cognitive and normative prescriptions than regulatory objectives. The second research question was: To what extent do the policies of each country address the normative, cultural-cognitive and regulatory institutional policy requirements?

EXHIBIT 9.1   EXCERPTS OF GHANA'S
                     WOMEN'S ENTREPRENEURSHIP
                     POLICY PRESCRIPTIONS

Examples of normative policies
'Facilitate allocation of resource by public and private sector institutions to set up a regular gender awareness and sensitization programme, to improve the culture for understanding gender roles and relationships in formal and informal decision making in homes, in communities and at work places.' (National Gender Policy, p. 32)

'Bring Ghanaian women entrepreneurs to the negotiation tables on African Market issues and marketing linkages ... Ensure that women entrepreneurs are involved in the processes and consensus building for exporters of products in the African Growth and Opportunity (AGOA) Act/issues ... Facilitate the representation of women on Boards of Regional and International trade organizations.' (National Gender Policy, p. 31)

Examples of cultural-cognitive policies
'Further, the ministry will promote innovation in women micro and small enterprises (MSEs) especially in the rural areas. Special programmes will be designed to encourage rural women engaged in micro- and small-scale production to adopt new and appropriate technologies conducive to their fields of operation.' (National Science Technology and Innovation Policy, p. 56)

'Promotion of access to skill-based trainings for the Youth ... A total of 15,000 youth (*at least 40% women*) will be targeted for training by 2021.' (National Agriculture Investment Plan, p. 44)

Examples of regulatory policies
'Implement specific measures and standards to protect the health of working women during pregnancy, after childbirth and while breastfeeding.' (National Employment Policy, p. 33)

'Facilitate advocacy groups to promote legislation enabling fathers to be granted paternity leave.' (National Gender Policy, p. 27)

With respect to the normative policies, eight of the nine documents were generic in nature while one, the Energy Policy, was sector specific. This finding suggests that the normative policies have a wider scope of application and, when properly enforced, will benefit a broader range of women entrepreneurs in the country. The normative policies include commitments to providing an equal voice to women in general and to women entrepreneurs, gender equity and entrepreneurship awareness creation. Despite the commitment to achieve gender equality, several policy prescriptions did not demonstrate equality. For instance, the following policy statement in the CPESDP shows the country's commitment to devoting 30 per cent of credit funds to women's enterprises rather than 50 per cent which would represent an equal proportion: '... implement a policy of reserving 30 percent of poverty alleviation/credit funds of MMDAs to service women's enterprises ...' (CPESDP, p. 5).

Moreover, although entrepreneurship awareness creation was featured in the CPESDP and the National Agriculture Investment Plan, only the Ministry of Business Development's Medium-Term Expenditure Policy Framework (MTEF) paid special attention to female entrepreneurship by making provision for a women's entrepreneurship conference. This conference can also be regarded as a platform for giving an equal voice to women entrepreneurs. However, since most women entrepreneurs operate in the informal sector and have lower educational qualifications (Boohene, 2009; Hampel-Milagrosa, 2011), an entrepreneurship conference will not suffice for the majority of them.

Our analysis also showed that there were cultural-cognitive policy prescriptions in the domain of women's empowerment. Eight of Ghana's 13 policy instruments were committed to the social empowerment of women, 12 made provisions for the economic empowerment of women entrepreneurs and one instrument addressed women entrepreneurs' leadership empowerment. The National Gender Policy and the MTEF made provisions for their interpersonal/relational empowerment, but there were no specific policies on the psychological empowerment of women entrepreneurs, in terms of building their self-esteem, risk-taking propensity and achievement motivation (Kuada, 2009; Wrigley-Asante, 2012). Thus, Ghana's cultural-cognitive women's entrepreneurship policies were more oriented to the social and economic empowerment of women entrepreneurs with an emphasis on entrepreneurial and skills training and funding.

Although research shows that Ghanaian women entrepreneurs are able to access informal sources of finance due to their strong social networks (Kuada, 2009; Schindler, 2010), there is an urgent need to build their leadership, relational and psychological capital to enable them to venture into and effectively navigate more productive sectors of the formal economy. Adom and Williams (2012) found that women who initially enter informal entrepreneurship out of necessity become more opportunity-driven entrepreneurs over time and make significant contributions to household and national welfare (Seshie-Nasser & Oduro, 2018). This highlights the need to empower more women entrepreneurs to operate in the formal economy without fear or favour.

Another major finding is that several policies, for example, the MTEF and the Ghana Industrial Policy, indicate government's commitment to intensify infrastructure development in support of entrepreneurship. For instance, the MTEF states: '... After being shortlisted for incubation the enterprises will be supported with seed capital, 12 months' mentorship, networking and use of hub space, facilities and resources to grow the business.' Nonetheless, there were no specific provisions for female enterprises. The lack of specific quotas for female enterprises reflects inadequate attention to the infrastructural challenges confronting women entrepreneurs (Bamfo & Asiedu-Appiah, 2012; Peprah et al., 2019).

The third policy pillar constitutes regulatory policies (Exhibit 9.1). Our analysis of the four policy instruments (MTNDPF, National Gender Policy, National Social Protection Policy and National Employment Policy) that included regulatory women's entrepreneurship policies revealed that, although the National Gender Policy clearly communicated social intervention policies on childcare support, paid family leave and provision for maternity/paternity leave, these policies only apply to women in paid employment. For example, the National Gender Policy sought to 'Liaise with labour market leaders to facilitate balancing of life responsibilities including financial support to car-egivers by providing child friendly facilities at the workplaces ... Promote and accelerate the implementation of unpaid work module ... .' (National Gender Policy, p. 32).

Given that the majority of women entrepreneurs are self-employed in the informal sector (Seshie-Nasser & Oduro, 2018; Wrigley-Asante, 2012), this focus on paid employment puts them at a disadvantage, as they lose out on the social and economic incentives extended to workers. Moreover, although high tax rates have been found to limit women entrepreneurs' performance in Ghana (Bamfo & Asiedu-Appiah, 2012; Peprah et al. 2019), the commit-ment to reduce the tax burden on vulnerable persons as communicated in the MTNDP does not explicitly indicate a focus on women entrepreneurs, nor is the extent to which taxes are reduced specified.

Another key finding is that, unlike the normative policies on gender equal-ity and cultural-cognitive policies on social and economic empowerment captured in the two main national generic policy instruments – the CPESDP and the MTNDPF – and further communicated in other policy documents, the regulatory policies on social interventions were only addressed in the National Gender Policy. The MTNDPF and the National Employment Policy addressed issues relating to the formalization of women-led enterprises, while the National Social Protection Policy focused on labour rights issues that affect women entrepreneurs. This shows that regulatory women's entrepreneurship policies have not received sufficient attention from policymakers, as they are absent from the operational/ministerial policies.

Overall, few of Ghana's women's entrepreneurship policies were prescrip-tive while most were measures aimed at creating the conditions for specific policies to emerge in the future. Illustrating this point, the National Gender Policy sought to: 'Review and promote leadership development channels for women across the regions ... Promote political leadership mentoring for women at least from the tertiary levels of education' (NGP, p. 29). The Ghana Trade Policy also indicates that: 'The Government will identify and target spe-cific sectors for development on the basis of export potential, domestic market requirements, increased employment and income for disadvantaged groups such as women, rural communities and the poor' (Ghana Trade Policy, p. 19).

South Africa's Women's Entrepreneurship Policies

We also analysed South Africa's women's entrepreneurship policy prescrip-tions in the selected policy instruments. As noted previously, unlike Ghana, South Africa has a national policy framework for the development and promo-tion of small businesses, and women's entrepreneurship represents an integral part of that policy. One of the national policy's key objectives is to promote women's entrepreneurship in all sectors of the economy and in different geographical locations (White Paper on Small Business Development, 1995). In particular, objective 4 of the White Paper is to 'Support the advancement of women in all business sectors' (p. 15). The government's commitment to the small business sector is also reflected in the establishment of the Department of Small Business Development, which has a mandate to implement, manage and oversee the national policy's objectives as reflected in its Strategic Plan for 2020–2025.

Furthermore, South Africa's national policies are co-ordinated such that they align with the mandate of the White Paper on Small Business Development in supporting the advancement of entrepreneurship, including women's entrepreneurship. For example, the mandate of the Financial Sector Charter is to address inequalities in the financial sector by ensuring that women-owned enterprises, and particularly enterprises owned by black women, can easily access sources of finance. The B-BBEE Act also promotes women's participation in government procurement opportunities and senior leadership positions in organizations.

Analysis of the White Paper on Small Business Development revealed that the national policy is comprehensive and offers a broad scope of application in order to promote women's entrepreneurship. Simultaneously, however, the policy framework acknowledges the challenges that hamper growth in the small business sector. According to Section 2.3.1 of the framework, these include an 'unfavourable legal and regulatory environment, access to markets, finance and affordable business premises, lack of business skills and managerial expertise, access to technology, lack of business infrastructure in impoverished areas and, the tax burden' (p. 9). The policy also notes that women encounter gender barriers due to oppressive and discriminatory socio-cultural norms and practices that are deeply rooted in society, including the small business sector. As a result, women's entrepreneurship is one of the policy's key priority areas.

Similar to Ghana, normative, cultural-cognitive and regulatory policy prescriptions for women's entrepreneurship were identified in South Africa. Analysis of the White Paper on Small Business Development revealed wide-ranging coverage of the three policy pillars of institutional theory (see Exhibit 9.2 for excerpts from the policy prescriptions). While all the policy documents addressed the three pillars within their policy prescriptions, the extent to which they did so depended on their respective objectives.

EXHIBIT 9.2   EXCERPTS OF WOMEN'S
                   ENTREPRENEURSHIP POLICY
                   PRESCRIPTIONS IN SOUTH
                   AFRICA'S WHITE PAPER ON
                   SMALL BUSINESS DEVELOPMENT

Examples of normative policies
'School curricula and other school-related activities should give more
scope for teaching entrepreneurial attitudes and general awareness about
self-employment opportunities.' (Section 4.7.2)

'In addition, literacy and entrepreneurial awareness are essential to enabling people to advance from survivalist activities into more extensive and
better-earning enterprises.' (Section 4.7)

Examples of cultural-cognitive policy
'The acquisition of relevant vocational, technical and business skills is gen-
erally regarded as one of the critical factors for success in small enterprises.'
(Section 4.7)

Examples of regulatory policies
'Given the critical role collateral plays in the attraction of conventional
bank credit, attention will be given to the recognition of other types of se-
curities and collateral substitutes, especially in the rural areas where land is
communally held and with respect to women entrepreneurs.' (Section 4.5.7)

'Establishing a user-friendly environment also calls for the simplification
and standardisation of documents of business registration and licensing,
financial and loan applications, purchasing and sub-contracting (tender)
document, and export documentation and other commercial documents.'
(Section 4.2.5)

The normative policy prescriptions assist women in achieving gender equity
and having an equal voice in the small business sector, while increasing their
awareness of entrepreneurship opportunities (Foss et al., 2019; Panda, 2018).
As an example, Section 9.6 of the WEGE Bill seeks 'to empower women and
eliminate gender discrimination by introducing economic and land reform initiatives that promote their rights and benefits in society' (p. 60). To eliminate
gender inequality and discrimination in entrepreneurship, one of the objectives
of the B-BBEE Act is to 'increase women's participation in management and
business ownership by 40–50%' (p. 12).

Similarly, the Financial Sector Charter seeks to address gender inequality in this sector by ensuring that 'black women-empowered enterprises with more than 30% ownership …' (p. 2) can access business funding. In both cases, business ownership of less than 50 per cent is problematic as it perpetuates gender inequality in workplaces and entrepreneurship. Such policy prescriptions favour males, as they give them more control of the small business sector. In contrast, the WEGE Bill advocates that, 'targets for women in all laws and policies on empowerment shall be at least 50%' (p. 60). Further evidence of normative policy can be found in the SANPFWEGE policy that advocates for 'training of policymakers and managers to improve their knowledge, skills, and attitudes in gender analysis and gender equality' (p. v). Measures of this type are critical for driving the gender equality agenda in South Africa.

The analysis also found evidence of cultural-cognitive policy prescriptions for women's entrepreneurship in the policy instruments. These policy prescriptions seek to build women's capacity to participate fully in entrepreneurship and to improve their entrepreneurial outcomes (Terjesen et al., 2016) by empowering women in all the domains of empowerment (economic, social, psychological, relational and leadership) (Malhotra et al., 2002; Peprah et al., 2019). For example, Section 4.7.3 of the White Paper on Small Business Development seeks to address the social and psychological domains of empowerment by ensuring that 'education and training help break the traditional gender roles in business and skill categories' (p. 32).

Similarly, the White Paper on Science, Technology and Innovation states that 'the education system must equip students with the necessary skills required for engaging in successful entrepreneurship' (p. 51). The Provincial Tourism Sector Charter also acknowledges that 'women operate at the bottom of the tourism sector economic value chain' (p. 1) and that, 'training on business skills and personal development should assist them to develop competitive advantage for their businesses' (p. 1).

Within the realm of women's economic and social empowerment, the SANPFWEGE advocates for 'more resources (e.g. access to land and finance) to be allocated to women in rural and urban areas, and equipping them with the necessary skills to enable them to use the land more productively' (p. viii). Consistent with this, the NDP highlights the significance of 'access to land and financial resources for rural women entrepreneurs as well as enhancement of their skills and capabilities' (p. 219). For the relational empowerment domain, it is recommended that women entrepreneurs in the tourism sector attend conferences as a platform for networking and discussing how they are 'overcoming barriers to gender empowerment' (p. 1). While such conferences could contribute to women's relational empowerment, most women do not benefit as they operate at the bottom of the sector's value chain.

The regulatory policy prescriptions for women's entrepreneurship seek to establish rules, ensure conformity to and, where necessary, reward or punish citizens in an attempt to promote future favourable behaviour (Scott, 2014) as a means for increasing the level, quality and outcomes of entrepreneurial activities (Terjesen et al., 2016). An assessment of the selected policy documents showed alignment with the White Paper on Small Business Development. Thus, the SANPFWEGE highlights 'the enactment of laws that consider the needs and aspirations of women' (p. viii). Similarly, the White Paper on Science, Technology and Innovation notes the necessity of 'supporting women and black entrepreneurs with the commercialization of intellectual property' (p. 35). Nevertheless, although the selected documents address aspects of the regulatory pillar, the policy prescriptions are not very clear on how childcare provisions support women's entrepreneurship as suggested by prior research (e.g. Panda, 2018; Ratten & Tajeddini, 2018).

Overall, South Africa's women's entrepreneurship policies demonstrate a broader application of all three pillars of the institutional framework. The policy prescriptions, included in our selected policy documents, align well with the White Paper on Small Business Development which represents a foundation for the development of entrepreneurship in South Africa, including women's entrepreneurship. The policy prescriptions are comprehensive and have the potential to change the landscape of women's entrepreneurship if adequately implemented and enforced.

CONCLUSIONS AND RECOMMENDATIONS

Motivated by the need to promote and develop women's entrepreneurship in Ghana and South Africa, coupled with the scarcity of research on women's entrepreneurship policies in these countries, this study sought to address two research questions: First, what kind of women's entrepreneurship policies exist in Ghana and South Africa? Second, to what extent do the policies of each of these countries address the normative, cultural-cognitive and regulatory institutional policy requirements? Using an analytical framework for women's entrepreneurship policy, which we developed from Scott's institutional policy framework, we analysed qualitative data from relevant policy instruments. Our results show that both countries employ normative, cultural-cognitive and regulatory policies.

Although Ghana has the aforementioned policy pillars, the policies themselves are fragmented in different policy documents. Further, the policies are less prescriptive and do not entirely address the normative, cultural-cognitive and regulatory policy requirements. It is, therefore, imperative that the Ghanaian government devotes adequate attention to women's entrepreneurship in the ongoing process of developing a national entrepreneurship policy or, alternatively, considers the development of a separate national women's entrepreneurship policy.

In either case, Ghanaian national policy should broaden the normative and cultural-cognitive policies beyond conferences, training and funding to include infrastructure development and relational, psychological and leadership empowerment of women entrepreneurs. These can be achieved through further measures designed to address discrimination against females, including long-term community education/sensitization programmes; equal access to incubation/acceleration facilities and other forms of resources; and leadership and mentorship programmes. Further, efforts to achieve the goals of generic policies, especially regulatory policies, should be intensified to pave the way for specific prescriptive policies on childcare support, maternity/paternity support and tax relief for women entrepreneurs.

South Africa's three policy pillars of the institutional framework have a broader scope, although they are spread across different national policy and strategic documents. The policies are comprehensive and co-ordinated and have the potential to transform the women's entrepreneurship landscape if adequately enforced and properly implemented. Whether or not South Africa should develop a separate national policy for women's entrepreneurship is a debate that calls for rigorous research and consultation, in conjunction with monitoring and evaluation of the current support programmes for women in the small business sector. A separate women's entrepreneurship policy would be a step forward in achieving a co-ordinated approach to further promote and develop competitive and sustainable women's entrepreneurship. Such a policy document could assist in bringing together elements from all the policy prescriptions supporting women's entrepreneurship into one document for ease of implementation and co-ordination.

This study contributes to women's entrepreneurship research by employing an institutional theory framework for analysing Ghana's and South Africa's women's entrepreneurship policies, and for reviving the debate on women's entrepreneurship policies in Africa. A limitation of this study is that it relies on data from a select group of policy documents chosen by the authors. Future studies could (1) extend the data sources to include laws and other national policy documents that were omitted; (2) focus on country-specific analysis of the comprehensiveness of women's entrepreneurship policies in relation to specific barriers to women's entrepreneurship; and (3) examine implementation of the policies and their effectiveness in addressing barriers to women's entrepreneurship.

REFERENCES

Adom, K., & Williams, C. C. (2012). Evaluating the motives of informal entrepreneurs in Koforidua, Ghana. *Journal of Developmental Entrepreneurship, 17*(01), 1250005-1–1250005-17.

Ahl, H., & Marlow, S. (2017). Postfeminist times: New opportunities or business as usual? Paper presented at the 2017 RENT conference, Lund, 16–17 November.

Alkhaled, S., & Berglund, K. (2018). 'And now I'm free': Women's empowerment and emancipation through entrepreneurship in Saudi Arabia and Sweden. *Entrepreneurship & Regional Development, 30*(7–8), 877–900.

Bamfo, B. A., & Asiedu-Appiah, F. (2012). Investigating the challenges and prospects of female entrepreneurs in Ghana. *International Journal of Business and Management Studies, 1*(1), 43–54.

Baughn, C. C., Chua, B. L., & Neupert, K. E. (2006). The normative context for women's participation in entrepreneurship: A multicountry study. *Entrepreneurship Theory and Practice, 30*(5), 687–708.

Boohene, R. (2009). The relationships among gender, strategic capabilities, and performance of small retail firms in Ghana. *Journal of African Business, 10*(1), 121–138.

Bosma, N., Hill, S., Ionescu, A., Kelley, D., Levie, J., & Tarnawa, A. (2020). *Global entrepreneurship monitor 2019/2020 Global report*. Global Entrepreneurship Research Association.

Botha, M. (2006). *Measuring the effectiveness of the women's entrepreneurship programme, as a training intervention, on potential, start-up and established women entrepreneurs in South Africa* (Doctoral dissertation, University of Pretoria).

Brush, C., Edelman, L. F., Manolova, T., & Welter, F. (2019). A gendered look at entrepreneurship ecosystems. *Small Business Economics, 53*(2), 393–408.

Creswell, J. W. (2014). *Research design: Qualitative, quantitative and mixed methods approaches (4 edn)*. Sage.

Derera, E., Chitakunye, P., & O'Neill, C. (2014). The impact of gender on start-up capital: A case of women entrepreneurs in South Africa. *The Journal of Entrepreneurship, 23*(1), 95–114.

Eesley, C. E., Eberhart, R. N., Skousen, B. R., & Cheng, J. L. (2018). Institutions and entrepreneurial activity: The interactive influence of misaligned formal and informal institutions. *Strategy Science, 3*(2), 393–407.

Foss, L., Henry, C., Ahl, H., & Mikalsen, G. H. (2019). Women's entrepreneurship policy research: A 30-year review of the evidence. *Small Business Economics, 53*(2), 409–429.

Gimenez-Jimenez, D., Calabrò, A., & Urbano, D. (2020). The neglected role of formal and informal institutions in women's entrepreneurship: A multi-level analysis. *Journal of International Entrepreneurship, 18*(2), 196–226.

Godlewska, M. (2019). Do interactions between formal and informal institutions matter for productive entrepreneurship? *Economics and Law, 18*(1), 17–28.

Goltz, S., Buche, M. W., & Pathak, S. (2015). Political empowerment, rule of law, and women's entry into entrepreneurship. *Journal of Small Business Management, 53*(3), 605–626.

Hampel-Milagrosa, A. (2011). *The role of regulation, tradition and gender in doing business: Case study and survey report on a two-year research project in Ghana*. The German Development Institute.

Hart, D. (2003). Entrepreneurship policy: What it is and where it came from. In D. M. Hart (Ed.), *The emergence of entrepreneurship policy. Governance, start-ups and growth in the US knowledge economy* (pp. 3–19). Cambridge University Press.

Henry, C., Orser, B., Coleman, S., Foss, L., & Welter, F. (2017). Women's entrepreneurship policy: A 13-nation cross-country comparison. *International Journal of Gender and Entrepreneurship, 9*(3), 206–228.

Herrington, M., & Kelley, D. (2012). *African entrepreneurship: Sub-Saharan African regional report.* International Development Research Centre.

Kabeer, N. (2005). Gender equality and women's empowerment: A critical analysis of the third Millennium Development Goal 1. *Gender & Development, 13*(1), 13–24.

Kuada, J. (2009). Gender, social networks, and entrepreneurship in Ghana. *Journal of African Business, 10*(1), 85–103.

Langevang, T., Gough, K. V., Yankson, P. W., Owusu, G., & Osei, R. (2015). Bounded entrepreneurial vitality: The mixed embeddedness of female entrepreneurship. *Economic Geography, 91*(4), 449–473.

Lascoumes, P., & Le Galès, P. (2007). Introduction: Understanding public policy through its instruments – from the nature of instruments to the sociology of public policy instrumentation. *Governance, 20*(1), 1–21.

Malhotra, A., Schuler, S. R., & Boender, C. (2002, June). Measuring women's empowerment as a variable in international development. In *Background paper prepared for the World Bank Workshop on Poverty and Gender: New Perspectives*, 28.

Maru, L., & Chemjor, R. (2013). Microfinance interventions and empowerment of women entrepreneurs' rural constituencies in Kenya. *Research Journal of Finance and Accounting, 4*(9), 84–95.

Meyer, N., & Hamilton, L. (2020). Female entrepreneurs' business training and its effect on various entrepreneurial factors: Evidence from a developing country. *International Journal of Economics and Finance Studies, 12*(1), 135–151.

Neergaard, H., & Thrane, C. (2011). The Nordic welfare model: Barrier or facilitator of women's entrepreneurship in Denmark? *International Journal of Gender and Entrepreneurship, 3*(2), 88–104.

North, D. C. (1990). *Institutions, institutional change and economic performance.* Cambridge University Press.

North, D. C. (2016). Institutions and economic theory. *The American Economist, 61*(1), 72–76.

Overå, R. (2003). Gender ideology and manoeuvring space for female fisheries entrepreneurs. *Institute of African Studies Research Review, 19*(2), 49–62.

Overå, R. (2017). Local navigations in a global industry: The gendered nature of entrepreneurship in Ghana's oil and gas service sector. *The Journal of Development Studies, 53*(3), 361–374.

Panda, S. (2018). Constraints faced by women entrepreneurs in developing countries: Review and ranking. *Gender in Management: An International Journal, 33*(4), 315–331.

Peprah, V., Buor, D., Forkuor, D., & Sánchez-Moral, S. (2019). Characteristics of informal sector activities and challenges faced by women in Kumasi Metropolis, Ghana. *Cogent Social Sciences, 5*(1), 1656383.

Ratten, V., & Tajeddini, K. (2018). Women's entrepreneurship and internationalization: Patterns and trends. *International Journal of Sociology and Social Policy, 38*(9/10), 780–793.

Sallah, C. A., & Caesar, L. D. (2020). Intangible resources and the growth of women businesses: Empirical evidence from an emerging market economy. *Journal of Entrepreneurship in Emerging Economies, 12*(3), 329–355.

Sarfaraz, L., Faghih, N., & Majd, A. A. (2014). The relationship between women entrepreneurship and gender equality. *Journal of Global Entrepreneurship Research, 4*(1), 1–11.

Schindler, K. (2010). Credit for what? Informal credit as a coping strategy of market women in Northern Ghana. *The Journal of Development Studies, 46*(2), 234–253.

Scott, W. R. (2014). *Institutions and organizations: Ideas, interests, and identities.* Sage.

Seshie-Nasser, H. A., & Oduro, A. D. (2018). Women-owned businesses and household welfare. *International Journal of Gender and Entrepreneurship, 10*(4), 310–331.

Terjesen, S., Bosma, N., & Stam, E. (2016). Advancing public policy for high-growth, female, and social entrepreneurs. *Public Administration Review, 76*(2), 230–239.

World Bank (2018). *An operational guide to women's entrepreneurship programs in the World Bank.* The World Bank.

Wrigley-Asante, C. (2012). Out of the dark but not out of the cage: Women's empowerment and gender relations in the Dangme West district of Ghana. *Gender, Place & Culture, 19*(3), 344–363.

Yousafzai, S. Y., Saeed, S., & Muffatto, M. (2015). Institutional theory and contextual embeddedness of women's entrepreneurial leadership: Evidence from 92 countries. *Journal of Small Business Management, 53*(3), 587–604.

Index

Printed and bound by CPI Group (UK) Ltd, Croydon, CR0 4YY

25/03/2025

14647009-0002